An Introduction to the Study of Education

D0209584

DISCARDED

Edited by

David Matheson

and

Ian Grosvenor

David Fulton Publishers

London

To Pauline, Julie and Benjamin
DM

To Sue, Tom and Rachel
IG

David Fulton Publishers Ltd
Ormond House, 26–27 Boswell Street, London WC1N 3JD

First published in Great Britain by David Fulton Publishers 1999

Note: The rights of David Matheson and Ian Grosvenor to be identified as the editors of this work have been asserted by them in accordance with the Copyright, Designs and Patents Act 1988.

Copyright © David Fulton Publishers 1999

British Library Cataloguing in Publication Data
A catalogue record for this book is available from the British Library

ISBN 1–85346–612–3

All rights reserved. No part of this publication may be reproduced, stored in a retrieval system or transmitted, in any form, or by any means, electronic, mechanical, photocopying, recording or otherwise, without the prior permission of the publishers.

Typeset by FSH Print & Production Ltd
Printed by The Cromwell Press Ltd, Trowbridge, Wilts.

Contents

Preface

'Now what I want is, Facts. Teach these boys and girls nothing but Facts. Facts alone are wanted in life. Plant nothing else, and root out everything else. You can only form the minds of reasoning animals upon Facts: nothing else will ever be of any service to them...Stick to the Facts, sir!'

Thomas Gradgrind in Charles Dickens' *Hard Times. For these Times* (1854)

Education is rarely out of the news. There has been a recent debate about whether primary schools should concentrate on the 3Rs or should offer a broad curriculum. The framework of this debate is not new. In the 1860s inspectors visited schools in England (and elsewhere) to test standards of reading and writing and schools were then paid according to results. The curriculum offered was condemned by one inspector as 'mechanical and lifeless'. The issue of payment by results has not gone away, there has been an outcry from teachers about recent plans to introduce performance related pay. Education for Citizenship and the teaching of democracy in schools was an area of debate in the 1930s and became a dominant concern once more in the 1990s because of worrying levels of apathy, cynicism and ignorance about public life. What should children be taught? Do the education systems of other countries offer useful comparisons? Certainly, in the 1990s the experiences of pupils in the UK in terms of numeracy scores were unfavourably compared with pupil performance in Pacific Rim countries, usually with little or no account being taken of the context within which various school systems operate or of the expectations put upon them. In international surveys, such as the *Third International Mathematics and Science Survey*, UK pupils seem to perform at levels well below those shown in many other industrialised countries and UK commentators demand to know what is 'wrong'. The media appear to revel in tales of schools, pupils and other learners 'failing', however failure is defined. That education should be so newsworthy should not be surprising: after all, a substantial part of the national budget of any country in the world goes on providing education of one form or another. For the same reason, it should be no surprise that education is the stuff of controversy and debate, some of it well informed, some of it simply prejudice. At the time of writing, February 1999, we have on-going debate over standards in schools, widening participation in higher education, lifelong learning and many more domains besides. Indeed, it is hardly possible to watch the news on television or to listen to the radio without hearing some mention of a debate, a controversy or an argument in education.

The purpose of this introductory text is to provide student readers with 'facts' about some of the key issues in contemporary education, but it has also been designed to provoke discussion by offering opinions and perspectives on current debates. It is intended to help the readers to begin thinking about some of the issues in education and to help them (through the suggested further reading at the end of each chapter) to develop their understanding further.

The reader is encouraged to consider education as more than just school and to consider school as more than just a curriculum. We therefore have chapters discussing issues such as the role of ideology in education, the function played by social class, 'race' and gender, the rights of children and responsibilities of adults to see that those rights are respected. Pre-school is considered as a distinct entity, not merely a precursor to compulsory schooling. In the latter stages of the book, we consider some aspects of post-school education, moving from access to higher education through the university to lifelong learning itself which effectively brings us full circle since the tools for lifelong learning are very often acquired (or not) at the level of school or even before.

However, the scene has to be set. Before we can discuss education, it makes sense to have some idea about what it is and what it is for.

From purpose...

The first object of education is not so much to impart knowledge as to inculcate sound principles, form good habits, and to develop all human faculties, physical, moral, and intellectual.

Arthur Hill, *Hints on the Discipline Appropriate to Schools* (1855)

To stimulate life – leaving it free to develop, to unfold – herein lies the first task of the educator.

The Montessori Method (1912)

...education means the enterprise of supplying the conditions which ensure growth, or adequacy of life, irrespective of age...

John Dewey, *Democracy and Education* (1915)

Education is about the empowerment of individuals. It is about discovering, and providing the conditions which encourage the fuller development of abilities and skills in every sphere of human activity – artistic, scientific, social and spiritual.

Brian Simon, *The History of Education: Its Importance for Understanding* (1993)

to study...

...education must be raised to the level of a science which must spring from, and be based upon, the deepest possible knowledge of human nature.

J. H. Pestalozzi, *Address to my House* (1818)

It is, unquestionably, a singular circumstance, that, of all problems, the problem of Education is that, to which by far the smallest share of persevering and rigorous analysis has yet been applied.

Sir Thomas Wyse, *Education Reform* (1836)

and controversy...

Education is an immature discipline and, because of the very strong element of politics, ideology and connection with wider social aims that are always part of the theory of how to teach, that will remain the case and educational theory will always be highly disputable.

Lord Skildelsky, *Hansard* (1993)

The competent teacher of today has a complex pattern of understandings that come partly from training and from reading, but largely from experience and from professional discourse with colleagues...Educational research...informing educational judgements and decisions in order to improve educational action, serves practitioners and policy-makers by contributing to the development of their personal theories...

Michael Bassey, *Creating Education Through Research* (1995)

Is education a discipline worthy of study? Is it a discipline at all?

Chris Woodhead, *Guardian/Institute of Education Debate* (1998)

David Matheson, Northampton
Ian Grosvenor, Birmingham
February 1999

Contributors

Nigel Grant	Emeritus Professor of Education, University of Glasgow
Ian Grosvenor	Lecturer in Education, University of Birmingham
Dave Hill	Lecturer in Education, Nene-University College Northampton
David Limond	Lecturer in Education, Nene-University College Northampton
Jane Martin	Lecturer in Sociology, Nene-University College Northampton
Catherine Matheson	Researcher in Education, City University, London
David Matheson	Lecturer in Education, Nene-University College Northampton
Ian Menter	Head of School of Education, University of North London
Richard Rose	Lecturer in Education, Nene-University College Northampton
Peter Wells	Lecturer in Education, Nene-University College Northampton
J. Eric Wilkinson	Professor of Education, University of Glasgow

Acknowledgements

This book is the result of many years, accumulated between the contributors, of listening to students. We wish to thank them for sharing their knowledge, insights and critical thinking with us. In particular, we thank the students of Nene-University College Northampton, the University of Birmingham, the University of Glasgow, the University of North London and Newman College Birmingham.

Chapter 1

What is education?

David Matheson and Peter Wells

The roots of education are bitter, but the fruit is sweet.

Aristotle

Introduction

For all the evident diversity in our society (however we seek to define it), there are a number of things which all, or virtually all, of us have done or will do in the future, assuming we survive long enough. Among these near-universal activities is that of being educated. We all learned somehow to do the things we do, to know the things we know, to possess the skills we display when the occasion arises. For most of us, when the word *education* is mentioned we feel intuitively that we know what it is. Whether we think automatically of school as education (a point we return to later in this chapter and in the final chapter of this volume) or we cast our thoughts into non-school domains, we still have the notion that we know what is education. The aim of this chapter is to look into some of the meanings that can be attached to the word *education* and to take a few of the logical steps beyond asking what education is and look at what education is for.

Some thoughts on theories

The definitional problems of any concept arise from, or are illuminated by, the theory or theories which seek to underpin that concept. The theory may have been constructed as the concept developed or it may have been elaborated during or after the event. In the case of education, theories have been used to describe and define past practice with a view to informing future practice. But, before proceeding further, it is perhaps helpful to spend a moment on looking at the notion of theory itself.

The simplest sort of theory is the basic personal theory which is really just a notion based on some personal experience, e.g. 'every time I leave my umbrella at home, it rains'. There is actually no causal link between the two phenomena but superficially there may appear to be. On a more serious level, we have descriptive and prescriptive theories. A *descriptive* theory is a scientific theory. An example is the Theory of Evolution (strictly speaking, it should be theories since there are a few different ones). There is no absolute proof that evolution ever happened, rather there is strong evidence that, out of all the possible ways for the biosphere to have got to where it is at this moment, the most likely is through an evolutionary process. The scientific theory of this kind describes what likely happened. 'If I drop a stone in the Earth's gravitational field, it will fall' is an illustration of the Theory of Gravity. Where you can repeat an experiment and always get the same result, then a theory may become a Law. There is of course the problem of just how objective science is and how similar two results must be to be judged the same, but these we must leave as interesting tangents but tangents just the same.

In Social Sciences, theories tend to be *prescriptive*. In other words, the theorist sets out various conditions and argues that, if these are fulfilled, then a particular result will ensue. One might argue that if every child attended a comprehensive school then greater social cohesion should result. This would be a simple example of a prescriptive theory. The strength of the theory would be dependent on the evidence given to back up my claim. As we shall see in the course of this book, there are many theories concerning education. First, however, we need to look at some of the definitional problems surrounding the concept of education.

Defining education

The definitional problems surrounding education are immense and we can do little more than scratch the surface here. However this will at least cast some light on the diversity of definitions which exist in the literature and we shall indicate some of the problems with each.

Firstly, there is the 'plastic' sense of *education*; in other words, it is flexible in its use. The term is used sociologically in the sense of bringing a person to adopt the customs of a society or to alter his/her interactions with that society. It can also be used institutionally, in that whatever happens in a school, college or university is education. This institutional sense brings its own immediate difficulties.

It is a commonplace that the terms *school* and *education* are used interchangeably, although, as Abbs remarks, 'education and school can refer, and often do refer, to antithetical activities' (Abbs 1979: 90). For Illich, school is the antithesis of education and one of the main functions of school is to provide custodial day care for young people (Illich 1986). The synonymous use of school and education is however hardly surprising when we consider that most of us will have experienced in schools what is arguably the most important part of our formal education. After all, it is there that we tend to have learned to read, we have developed our skills in social interaction, we have encountered authority which does not derive from a parent and we have been required to conform to sets of rules, some of which might have been explained, some of which may not. School leaves its mark on us and on our personal conception of education but this risks rendering us at least myopic to other possibilities.

Much of the literature on learning and education also proceeds from the standpoint that we *know* what education is and then carries on to discuss it in terms of an absent definition. For an example of the logical difficulties which can result we need only look to the UNESCO report Learning to Be (Faure *et al.* 1972) which sets the scene for much of the lasting debate on lifelong education. For their first forty pages or so, Faure *et al.* implicitly assume that education equals formal learning (*school* in an American sense) and, having discussed other points, suddenly condemn the very dogma they earlier appeared to accept.

Cyril Houle, with a measure of circumspection characteristic of his writing, defines education as:

> The process by which individuals (alone, in groups or in institutional settings) seek to improve themselves or their society by increasing their skill, their knowledge, or their sensitiveness. Any process by which individuals, groups or institutions try to help individuals improve themselves in these ways. (Houle 1972: 231)

Cropley (1979) comments that 'education... focuses on the experiences which influence learning' and this illustrates in its very woolliness just how difficult it is to pin down a definition of education without stumbling into the difficulties which we discuss below with regard to R. S. Peters' somewhat more developed and highly influential definition of education.

The looseness of the definitions of Cropley and Houle is remarkable but it is also remarkable that they are sufficiently wide as to encompass just about any activity in which one seeks to learn. This last point is perhaps quite critical. We are, as is developed a little further in the last chapter in this volume, effectively learning machines. We learn all the time. Therefore to avoid tautology, we must include intentionality, or at least purpose, in any definition.

Lawson writes that:

> A concept of 'education' which includes... learning within the home, the neighbourhood, from the mass media and from recreational agencies (etc)... is loose and lacking in 'cutting edge'... What we call 'education' can be regarded as planned, intentional preparation, it is an aid to coping, a way of short-circuiting personal experience by drawing upon the accumulated experience of others. (Lawson 1982: 47–8)

Taken to its logical conclusion, this argument would admit only formal education. Any form of unplanned learning is excluded from the concept of education. Thus the very essence of scientific discovery is excluded.

Contrary to popular belief, the discoverer in science rarely does so by methodical plodding, setting goals and attaining them, i.e. by what Lawson would term education. Instead s/he proceeds by intuitive leaps and by failing to attain goals. A case of the first is Einstein, much admired by certain logical positivists, and of the second, Michelson and Morley. These latter set out to find the speed of the medium through which light was thought to travel (the ether) and ended up by making the crucial discovery that the ether does not exist. In neither case would Lawson admit that 'education' had taken place. So we might learn from our mistakes, but, for Lawson, they can never educate us! However, as Lawson (1975) himself says, to call an activity or process 'educational' is typically to vest it with considerable status. This is exemplified by the proliferation of terms such as:

- liberal education
- lifelong education
- moral education

- vocational education
- multicultural education
- intercultural education

The list is endless. For our purposes, it is worthwhile considering whether *education* changes with these prefixes or whether there is something stable about the very idea of education.

What follows is an attempt to introduce a degree of stability around the term. This conceptualisation will acknowledge that *education* can be seen as something that is *achieved* and something that is indicative of a *process*. In other words, *education* has two components: the end and the means used to attain it. It is not simply an end-product or a qualification; it is also the manner in which this is attained.

Peters asserts that 'education implies that something worthwhile is being or has been intentionally transmitted in a morally acceptable manner' (Peters 1966: 25). Leaving aside for the moment the notion of intentionality which we have mentioned above, Peters' statement clearly begs a number of obvious questions:

(a) To what does 'something' refer?

(b) What criteria does one use to ascertain whether this/these something(s) are valuable or worthwhile?

(c) What has morality got to do with this? What would (not) count as morally acceptable?

The 'something'

For Peters, the 'something' refers to knowledge and understanding (and may be argued to include also skills and attitudes). This in turn leads us to question the distinction between knowledge and understanding and we might also ask why the 'something' does not *just* concern knowledge. In passing, it will be helpful to distinguish between information and knowledge. To illustrate this, let us consider the Internet. This is probably the largest stock of information ever made available in the entire history of humanity. What is manifestly lacking from the Internet however is structure. Individual parts may have their own structure but the lack of overall structuration is evident immediately one tries to do a search of Internet sites. It is up to the user to apply a structure, to take what is needed and to assimilate it into existing structures of knowledge which s/he has in his/her head.

In this way, the Internet offers information (and vast quantities of it). It is for the user to create knowledge from it. An educative process, by Peters' argument, has structure built into it. It is not merely the transmission of snippets, or even large lumps, of information, but portions of cohesive wholes.

Knowledge consists of several components. Most notably these consist in their turn of: knowing *how* to do things and knowing *that* certain things exist or are true or have happened and so on. *Understanding* takes us beyond simply knowing and into the realms where we become better equipped to grasp underlying principles, are able to explain why things are the way they are or why they happen the way they do, and so on.

The role of knowledge and understanding in defining education becomes even more crucial when one considers Peters' view on what it means to be educated (see Barrow and Woods 1995: Chapter 1). For Peters, becoming educated is an asymptotic process: we can move towards it but we can never fully attain it. There are echoes here of the debates surrounding lifelong learning and lifelong education which are dealt with in Chapter 13.[1]

Becoming educated carries with it a number of notions such as the acquisition of *depth* whereby a person understands (increasingly) the underlying principles within an 'area of knowledge'. The educated person will acquire *breadth* in the sense that s/he will develop a cognitive perspective *within* an area of knowledge and *between* areas of knowledge. This implies the creation of linkages across the area of knowledge and into areas which may adjoin or not. This not only serves to distinguish knowledge from information but serves to encourage the adoption of differing perspectives on the same domain (an almost essential prerequisite to creative problem-solving).

An area of knowledge is, by definition, not an amorphous mass but has certain rules which bind it together. In this view of education, the educated person has to abide by these rules when acquiring knowledge, when handling knowledge and when using knowledge. To take one example, when learning another language, one accepts that the grammar and syntax of that language are rules to be obeyed (as best one can) if one wishes to actually communicate in that language. Failure to obey the rules will make communication difficult, if not altogether impossible. Against this has to be set the notion that fundamental creativity often comes about when the accepted rules in an area of knowledge are bent or ignored and a new, revised set has to be put in place. However, as we have seen, in some cases at least, creativity may be accidental and hence not strictly an educational act. There is also the argument whereby the act of creation may reveal underlying rules which supersede the old ones. In this case, the old rules are not rendered invalid; the new ones merely refine and develop them.

Educationally worthwhile and worthless knowledge

There are various criteria we might use to mark out *educationally* worthwhile or valuable knowledge from that which is worthless. We might do this in terms of need but in doing so one must take care not to confuse *needs* with *wants*. What I want is not necessarily what I need and vice versa. Again, it is a matter of perspective and relative importance. With this in mind, needs can be defined in terms of societal needs or individual needs. The question arises as to whether the needs of society are necessarily compatible with the needs of the individual. The answer one gives is very much contingent on one's view of the social goal of education and whether one views society as composed of individuals or whether one sees individuals subsumed into society. These notions are further developed later in this chapter and in later chapters in this volume.

There is also the cultural aspect to knowledge to consider. Whether we seek cultural replication, maintenance or renovation or even replacement will play a major role in one's definition of educationally worthwhile knowledge. Our view, not only of the society we have now, but also of the society we want to have, is critical both in determining educationally worthwhile knowledge and in determining what counts as knowledge at all. This is exemplified, in all too many parts of the world, by the way in which some minority (and sometimes even majority[2]) languages have been proscribed in schools. This happened, for example, to Welsh, Scottish Gaelic, Scots, Swiss and French patois, Breton, Catalan to name but a few cases in Europe. These languages were effectively designated as educationally (and often politically) unacceptable knowledge in often vicious bids to extirpate them.

Education as a moral enterprise

Peters contends that education must be conducted in a morally acceptable manner. If there were consensus as to what constitutes morality then this exigency would present few, if any, problems. Unfortunately in our present society we see what are termed moral values being challenged on a regular basis. No longer is the teacher seen, if ever s/he were, as an absolute authority on moral matters and this is the case across the whole range of teaching and learning. Our society increasingly sees itself as multicultural (as indeed it has been since the dawn of recorded history – see Grant 1997) and, as such, recognises that there can exist a multiplicity of value systems within one society. This poses the major problem of defining 'morally acceptable'. There are, however, some points of agreement within our society that certain 'educational' methods are simply unacceptable. At the extreme this precludes inflicting physical pain as a means of encouraging learning. Yet it was only in 1985 that corporal punishment was finally outlawed in state schools in the UK. While in theory in its latter years this punishment was reserved for recalcitrant miscreants, in practice it could be used, and was used, as an 'aid' to learning whereby, for example, a pupil might be hit for not spelling a word correctly.[3] Moral torture in the form of denigration, however officially decried, still continues as a not uncommon means of pupil regulation. This can range from sarcasm to denigration of speech patterns and the learners' cultural roots.

The literature, however, tends to highlight *indoctrination* as an immoral means of encouraging learning. Indoctrination is defined as the intentional implantation of unshakeable beliefs regardless of appeals to evidence (Barrow and Woods 1995). Indoctrination is seen as running counter to the very idea of education as it 'necessarily involves lack of respect for an individual's rationality [and hence] is morally unacceptable' (Barrow and Woods 1995: 80). These same writers illustrate their opposition to indoctrination by means of an imaginary Catholic school where all the teachers endeavour to have the pupils wholeheartedly and unequivocally share their belief in Catholicism. The fact that Barrow and Woods demonstrate some remarkable ignorance about Catholicism[4] is beside the point. Their focus is on major areas of belief, on whole-life beliefs, on what one might term *macro*-beliefs. What about the lesser ones, the *meso*-beliefs and the *micro*-beliefs? How did we learn that science is objective? That experts are to be trusted? That reading is a necessary prerequisite for any modern society? It does not demand much imagination to determine a welter of beliefs which we usually hold unshakeably and which have been intentionally transmitted to us. There is also the question of the level at which intentionality occurs. While a teacher may not intend to indoctrinate his/her learners, it is quite conceivable and indeed likely that the socio-political system within which that teacher operates demands that certain values and beliefs be transmitted (this is a theme returned to in the next chapter). If we are not only indoctrinated but also conditioned then perhaps the very thoughts we are capable of thinking are restrained and constrained.

Is it not an example of conditioning that we view mathematics as a linear mode of thinking? If you doubt this linearity then observe how people in general will add up a string of numbers or carry out a division: their personal method is always the same regardless of how appropriate it is to the circumstances or not and is determined by the culture in which they learned how to count.[5] Indeed, one may not be able to conceive that there are alternative ways of carrying out many calculations. In Chapter 10 in this volume Nigel Grant reminds us that we are generally better at identifying when others are indoctrinating. When it happens in our own education system we are more liable to call it 'moral education' or 'citizenship'. The question of moral (un)acceptability remains unanswered.

Perhaps a better question to ask is whether one can avoid *all* indoctrination in an educational process. Can one always present a learner with rationales as to why things are as we say they are? Will one always have learners who are capable of understanding such rationales? How does one rationalise to a three-year-old that to stick one's finger in the fire is not a good idea? By explaining the basic theories of thermodynamics and the interaction between skin and hot surfaces? By slightly scorching the child's finger? By telling the child that it will hurt and hope that one's authority as an adult/parent will be enough to have the child always believe that sticking a finger in the fire is not a good idea? Simply presenting notions as truth is much simpler than explaining them and may be much preferable to demonstrating possible consequences of an action one wishes the learner to avoid.

Explanation demands a level of understanding which may simply not exist in the teacher. However, even rationalising everything might be construed as 'indoctrination', in that one is presenting the learner and encouraging in him/her a pattern of behaviour and hence beliefs as to its acceptability. It seems that the teacher is in a cleft stick if s/he decides to avoid *all* indoctrination. Giving no teaching implies to budding learners either that learning has a low value or that they themselves have. If we offer teaching, we are offering a complete package of beliefs that go with it and implying, if not insisting upon, its acceptability and desirability and hence 'indoctrinating' (Sutherland 1994).

On the other hand, perhaps there is a major argument in favour of critical thinking. Indeed if one's position is that indoctrination *in all its forms and regardless of the intent* is immoral (i.e. if one accepts that Peters' definition of what constitutes education is valid at least in this respect) then the encouragement of critical thinking is essential. Expressed at its least subtle we have Postman and Weingartner's notion of 'crap-detection' whereby the 'crap detector ... is not completely captivated by the arbitrary abstractions of the community in which he (*sic*) happened to grow up in' (Postman and Weingartner 1976: 18). In other words, the crap detector is able to look past the symbolism and theatricals of his/her society and adopt a critical perspective. This is a notion which is most often associated with Paulo Freire and his idea of conscientisation. In dealing with Freire a word of caution is needed: Freire wrote in Portuguese and used the term *consciencização* which, since the Portuguese words for conscience and consciousness are the same, could be translated into English as either *conscience-raising* or *consciousness-raising*, so there is an element of ambiguity about the concept. However, Freire, a gifted linguist and a deeply religious man, was probably aware of this and hence the double meaning is more than likely deliberate.[6]

Conscientisation is a means of empowerment where the learner decides what is to be learned and does so in terms of what is meaningful to his/her own existence. The goal of this education is to make the learner more critically aware of the area under discussion, and hence more critically aware of him/herself and his/her environment. The political implications of such an educational goal and its associated pedagogy are immense. In this view of education, there is no received wisdom and everything is open to question. Nonetheless, the quandary outlined above remains, whereby offering teaching in any shape or form, or not at all, constitutes indoctrination but perhaps the development of the critical faculty is the most moral of options in that it encourages the learner to question even the basic premise upon which the learning experience is based.

Justifying education

Before we proceed to look at the role(s) that education can serve, it is necessary to first look at some justifications for having education at all. There are at least three of these:

Instrumental justification

Instrumental education is where there is a defined extrinsic goal such as a job, a qualification, providing skills needed in the economy. This can include providing for *all* learners a unifying experience – a commonality – that enables them to fit into society. Part of this is the idea that the person who is educated will do better for him/herself and indeed *be* better and that in this manner both the individual and the community will benefit (Hamm 1989: 166). In this light, education is seen as utilitarian. The end, in terms of qualification, acquired knowledge, skills and attitudes, is more important than the means.

Paternalistic [sic] *justification*

From this viewpoint the learner is incapable of making meaningful choices as to what educational experience would be of most benefit to him/her. Nonetheless, the educated see themselves as having a social duty to arrange the educational advancement of the uneducated, on the basis that once the latter are educated they will be grateful and their benefit to society will increase. This is clearly a subdivision of instrumentalism and at first glance seems to apply to young learners much more than to older ones. However, as we see in Chapter 13, there is a certain element of paternalism in many of the vocationally oriented strands to the lifelong learning debate, especially as we see it manifesting itself in the UK and USA in the various 'Welfare to Work' programmes which are being developed. There is the apparent notion that the government agency concerned somehow knows better than the unemployed person what that person needs in terms of skills in order to secure a new employment. An underlying idea in paternalism is that without intervention then educational experiences are unlikely to occur. This carries a clear notion of compulsion which, while we accept that younger people *require* education, has somewhat sinister overtones when applied to adults who, after all, are supposed to be responsible for their actions and capable of making their own decisions.

Intrinsic justification

With the intrinsic justification one does not need to justify education at all. Education and being educated are self-evidently good and desirable. Indeed as soon as one begins to pose questions about the value, purpose, scope, scale of education, etc. one is using the very 'things' that one is seeking to justify, namely, education. One is, for example, manipulating knowledge and understanding in order to frame reasons for and against a position. This kind of argument is either circular or incoherent. Hence, education is self-justifying.

What is education for?

What education is for is clearly dependent on how we choose to define education; how we choose to justify it and then how we determine the relationship between education and the society in which it operates. For the purposes of this section where we look at some of the social goals of education, we shall concentrate on the formal domain. Non-formal education and some issues arising from it are dealt with in the last chapter of this volume. Formal education, incidentally, is above all associated with school, further education and higher education. It tends to aim, at least at some levels, at a qualification and is often associated in the public mind with younger people. Non-formal education requires no entrance qualifications, may result in no exit qualifications and is more usually associated with adults. The boundaries between formal and non-formal education were never very strict and are becoming even more blurred as time goes on.

Since time immemorial, formal education has been used with a social goal in mind. Every society seeks to replicate itself and finds ways of transmitting what it considers worthwhile to its young and sometimes its not-so-young citizens. In Ancient Greece, for example, the Spartans used a formal school system to instil into their young men the ideas of absolute obedience to their military commanders, extreme courage and resistance to pain as well as, what were for the time, some of the most advanced notions of military strategy. The young women were trained in domestic arts and motherhood. By the same token, it was not uncommon for commentators to complain, as did Seneca during the Roman Empire, that 'we are training children for school, not for life'. From this it becomes clear that it has been held for a very long time that school *ought* to have a social function and that this social function has not always been clear and well-defined.

Since the Reformation, at least, the idea that formal education can be used to reproduce society, mould society or create a new society has been widely discussed and written about in the West. The Reformers sought to create a society based around the *reading* of the Bible which distinguished them from their Roman Catholic predecessors who emphasised the *interpretation* of the Bible given by the Old Church. The social upheaval of the Reformation was accompanied by attempts to literally create a new society based on a literate population. To this end, John Knox (1560), in his *First Book of Discipline*, proposed the creation of schools in every centre of population whose aims would be not only to teach basic skills such as reading and writing but also to act as a means whereby the more able boys and girls would learn sufficiently to allow entry to higher education. In this way, the intelligentsia would be kept in contact with the rest of the population and the upper echelons of society would be revitalised by new blood. This is similar, at least on a superficial level, to the ideas of the Italian communist leader, Antonio Gramsci (1891–1937), which are also discussed in Chapters 2 and 7.

Gramsci divided society effectively into those who lead and those who follow. The leaders are the bourgeoisie, the followers are the subaltern classes. This, incidentally, is at odds with some other Marxist writers who, while acknowledging the role of the bourgeoisie, place a ruling class over it. Gramsci questioned how and why the bourgeoisie could, according to him, maintain their grip on power when they were numerically inferior to the subaltern classes. The answer, decided

Gramsci, lay in formal education and in the concept of *hegemony*. He held that the bourgeoisie constructed school in such a way as to align it with their own cultural norms and expectations while simultaneously alienating the subaltern classes. In this respect, he maintained that traditional intellectuals, who had come through such a system, were organic to the bourgeoisie and would, in consequence, work consciously or unconsciously for its maintenance. This point of view has been repeated in various forms for many years.

Hegemony literally means power. In Gramscian terms, it refers to the relations engendered by power and most especially the role played by the oppressed in collaborating in their own oppression. 'It seems essential to Gramsci's notion of hegemony that the implication of rule by physical coercion, which the notion of dictatorship commonly entails, is absent' (Entwistle 1979: 12). Rather, hegemonic direction is by moral and intellectual persuasion. There is not enough space here to develop fully the notion of hegemony. But to help in understanding, try to consider the forces which control your life and the means by which this control is exercised – the concept of guilt may be a good starting point.

Hegemony is not static. It is part of a dynamic process which does not eliminate dissent. Often this is far from being the case. Indeed one of Gramsci's propositions is that hegemony acts to allow an appearance of liberty in order to absorb dissenting elements. Dissenters can serve to revitalise ideas, provided their actions are limited by the prevailing culture.

It is commonly asserted, especially by left-wing writers, that school exists to reproduce the present class structure. In this respect, the upward social mobility of a few is an example of the dynamism present in hegemony. The rise of a few not only gives hope to the rest that they might also rise, but also makes those that fail more likely to blame themselves. This, in any case, is the theory. The extent of its truth is open to debate.

Gramsci considered the structure and content of the schools which were producing the bourgeoisie. He noted a general absence of progressive methods (such as those of John Dewey and Maria Montessori – the latter was influenced by the former and in turn has been one of the greater influences on primary school pedagogy in the Western world). He observed the role played by Latin and Greek as means of developing logical thought and as means of developing in future bourgeoisie a sense of their own culture and history. The worker, for his/her part would have roots in technology and science in the Gramscian scheme of things. At the centre of the programme is history since 'the individual is a précis of the past' (Entwistle 1979: 41). He insisted that in order to know oneself one must know where one came from. One must also 'know others, their history, the successive efforts they have made to be what they are, to create the civilisation they have created and which we seek to replace with our own' (Gramsci in Entwistle 1979: 41). The acknowledgement of the contribution which bourgeois culture might make goes much further: 'Proletarian culture must be the result of the natural development of the stores of knowledge which mankind has accumulated under the yoke of capitalist society, landlord society and bureaucratic society' (Gramsci in Entwistle 1979: 44).

An important point which distinguishes Gramsci from most other left-wing writers on education is that he conceives of education as a job of work. Indeed he went as far as to insist that all education was vocational (Forgacs 1988).

For Gramsci, then, education was a form of social engineering which served to keep one group of people in dominant positions and another group in subordinate positions. The idea of using education for social engineering dates back at least to the nineteenth century when Robert Owen (1835) stated in his *New View of Society* that:

> Any general character, from the best to the worst, from the most ignorant to the most enlightened, may be given to any community, even to the world at large, by the application of proper means; which means are to a great extent at the command and under the control of those who have influence in the affairs of men. (Owen [1835] 1965: 85)

It is important to underline here that *character* refers not to individuals but to the communities that they form. The essential point however is that for Owen education had the power to shape collections of individuals into communities and to determine the nature of those communities. In other words, education has a major socialising function. This theme is taken up by Durkheim for whom 'education consists of the methodical socialisation of the young generation' (Durkheim 1956: 71). Durkheim also sees education as a means for social reproduction:

> Education, far from having as its unique or principle object the individual and his interests, is above all the means by which society perpetually recreates the conditions of its existence. (Durkheim 1956: 123)

This was the educational *status quo* which Gramsci recognised at his time but which he saw could be changed into a movement towards social renovation.

Formal education serves many functions besides those outlined above. It contains examinations of various kinds which serve to decide, in part at least, the choice of next destinations the learner can move on to. Depending on one's perspective, these can be seen as an opportunity for social mobility or as a means for further entrenching social divides and further ossifying the existing social structure. Formal education may liberate or enslave, expand horizons or confirm feelings of personal failure. These notions are dealt with in some depth in Chapter 7. But let us note that formal education is seen as a right but seldom as a privilege despite general consensus that it is essential in order for a person to learn how to function within our society.

In essence, this chapter has been about ideas regarding education and its purpose. Ideas when formalised into practice naturally have material impacts and some of these are picked up in later chapters. A negative perspective on such an impact is given by Common (1951) who presents us with perhaps the most cynical view of formal education as social control:

We learn reading and boredom, writing and boredom, arithmetic and boredom, and so on according to the curriculum, till in the end it is quite certain you can put us in the most boring job there is and we'll endure it. (Common in Meighan 1986: 75)

A positive perspective on the impact of education was given by Helvétius (1715–71) who claimed 'l'éducation peut tout' ('education can do everything') (Larrain 1979:25).

Suggested further reading

There is a vast literature concerning the topics we have discussed in this chapter. However a few texts stand out as especially suitable for the debutant. On the philosophical side there are Barrow and Woods (1995) and Walker and Soltis (1992) who introduce the reader to a wide variety of concepts in the philosophy of education without getting lost in jargon. The latter duo include a brief but fairly complete account of Freire and his conscientisation, although Freire (1972) is a clear and lucid account of the ideas behind conscientisation. Sociologically two texts stand out. Most recent is Meighan and Siraj-Blatchford (1998) which adopts a themed approach while Blackledge and Hunt (1993) is arranged according to major theories and theorists and takes the reader from Durkheim through various Marxisms to the micro-interpretive approach.

Notes

1 Peters, incidentally, uses the notion of the educated person to illuminate his understanding of what education is. However, this brings its own problems. If we consider the two present writers: one philosophises better than the other, one speaks French better than the other (to name but two educational differences between them). On this basis, which is the more educated? The question is not so much unanswerable as depending on the perspective adopted and the relative importance attached to these attributes.

2 *Majority* is a very relative term. In the UK, English speakers are in the majority but they are very much in the minority in Europe, however we want to define *Europe*, for this too is a relative term: do we mean the *European Union*? If so, then what about Switzerland and Norway? If Europe is that part of the world west of the Urals which sits on the European Continental Shelf (a traditional definition of Europe) then what about Iceland? The Icelanders *consider* themselves European and yet their country is a volcanic island in the middle of the Atlantic and very definitely *not* on the European Continental Shelf. Similarly, minority is relative. Both terms can also be considered in terms of power. See Gramsci's notion of hegemony later in this chapter and elsewhere in this book.

3 This was common practice in the primary school which one of the present writers attended in the 1960s.

4 This they do, among other things, by insisting that Catholics believe that the Pope is infallible (p.70). The reality is that the Pope is held under the doctrine of infallibility to be able to make infallible statements under certain circumstances and only on matters of doctrine.

5 British division is conducted in a manner often incomprehensible to those who learned to divide in the French manner. Similarly, Russian multiplication differs from the manners of multiplying in Western Europe. Regardless of the method, the answer is always the same.

6 Thanks for this information are due to Professor Emeritus Pierre of the University of Geneva who worked with Freire in Brazil and remained in contact with him until the end of the latter's life.

Bibliography

Abbs, P. (1979) *Reclamations*. London: Heinemann.

Barrow, R. and Woods, R. (1995) *An Introduction to the Philosophy of Education*. London: Routledge.

Blackledge, D. and Hunt, B. (1993) *Sociological Interpretations of Education*. London: Routledge.

Durkheim, E. (1956) *Education and Sociology*. New York: The Free Press.

Entwistle, H. (1979) *Antonio Gramsci: Conservative Schooling for Radical Politics*. London: Routledge.

Faure, E. *et al.* (1972) *Learning To Be*. Paris: UNESCO.

Forgacs, D. (ed.) (1988) *A Gramsci Reader*. London: Lawrence & Wishart.

Freire, P. (1972) *The Pedagogy of the Oppressed*. Harmondsworth: Penguin.

Grant, N. (1997) 'Intercultural education in the United Kingdom', in Woodrow, D. *et al. Intercultural Education: Theories, Policies and Practice*. Aldershot: Ashgate.

Hamm, C. M. (1989) *Philosophical Issues in Education*. New York: Falmer Press.

Houle, C. (1972) *The Design of Education*. San Francisco: Jossey Bass.

Illich, I. (1986) *Deschooling Society*. Harmondsworth: Pelican.

Larrain, J. (1979) *The Concept of Ideology*. London: Hutchinson.

Lawson, K. H. (1975) *Philosophical Concepts and Values in Adult Education*. Nottingham: University of Nottingham.

Lawson, K. H. (1982) *Analysis and Ideology: Conceptual Essays on the Education of Adults*. Nottingham: University of Nottingham.

Meighan, R. (1986) *A Sociology of Educating*, 2nd edn. London: Cassell.

Meighan, R. and Siraj-Blatchford, I. (1998) *A Sociology of Educating*, 3rd edn. London: Cassell.

Owen, R. [1835](1965) *A New View of Society and Report to the County of Lanark* (Gatrell, V. A. C. (ed.) Harmondsworth: Pelican.

Peters, R. S. (1966) *Ethics and Education*. London: Allen and Unwin.

Postman, N. and Weingartner, C. (1976) *Teaching as a Subversive Activity*. Harmondsworth: Pelican.

Sutherland, M. (1994) *Theory of Education*. Harlow: Longman.

Walker, D. F. and Soltis, J. F. (1992) *Curriculum and Aims*. New York: Teachers' College Press.

Chapter 2

Ideology in education in the UK
Catherine Matheson and David Limond

To ideologues one must attribute all the misfortunes which have befallen France.

Do you know what fills me most with wonder? The powerlessness of force to establish anything ... In the end the sword is always conquered by the mind.

Napoleon Bonaparte

Introduction

Every concept in education has varying and various interpretations but perhaps none more so than ideology. As this chapter will show, it is used in a variety of senses and to a variety of ends. To do this, we begin with a discussion of the concept of ideology and show how it has had multiple meanings from the time it was first coined. We then move on to discuss ideology in education and show some of the types of ideology that are used in understanding education, before illustrating some of these types.

The concept of ideology

Ideology is a 'highly ambiguous concept' (Meighan and Siraj-Blatchford 1998: 179), a 'most equivocal and elusive concept' (Larrain 1979:13) which has many meanings and usages and can be conceived either negatively and critically as a 'false consciousness' or positively as a 'world-view'. The former has a restricted meaning and tends to be used in a pejorative manner to describe a set of undesirable and even distorted beliefs, while the latter has a looser meaning and is used by philosophers and social scientists in neutral and analytical way. Ideology can also be viewed as a subjective psychological phenomenon emphasising the role of individuals and groups or as a more objective social phenomenon 'impregnating the basic structure of society' (Larrain 1979:14). Ideology can also be seen either, restrictively, as part of, or more loosely, as equal to, the whole of the cultural sphere or ideological superstructure of society.

The word 'ideology' originated with that group of *savants* or intellectuals in the

French Revolution who were entrusted by the Convention of 1795 with the founding and management of a new centre of revolutionary thought. These people were located within the newly established *Institut de France* which was committed to the ideas of the French Enlightenment and thus the practical realisation of freedom of thought and expression (Lichtheim 1967).

In its original sense, the word 'ideology' was first used in 1796 by the French philosopher Destutt de Tracy, a member of the *Institut de France* and one of the directors of the highly influential French literary review *Mercure de France*. It was, in the words of one of the *Mercure*'s regular contributors, Joseph-Jérôme Le François de Lalande, nothing more than a name for the 'science of ideas, their rules and their origins' (Lalande in Rey and Rey-Debove 1990: 957). Deriving ideas from sensations Destutt de Tracy undertook to study the 'natural history of ideas' in his *Eléments d'idéologie* (1801–15). He wanted to unmask the historicity of ideas by tracing their origins and setting aside metaphysical and religious prejudices but also wanted this unmasking to reveal a true and universal knowledge of human nature (Hall 1978). Ideology was presented as a science and set in opposition to prejudice and false beliefs because scientific progress was possible only if these could be avoided.

From the start, however, ideology was to have pejorative connotations, one reason being because de Tracy and those who practised it, the ideologues, were concerned with two logically incompatible concepts of 'ideology': the relation between history and thought and the promotion of 'true' ideas which would be true regardless of the historical context. Following Helvétius, who believed that education could do everything, the ideologues shared his enthusiasm for education (Larrain 1979). After the years of revolution they wanted to educate the French people and above all the young people so that a just and happy society could be established. De Tracy wanted his book to be a study programme for youngsters and explicitly acknowledged that a motive for writing it was the new law (1801) introducing public education.

The other reason for the pejorative connotation of ideology was Napoleon who was the first to use ideology in a truly negative sense. Initially he shared the objectives and goals of the *Institut de France* and even became an honorary member in 1797 (Lichtheim 1967). The *Institut* then facilitated Bonaparte's accession to power, which he achieved in 1799, by helping him win the support of the educated middle-class (Hall 1978). However, he abandoned the ideologues in 1803 when he signed his Concordat with the Church and deliberately set out to destroy the core of the *Institut*, the liberal and republican ideas of which greatly influenced the educational establishment. After the defeat in Russia in 1812, Napoleon then turned on them and attributed all of France's misfortune to the unrealistic, doctrinaire and ignorant of political practice 'ideologists' as he disparagingly called them (Lichtheim 1967).

It is from this pejorative use of ideology as an undesirable or misguided set of ideas that many modern uses of the word have grown. Continuing this tendency,

Marx and Engels used ideology pejoratively to mean a false belief or illusion. In *The German Ideology*, written in 1845–7 but only published in 1927, Marx and Engels, although not clearly defining the concept, use ideology to deride the proposition of the belief in the power of ideas to determine reality. For Marx [and Marxists] ideology was thus often seen as an attempted justification of a distorted set of ideas which consciously and/or unconsciously concealed contradictions in the interests of the dominant class or of a group and served to maintain disproportionate allocation of economic and political power to the ruling class or dominant groups (Marx and Engels [1845–7] 1970). Elsewhere Marx uses the term less pejoratively and gives a sociological interpretation of ideology (Marx [1859] in Meighan and Siraj-Blatchford 1998) where ideology can be defined as a broad interlocked set of ideas and beliefs about the world held by a group of people operating at various levels in society and in various contexts and which is demonstrated in their behaviour. This adds to the ambiguity of the concept of ideology not only because of the competing definitions but also because the set of beliefs operates with several layers of meaning (Meighan and Siraj-Blatchford 1998).

After a period of disuse the word was revived with the publication in 1927 of Marx and Engels previously unpublished *The German Ideology* which reinforced the Marxist and central sociological tradition view of ideology as 'distortion of reality' (Bullock *et al.* 1988). For Gramsci, and other Marxists, however, ideology is explained in terms of its social role, it is neither true nor false but 'the "cement" which holds together the *structure* [in which economic class struggle takes place] and the realm of the complex superstructures' (Hall 1978: 53).

For our purposes we shall consider ideology in its broad sense of set of beliefs as opposed to the narrow sense of a set of undesirable or misguided beliefs. Within contemporary sociology one distinguishes between 'particular' ideologies concerning specific groups and 'total' ideologies concerning a total commitment to a way of life. Every ideology is composed of three ingredients: an invariable mythological structure, an alternating set of philosophical beliefs and a historically determined chosen group of people (Feuer 1975). Where ideologies exist in competition there are several outcomes: domination, incorporation and legitimation. In the first instance, we have cultural domination or hegemony. In the second, we have radical ideas incorporated into the traditional ideology. In the last instance, an ideology may achieve acceptance of its beliefs by direct repression or by more indirect means of institutional control such as those of the media, education, religion, law or economy (Meighan and Siraj-Blatchford 1998).

Ideology, knowledge and the curriculum

A curriculum as a package of ideas, together with the manner in which it is delivered (its pedagogy) certainly fits the bill as an ideology. Curriculum heritage is the product of a philosophical tradition which can be traced through historical and contemporary curriculum practice, and in which we find the European triad of humanism (Plato, Erasmus and Locke), rationalism (Plato and Descartes) and naturalism (Rousseau). The first two elements of the triad underline respectively the importance of the human character and especially the feelings and the importance of reason but with both understanding is sought by submission of the individual to an external body of knowledge, while the third seeks understanding in the private, concrete and the natural (McLean 1995). As in much in ideology, the triad's elements are not mutually exclusive.

It is these first two approaches which have dominated curriculum development across Europe, and, as a consequence of European influence, across much of the world. In France there is the rational encyclopaedic educational ideology with state prescription of national occupational needs. In this collectivist tradition upper secondary schooling is subordinated to economic and social planning and general and vocational education are linked in content and control (collectivism). In the pluralist tradition we move towards individualist and humanist approach such as exists in the UK and Germany with a clear separation between general education and vocational training, but in Germany the curriculum is more infiltrated with rational encyclopaedic ideology than in the UK. We also have generalism (as in France and Germany) versus specialism or, some say, élitism in England and to a lesser extent in Scotland (McLean 1995). Naturalism, however, as we shall shortly see, is very present and has been highly influential, especially in primary schools.

Educational ideologies

An educational ideology is any package of educational ideas held by a group of people about formal arrangements for education, typically expressed by contrasting two patterns of opposed assumptions such as teacher-centred and child-centred methods (the *Plowden Report*, DES 1967) or traditional and progressive methods (Bennett 1976). Going beyond dichotomies, Davies (1969) and Cosin (1972) outline four ideologies of education: conservative or elitist which maintains cultural hegemony; revisionist or technocratic which is concerned with vocational relevance; romantic or individualist or psychological which focuses on individual development and derives from the work of Froebel, Herbart, Montessori, Pestalozzi and Piaget; and democratic socialist or liberal tradition or egalitarian which seeks equality of opportunity and the progressive elimination of élitist values (Meighan and Siraj-Blatchford 1998). These categories are not hermetic, nor are they entirely mutually exclusive; they overlap and indeed an educational ideology might belong to several categories simultaneously. Assuming one accepts these categories as valid at all, the category(ies) to which a particular ideology might be assigned is often a matter of perspective.

Any ideology can be compared with others on the basis of a series of theories functioning as part of an aspect of knowledge, learning, teaching resources, organisation, assessments and aims. The concept of ideology can be used as an analytical tool to compare various patterns of education. Ideologies operate at different conceptual levels and, if categorised into levels of operations, can be compared along the lines of whole education systems, competing ideologies within a national system, ideologies within formal education and ideologies of classroom practice. Ideologies are usually linked with, for example, ideologies of classroom practice being linked to other parts of the educational and political network. The levels at which ideologies operate can be seen nationally in terms of Education Acts; regionally in terms of Local Education Authorities; locally at the levels of educational establishments, rival groups within educational establishment, classroom, teacher/learner interaction, and rival groups within classroom (Meighan and Siraj-Blatchford 1998).

One could also distinguish between ideologies of legitimation or implementation, the former concerning goals, values and ends and the latter the means, and it can be a worthwhile exercise to consider the ideologies outlined below in this light.

Educational ideologies and politics

By definition, education is a political activity, although not necessarily a party political activity. Politics is to do with power and the distribution of power. Education, put simply, is to do with knowledge (in terms of *knowing that* and *knowing how*). If 'knowledge is power' then education is political. If Gramsci's theory of hegemony (see Chapter 1) is accurate, then politics is an educational activity. This does not mean that the one subsumes the other; rather it means that they overlap and have aspects in common.

Nonetheless to speak of an educational ideology is *not* to speak of a party political ideology acted out in an educational context. It is not at all obvious that any particular political ideology, be it party political or not, carries detailed or specific educational implications. There is a general assumption, borne out in fact, of a strong correlation between left-wing politics and support for child-centred pedagogies but this does not necessarily follow. That is to say, it so happens that many on the British left wing have often been attracted to child-centred methods but it has not always been so and it need not ever be so. We can see how it might be otherwise by considering the matter both in theory and in practice. Well before the advent of the child-centred Plowdenism which we discuss below there was the more general progressive movement (or ideology) in education which was especially strong in the 1910s and 1920s. Amongst its most trenchant critics was the Italian communist Antonio Gramsci for whom all such ideas smacked of naïve romanticism. Gramsci advocated 'Conservative Schooling for Radical Politics' (Entwistle 1979).

For Gramsci it was all very well for parents of children who were marked for social success to indulge them in and through progressivist schooling. But it was surely self-evident that the extended childhood favoured by the progressivists was possible only in cases where wealth and social position purchased and secured liberty. For others it was necessary that schooling be as concentrated an intellectual experience as possible – and thus a disciplined experience. Those who would need to earn their living by industrial or agricultural labour ought not to have their time wasted, but, more than this, if they were to be active players in any campaign for reform or revolution, they must learn as much as possible as quickly as possible. They must be sure to be highly literate – how else were they to know what was being done in their names by those ruling over them? They must be sure to have a detailed understanding of history, politics, economics and allied subjects – how else were they first to understand and then to change their circumstances? They must master the methods of science – how else were they to supplant superstition, fear and ignorance in their lives and in the lives of those around them? There could be no time for 'picking up' such knowledge by indirect means. There could be no time for playful experimentation (Forgacs 1988). Patience may be a virtue but it is a luxury that is not always available nor appropriate. Indeed, the lack of time for playful experimentation was one of the major reasons behind the Soviet Union abandoning in 1931 the very progressive and child-centred Dalton Plan which had been introduced from the USA shortly after the Russian Revolution. The Soviet Union needed to industrialise rapidly and discovery methods with self-directed learning were simply not delivering the expertise quickly enough (Grant 1979).

Clinging to certain political ideologies can lead people to draw conclusions about education but there are few, if any, necessary educational implications in the major political ideologies. Yet, it was political consensus in the closing years of the Second World War that advocated and then brought into being a form of selective secondary school. Selective secondary school is currently associated with right of centre politics and the Conservative Party has been for over a decade one of the most vocal critics of comprehensive schools as conceived in the UK. Yet, in 1967 the Party's leader, Edward Heath, could state that 'it has never been a Conservative principle that in order to achieve (selection or grouping by ability) children have to be segregated in different institutions' (Heath in Finn *et al.* 1978: 176).

Political ideas and ideologies evolve and their expression in educational circumstances evolves also. Indeed the apparently *same* educational ideology can be adopted simultaneously by different political ideologies. This is the case not only with selective and comprehensive secondary schools but also with such concepts as equality of opportunity and the meritocracy. What must be borne in mind, however, is that an educational ideology need not equally apply to the entire education system.

Some examples of educational ideologies

An elitist ideology: the public school ethic

There is perhaps no better illustration of an élitist educational ideology than that which is held to underpin the education of the ruling class in a country. This kind of ideology is important not only for the manner in which it might be held to form the ideas, behaviour and *mores* of the ruling class but also for the impact it has on the education of the 'lower orders'. This can be by mimicking, an aspect seen in the copying of some parts of the public school curriculum and some of ways of conducting an educational experience which occurs not only in mere private (i.e. non-state schools) but also in some state schools. Its impact can also be by contrast: schools which do not wish to be identified with elitism may seek to reject the entirety of the public school ethic without considering whether *any* of it is appropriate to their circumstances. This relates to the adoption and rejection of particular ideologies by particular political groups (and the subsequent rejection of *this* rejection by some members of those very same groups).

Everyone knows something of the public school ethic. Its motto is from Wellington who supposedly had it that 'the battle of Waterloo was won in the playing fields of Eton'; its anthem is a refrain borrowed from the poet Newbolt – 'Play up! play up! and play the game' and its principal values are those of physicality and character. The fact that it does not bear the name *ideology* is perhaps only indicative of the pejorative sense in which that word may be used. As a package of ideas, beliefs and determinants of behaviour, the public school ethic is an ideology in all but name. Nonetheless, it is worth remembering that another word for ethic is philosophy, a term with much more positive, indeed rational, connotations than has ideology. The fact that the public school ethic is an accretion of ideas, values and associated practices which have grown up over time rather than being precisely worked out seems to allow us to say that it is not truly an ethic or a philosophy at all because it lacks the required rigour. However we are stuck with the name so that we can do no more than proceed with caution when applying it.

Public in the sense of taking place not in space rented in private houses but in public buildings, the public schools pre-date the emergence of the British Empire. In one form or another the most distinguished date to the High Medieval period. However it was in the Imperial period that they became most clearly defined and refined their role, nature and ethic.

Two aspects of the public schools' ethic stand out – their favouring of character over intellect and their promotion of physicality. These themes most obviously come together in the fascination with games. Strenuous sporting activity was obviously physical but it was more than that because if you were to 'play the game' and 'keep your head' then it was necessary to develop a certain sort of character. This would be one in which self-control and discipline would be at a premium, where the 'stiff upper lip' would be of the highest currency and orders would be followed to the last. Such a character type as this was of clear imperial advantage. It was well suited to the needs of the military with its concern for discipline allied to a capacity to be uncomplainingly tolerant of inconvenience and even suffering, but equally suited to other forms and aspects of Imperial service from missionary work to exploration and administration. The Empire has effectively gone but the public school ethic endures. It endures in modified form to be sure but it does endure. The public schools survive not just because the public school ethic has a firm and unyielding hold on popular imagination but especially because they continue to educate the ruling class.

Some romantic or psychological ideologies

The romantic or psychological ideology, derived from the naturalism of Rousseau, was central to the establishment of progressive schools and has had considerable influence on some forms of curriculum revision and on the primary schools. Working within this ideology was perhaps the greatest influence upon the modern primary school curriculum: John Dewey who argued against the subservience of the child to a curriculum devised for him/her by adults with its logical division of subject matters and little notice taken of the child's interest. For him, 'the child is the starting point, the centre, the end. His/[her] development, his/[her] growth, is the ideal' (Dewey 1906: 21 in Curtis 1965: 162). This centrality of the child to the schooling process can perhaps be said to have reached its zenith in the UK with the *Plowden Report* (DES 1967).

Although often in bastardised form and often half-heartedly implemented, Plowdenism can be seen as the British, or more specifically English, culmination of the romantic or individualist/psychological tradition. Plowden was arguably a strong influence in British primary classrooms until the advent (in England and Wales) of the National Curriculum with its emphasis on cognitive performance, the generalised movement across the UK away from individualised schooling and the various calls from politicians for schools to get 'back to basics'. To its critics it is a ragbag of pernicious lies and misunderstandings. To its supporters it is a way and a truth which has never been fully tested in practice because it has often been misunderstood or overlaid only very thinly as a veneer on existing practices and principles.

In its own terms, Plowdenism emphasises such things as, 'Learning...[but] not [by]...direct teaching...[and] working harmoniously according to an unfolding rather than a preconceived plan' (Maclure 1973: 313). Plowden's was the pedagogy of learning by doing, being busy, finding out, following one's interests or enthusiasms, the pursuit of 'relevance' to oneself as the essential criterion of intellectual worth in any piece of knowledge and liberty and mobility in the classroom as preparation for (personal and political) liberty and (social and economic) mobility in life. It was influenced by developmental psychology such as that of Piaget. The aim was to find how the child grows and changes, then base all schooling on the needs of those processes because anything else will be counterproductive in practice if not also morally wrong. The metaphors in Plowdenism were all of growth and nurture.

In all, Plowdenism bears a striking resemblance to Montessorism, the theories of Maria Montessori articulated in *The Montessori Method* (1912) and *The Advanced Montessori Method* (1917). The former deals with mentally or socially handicapped children and the latter applies the deriving principles to normal children. In other words, Maria Montessori advocates a psychological method implying that 'the educative process is adapted to the stage of mental development of the child, and to his/her interests and is not wholly subordinated to the necessities of a curriculum or to the teacher's scheme of work' (Rusk 1954: 262). Like that of Plowdenism, Montessori's own child-centred progressive pedagogy with emphasis on freedom and auto-education is associated with the names of Rousseau, Pestalozzi, Froebel, Herbart, Dewey and Piaget. Such a pedagogy aims to replace traditional pedagogy, whereby the teacher maintains discipline and immobility and engages in loud and continual discourse, 'by didactic material which contains within itself the control of errors' and thus 'makes auto-education possible to each child' (Montessori 1912:371). She later added that 'to make the process one of self-education, it is not enough that the stimulus should call forth activity, it must also direct it' (Montessori 1917:71).

Montessori's emphasis on interest as a driving force for the learner finds a modern echo in Malcolm Knowles' (1998) idea of andragogy (although, unlike Montessori, Knowles thought primarily of adult learners). Interest as a motivator has, however, a much longer heritage and was defined as 'the doctrine of interest' by Herbart who derived the idea from Rousseau but expanded upon it (Herbart 1816 in Rusk 1954:210).

Herbart asserts that 'that which is too simple must be avoided' and 'instruction must be comprehensible and yet difficult rather than easy, otherwise it causes *ennui* [boredom]' (Herbart 1901 quoted in Rusk 1954:225). Herbart further asserts that 'the principle of interest braces [pupils] up to endure all manner of drudgery and hard work, the idea being 'of making drudgery tolerable by giving it a meaning' (Adams quoted in Rusk 1954:225). The doctrine of interest, however, is to be found in Plato's *Republic*, Rousseau's *Emile* and Pestalozzi's correspondence. Herbart also advocated the principle of recapitulation or spiral curriculum which is a doctrine common to many educators from Plato to Montessori and Dewey. For Herbart, there is no education without instruction and conversely no instruction which does not educate (Rusk 1954). Paradoxically, for an educational ideologist in the romantic tradition, Herbart ascribes to the teacher a centrality which is largely absent from those whose ideas derived from his (Dewey 1923).

A revisionist ideologist: Herbert Spencer

Herbert Spencer challenged the traditional curriculum and 'liberal education' by classifying the subjects with scientific subjects being seen as most important because the knowledge which enables one to earn a living should come first in the curriculum and literary subjects should occupy the lowest place on the scale' (Curtis 1965). Spencer further asserted that 'education of whatever kind, has for its proximate end to prepare a child for the business of life – to produce a citizen who, while he [she] is well conducted, is also able to make his [her] way in the world' (Spencer 1911 in Curtis 1965:154).

Spencer presents several facets of the doctrine of relevancy (i.e. relevant to the economy and relevant to the learner's future quality of life). The importance of this former facet in educational and economic debate should not be understated. Other than its returning to the forefront of debates with a great frequency (e.g. in Callaghan's 1976 Ruskin College speech), the doctrine begs a great number of questions. How might it be determined *how* a learner is going to earn his/her living? How can we know what economic needs there will be in the future? To what extent does formal education not already instil *pre*-vocational skills? Spencer wrote at a time of economic stability when the future appeared largely to be a direct continuation of the past. Our future now appears much more uncertain (see Chapter 13) but is this reason sufficient to discard Spencer's ideas? Even relevancy to the economy is relative as is discussed at length by White (1997). There are also questions which arise out of the second facet: the business of life also appears to be in mutation but are there underlying skills and values which the learner need acquire in order to be successful (by some measure or other) in the ways of the world? We no longer have the consensual moral frameworks that we arguably had at times in the past. Therefore what skills or values need the learner acquire? And who is to decide these? In sum, to apply the doctrine of relevance, be it to the economy's future (or actual) needs or to the learner's future (or actual) needs, we are obliged to decide who is to decide these needs, on what basis (i.e. on what criteria) and to what end(s). Fundamentally, we need decide what education is for.

Liberal or egalitarian ideology

The democratic intellect

Although most associated with the work of George Elder Davie, as he freely acknowledges, the term *democratic intellect* arises from a remark of Walter Elliot, sometime Conservative Secretary of State for Scotland, who characterised Scotland's post-Reformation and Enlightenment history as being marked by what he called 'democratic intellectualism' (Davie 1961:75). By this he seems to have intended a variety of thoughtful citizenship, a living tradition of reasoned participation and thriving debate. Davie's contribution has been to account for the origins and operation of this twin tendency towards participation (democracy) and reason (intellectualism) by arguing that – until the middle of the nineteenth century at least – the Scottish universities nurtured and promoted a set of highly distinctive academic values. The mechanism of this nurturing and promotion was their concentration on teaching philosophy in a system that only went into decline when forced to change from the 1840s and 1850s (Bell and Grant 1977).

To understand this point fully it is necessary to think of philosophy not as a discreet academic subject but more as an approach or concern. When Davie contends that the Scottish universities valued philosophy above all else he means that – in all subject areas – they demanded and encouraged from students inquiry into issues and ideas or, in more technical language, morals and metaphysics. This is a point perhaps more easily understood by example than in general terms. Thus we may consider Davie's account of Scottish and English interest in classical authors. In English universities (and at the start of the nineteenth century England had only two, while Scotland, with a tenth of England's population, had four) the emphasis was on inculcating a precise – even pedantic – grasp of Latin and Greek grammar. This was to be acquired by learning detailed rules and formulae for correct expression and also by immersion in authors of antiquity the better to learn how to emulate their style. In Scotland by contrast the emphasis was rather more on knowing what these authors had said with a correspondingly reduced concern as to *how* they said it. Insofar as this was the case it was far more acceptable in Scottish universities to read classical authors in translation. The ideas expressed in their words mattered more than the words themselves, thus the Scottish interest was philosophical rather than literary. In other subjects too there was a philosophical tone. What mattered in the study of mathematics was not – as in England and especially at Cambridge which was long famous for its mathematicians – technical mastery of rules, proofs and demonstrations but some grasp of such things as the nature of numbers (do they exist in time and space? if so, how?) and our knowledge of mathematical truths (do we encounter them or in some sense create them?). There was specific teaching of philosophy as a subject in its own right (a compulsory subject indeed) but the weaving of philosophical concerns into all other subjects was of far greater significance. Asking and (if possible) answering philosophical questions was always of prime importance in a system which favoured debate over decision (hence more asking than answering) and enlightenment over erudition (hence more morals and metaphysics than literature and language) (Beveridge and Craig 1989). In many respects, the notion of the Democratic Intellect has much in common with one of the missions which Newman (1852) set for the university: the cultivation of an educated scepticism through learning to philosophise.

Social democracy

In the period 1944 to 1970 educational policy was based upon the ideology of 'social democracy' constructed by three social groups who formed a coalition: the Labour Party (although supported in much of this by the Conservative Party), educationalists working in sociology and economics and the teaching profession. The key features of the ideology of 'social democracy' were: a commitment to educational progress through state policy and a concern with access and equality of opportunity. Reform was via the state (the state being seen as neutral) and was for the benefit of all sections of society, especially the underprivileged. A focus of attention in social democracy was working-class under-achievement and wastage of ability and, as a consequence, the idea of non-selective comprehensive schools slowly emerged. Teachers, for their part, pursued professional status and demanded autonomy and control of the curriculum. The notion was promoted, and accepted, that teachers knew best what was best for their pupils.

A clarion call of social democracy was equality of opportunity in education, a notion fraught with conceptual difficulties. In a simple form, equality of opportunity can be seen as open and fair competition for economic rewards and social privileges. The problems arise when one tries to determine what is open and fair. The way in which this meaning shifted in the UK is demonstrated by the move by socialists from supporting selective secondary schools in the 1940s and 1950s to calling for a total end to selection for secondary school from the 1960s onwards. Both the generalisation of selective secondary school and the abolition of selective secondary school were justified on the grounds of equality of opportunity. However, coupled with equality of opportunity was also equality *per se* (Finn *et al.* 1978). Arguably, equality of opportunity equalises the chances people have to become unequal. It is therefore incompatible with any notion of equality as reducing privilege, except perhaps privilege of birth. Equality of opportunity does however give rise to the notion of the meritocracy whereby everyone has, in theory, the same chances to go as far as their talents will take them. As this inevitably leads to the creation or at least the sustenance of an élite, it is perhaps best described as an élitist ideology hiding away in an apparently egalitarian one. This only goes to show the lack of mutual exclusivity of the four categories of educational ideology mentioned above.

In the 1970s the ideology of social democracy was finally challenged largely because of its failure to promote economic growth and growing concerns about falling standards and indiscipline in schools. James Callaghan's 1976 speech in Ruskin College, Oxford, effectively sounded the death knell for social democracy in education. Callaghan called for more control of teachers and more accountability from schools. Education, he claimed, should be seen as a means for training young people for work. The effect was the official beginning of the process that led into the National Curriculum in England and Wales with its concomitant national testing, OFSTED and the full trappings of direct state control over school (Chitty 1993).

Conclusion

This has only been a brief look at the role of ideology in education and, of necessity, it has been an eclectic look. There is a multitude of other educational ideologies that might equally merit inclusion, but space does not permit this. We have not specifically discussed the ideological precepts which underpin the National Curriculum although some of these are dealt with in other chapters. We have omitted the ideology of the market which has set schools and universities in competition with each other in a bid to attract students and other sources of funding. Other chapters in this volume take up again the theme of ideology in education under different guises. There are educational ideologies based on gender, 'race', social class, age, culture, the nature of learning itself, to name but a few which are touched upon.

It is, however, worth remembering that few, if any, ideologies actually bear the name openly. Rather we have various collections of notions, ideas and beliefs which may apply better to one level of education than to another (and this can mean, for example, applying better to a macro-perspective than to a micro-perspective or apply better to one level than to another) by which not only is behaviour influenced or even determined, but the very ways in which we think about phenomena may themselves be set. In this light, it can be worth wondering why comprehensive *secondary* school can rouse so much passion but comprehensive *primary* school never has. Is this through a rational choice on our part or is it through our internalisation of an ideological precept which precludes the stimulation of heated debates over the possibility of non-comprehensive primary school?

As the development of the social democratic ideology shows us, ideologies are not static. They evolve and they may expire, as did Scottish democratic intellectualism, although arguably this ideology has a few remaining vestiges in the form of the Scottish Ordinary degree which, unlike its English counterpart, is not (usually) a failed Honours degree but a general, as opposed to a specialised, degree. Meritocracy has survived the demise of social democracy while equality of opportunity persists. Whether any of these, or the other ideologies mentioned, were ever true (or valid as the case may be) is another issue but one we shall not pursue. Truth/validity depends on perspective. For its supporters, meritocracy is the hope held out for social mobility. For its detractors, meritocracy is little more than a pernicious lie, whereby a few from humbler origins might be permitted to succeed in order that those that fail blame themselves.

What is important in all these ideologies is not their truth or validity but rather the impact they have had and in some cases continue to have.

Suggested further reading

A good further introduction to educational ideologies is to be found in Meighan and Siraj-Blatchford (1998). Blackledge and Hunt (1985) detail and critique various sociological perspectives and the ideologies within they function. The work of Billig and his colleagues (1988) shows how ideologies operate in practice as more or less consistent packages of ideas (often less rather than more).

Bibliography

Bell, R. and Grant, N. (1977) *Patterns of Education in the British Isles*. London: Unwin Education Books.

Bennett, S. N. (1976) *Teaching Styles and Pupils' Progress*. London: Open Books.

Beveridge, C. and Craig, R. (1989) *The Eclipse of Scottish Culture*. Edinburgh: Polygon.

Billig, M., Condor, S., *et al.* (1988) *Ideological Dilemmas: A Social Psychology of Everyday Life*. London: Sage Publications.

Blackledge, D. and Hunt, B. (1985) *Sociological Interpretations of Education*. London: Routledge.

Bullock, A., Stallybrass, O., Trombley, S. (eds) (1988) *The Fontana Dictionary of Modern Thought*. London: Fontana Press.

Chitty, C. (1993) *The Education System Transformed*. London: Baseline Books.

Cosin, B. (1972) *Ideology*. Milton Keynes: Open University Press.

Curtis, S. J. (1965) *Introduction to the Philosophy of Education*. Foxton: University Tutorial Press.

Davie, G. E. (1961) *The Democratic Intellect: Scotland and her Universities in the Nineteenth Century*. Edinburgh: Edinburgh University Press.

Davies, I. (1969) 'Education and social science', *New Society*, 8 May.

Department of Education and Science (DES) (1967) *Children and their Primary Schools (The Plowden Report)*. London: HMSO.

Dewey, J. (1906) *The School and the Child*. Glasgow: Blackie.

Dewey, J. (1923) *Democracy and Education*. New York: Macmillan.

Entwistle, H. (1979) *Conservative Schooling for Radical Politics*. London: Routledge.

Feuer, L. S. (1975) *Ideology and the Ideologists*. Oxford: Basil Blackwell.

Finn, D., Grant, N., Johnson, R. (1978) 'Social democracy, education and the crisis', in *Centre for Contemporary Cultural Studies On Ideology*. London: Hutchinson.

Forgacs, D. (ed.) (1988) *A Gramsci Reader*. London: Lawrence & Wishart.

Grant, N. (1979) *Soviet Education*. Harmondsworth: Penguin.

Hall, S. (1978) 'The Hinterland of Science: Ideology and the "Sociology of Knowledge"', in Centre for Contemporary Cultural Studies *On Ideology*. London: Hutchinson.

Husén, T. (1974) *The Learning Society*. London: Methuen.

Knowles, M. (1998) *The Adult Learner*. Houston, TX: Gulf Publishing.

Larrain, J. (1979) *The Concept of Ideology*. London: Hutchinson University Library.

Lichtheim J. (1967) *The Concept of Ideology and Other Essays*. New York: Vintage.

McLean, M. (1995) *Education Traditions Compared*. London: David Fulton Publishers.

Maclure, J. S. (1973) *Educational Documents England and Wales 1816 to the Present Day*. London: Methuen.

Marx, K. and Engels, F. [1845–47] (1970) *The German Ideology*. London: Lawrence & Wishart.

Meighan, R. and Siraj-Blatchford, I. (1998) *A Sociology of Educating*, 3rd edn. London: Cassell.

Montessori, M. (1912) *The Montessori Method*. London: Heinemann.

Montessori, M. (1917) *The Advanced Montessori Method*. London: Heinemann.

Newman, J. H. ([1852] (1968 with introduction and notes by M. J. Svaglic)) *The Idea of a University*. New York: Rinehart.

Rey, A. and Rey-Debove, J. (1990) *Le Petit Robert*. Paris: Dictionnaires Le Robert.

Rusk, R. R. (1954) *The Doctrines of the Great Educators*. London: Macmillan.

White, J. (1997) *Education and the End of Work*. London: Cassell.

Chapter 3

Historical patterns in the development of education in England, Wales and Scotland

David Limond

> History should be placed in our memory as the first foundation of learning.
>
> Hugh of St Victor

Introduction

In what follows I shall limit myself to the discussion of British schools in roughly the period from 1870 to the 1990s. Since higher education is discussed in various aspects in Chapters 11 and 12, I shall say nothing further about it. Education can, of course, be construed in a number of fashions from the formal through the non-formal to the informal. For the purposes of this chapter, I shall limit myself to school, that part and form of education of which we are all perhaps most aware and endeavour to give an overview of some of the major issues and debates which arose in the period from 1870 to the 1990s.

The beginnings of state schooling in Britain

The state of educational provision and organisation in Britain in 1870 is not easily summarised or described. In many respects it was confused and contradictory in its nature and the acquisition of formal schooling was, for most, a haphazard business at best. Elementary education was as much as the majority of people could expect but elementary education in the late nineteenth century was not synonymous with primary education as we think of it in the late twentieth century. To say that some stage of a process is primary implies that there will be at least one other stage. After the meal's first course comes the second. In contemporary understanding, primary education prepares for the secondary education which necessarily comes thereafter. Elementary education by contrast was expected and intended to be complete and entire in itself. It was to be elementary both in quantity and quality. The other schools then in operation (known generally as burgh schools in Scotland and grammar schools elsewhere) were also complete in themselves, educating to a higher standard and for a longer time than the elementary schools but not existing to complete or continue the work of those schools. The name *grammar school* suggests clearly the essence of the curriculum in these institutions – Latin grammar.[1] Equally the name burgh school suggests their typical location. They were most often to be found in large towns, usually belonging to the councils running them. However named they all considered themselves the heirs of ancient traditions of classical learning. (A comparable institution in Germany and elsewhere often styled itself with a name, *gymnasium*, [Greek – a place for training] intended to emphasise their links with the world of classical antiquity). Preparing pupils in basic English literacy was the very least of their concerns while it was almost the sole concern of the elementary schools. The true function of grammar schools was to initiate their pupils into classical culture through its languages – most usually Latin – and thus elevate them to the assumed heights of taste and sensibility of the ancient world. At the same time this initiation was expected to impart the greatest possible understanding of the principles of virtue and nobility and the skills of leadership and government.

By 1870 three organisations in particular were involved in the provision of elementary schools – the *British and Foreign School Society* and the *National Society for the Promotion of the Education of the Poor in the Principles of the Established Church*, which both founded in the early years of the nineteenth century, operated in England and Wales while the Church of Scotland was the major provider in Scotland. The British and Foreign Society was funded by donations from non-Conformist churches and the National Society was the educational wing of the Church of England. In the schools of the latter there was strict adherence to the tenets of the Anglican church with little scope for deviation. Parents who were not in communion with the Church of England might send their children to National Society schools but they had to expect that every effort would be made there to convert those children to Anglican ways. As the Reverend William Johnson, Clerical Superintendent of the National Society said in the *Report of the Parliamentary Committee on the State of Education* in 1834: 'I should not think myself justified according to the understood principle and practice on which…the directing committee of the society act, to allow children to go to a dissenting [i.e. non-conformist] place of worship' (Maclure 1973: 29).

Always better financed and, perhaps more importantly, better organised, the National Society was far larger than its rival. Returns from the 1851 Census suggest that there were almost 250 000 pupils attending British and Foreign Society schools but nearly four times as many in those of the National Society. By 1870 there were more than 900 National Society schools in Wales alone as against only 300 operated by the British and Foreign Society. Further, the British and *Foreign* Society – much as its name suggests – was at least as much interested in sending educational missionaries abroad to work in the Empire as it was in making provision for schools in Britain. Its general lack of organisation was thus compounded by its divided attention so that by 1870 the British and Foreign Society, despite being slightly older, was very decidedly the junior player in elementary education provision in England and even in Wales which has long been characterised by its tendency towards non-Conformist religion (Corner 1984).

In Scotland the Church of Scotland had done its best to run a system of elementary schools since the middle of the sixteenth century. These were paid for by local rate payers (heritors) and such payment was a duty enforced by law but they were not state schools in the strictest sense in that the state neither funded nor in any way ran them. But from 1839 when the Privy Council (originally a select group of parliamentarians giving private – privy – advice to the monarch) was given responsibility for overseeing limited grant-in-aid monies for schools in England, Wales and Scotland the state took a greater role in funding schools and a corresponding regime of inspection began. Her Majesty's Inspectors of Schools had initially slim resources for their task – only one inspector was appointed for the whole of Scotland when inspections began in 1840 – but state control and bureaucracy were now established themes in the life of Britain's elementary schools.

The Privy Council's committee with responsibility for education was soon issuing instructions on the running of schools in many major and minor details. In 1851 for example it produced model plans for the construction of new schools which effectively regulated many aspects of their design. In 1860 its various regulatory documents were brought together in a Code, adherence to which was mandatory for those schools receiving state funding and in 1862 this was replaced with a Revised Code. (Although this did not operate in Scotland in its entirety until 1872.) At the heart of the Revised Code was the system of funding known as payment by results. Despite growing increasingly complicated over the years of its operation as more subjects became eligible for inspection, the essence of payment by results was simple. To establish that schools were indeed providing value for money pupils were to be inspected as to their progress and apparent abilities in certain subjects. If they proved to be functioning as well as was expected (and the Revised Code stipulated expectations for pupils at every stage and in some detail) the school would receive funds to continue its work. Funds were withheld in proportion to the numbers of pupils judged to be making insufficient progress.

Despite this degree of state funding and regulation there still did not exist anywhere in Britain anything which could be called a state system of education. The state simply made funds available for certain educational purposes and attached certain conditions to that funding, it showed no great lead in directing elementary education and certainly did little to interfere with the grammar schools. Even the Elementary Education Act of 1870, which applied only in England and Wales, did not – as was demanded by some at the time – replace the existing patchwork of provision with a newly created countrywide system making for uniform quantity and quality. Instead, it provided for an extensive survey of schools throughout England and Wales and only in those areas where existing provision was inadequate would new schools be built and run by School Boards (representative bodies elected locally) with a combination of local and state funds to finance their efforts. Wherever groups such as the National Society were seen to be working well, to be providing sufficiently many places in reasonably maintained buildings, staffed by generally competent teachers they were left to continue much as before. Elsewhere however, if provision was inadequate, elections were held for Boards and these new bodies were charged with building as many new schools and taking such steps as might be required to achieve something like adequate provision. The word most often used to describe this Act, designed by William Edward Forster, although significantly amended in parliament so as to be far weaker than he had originally planned, was a 'compromise' between those who wanted to see a state-provided system of schooling, which would be essentially secular, and those who wanted to maintain the provision of the 'voluntary' schools run by religious organisations such as the British and Foreign and National societies. It was also a compromise between those (including Forster himself) who wanted to make it a duty for parents to see their children educated to the age of thirteen at least and those who saw this as an interference with parental rights or who feared the costs of such a compulsory system or who simply imagined that too much education for too many was a dangerous thing. Compulsion only came about in a separate Act of 1876 – and even then it was only legally possible for Boards to compel parents to send their children to school. Not until 1880 were English and Welsh Boards required to compel attendance, although most had moved to doing this by then.

If educational change in the 1870s in England and Wales came about by compromise, the comparable Act in Scotland two years later seemed to be a continuation of the generally more interventionist approach which had been conspicuous there for some time. There was no compromise between state provision and the voluntary principle and there was no compromise on attendance. Remember that the Church of Scotland was running as many schools as it could manage by 1872 but was doing so with more state backing than was the case in England and Wales. This picture was only slightly complicated by the operation of schools run by the Free Church which had split from the Church of Scotland in the mid-nineteenth century. (The existence of separate Catholic schools in Scotland as in England and Wales does make for a further complication but that is a subject better dealt with at a later point.) What happened in Scotland in 1872 was thus a model of simplicity compared with the changes which took place in England and Wales. From 1872 onwards there were effectively no more elementary schools operated by Protestant churches in Scotland. Either in 1872, or fairly shortly thereafter, all elementary schools in Scotland other than Catholic schools became the responsibility of the thousand or so School Boards created by the 1872 Act.

There was also no compromise where attendance was concerned. A duty to see their children educated was placed on parents straightaway in 1872 and Boards had a responsibility to enforce that compulsion. From 1878, as elsewhere in Britain, there was provision for parents to demand that their children were schooled only 'half-time' after a few years of full-time attendance – subject to successful completion of a test in basic literacy and numeracy. Children thus 'released' from full-time schooling were 'free' to mix work with some continued attendance. In this respect the 1872 Act was compromised in principle but such half-time schooling was ended in Scotland from 1901 and in England and Wales from 1922. Nonetheless in the first years of the 1870s state schooling in Britain (schooling in which the state took a systematic interest) had truly begun.

Formalising the system

There were further significant Education Acts in Scotland and in England and Wales in 1918 by which time the most obvious administrative difference between the two systems was that schools in the former continued to be run by authorities described as *ad hoc*, while those in the latter were not. In both systems the Boards established in the 1870s had been alike in an important respect, their members were elected solely to have responsibility for education. Being *ad hoc* in the sense that they were elected for this purpose alone, members of such Boards might be expected to be, or at least become, highly expert in educational matters. On the other hand they might operate in ignorance of relevant matters of concern locally so that they could have no strategic view of educational, social, economic and other needs in their area. The Bryce Report of 1895 (fully: the *Report of the Royal Commission on Secondary Education*, headed by James Bryce) drew a distinction between 'professional scholastic opinion' which it contended was often 'fearful' of local education passing from the specialist Boards into the hands of local authorities and 'what we may term the administrative and political mind' (Maclure 1973: 143) which favoured unified authorities.

The Report conceded that each attitude was explicable enough and certainly there were sufficient merits in the two approaches to allow one (unified authorities) to be adopted in England and Wales and the other (the *status quo* of Boards) to be retained in Scotland. Thus while England and Wales diverged from Scotland in 1902 when administrative reform was adopted south of the border – placing education in the hands of County Councils – the systems were to be reunited in 1918 when Scotland's Boards were finally abolished. Although the authorities which replaced the Boards in Scotland in 1918 remained *ad hoc* for some ten more years they were larger, covering whole counties or cities, and thus had the strategic view which the old Boards had lacked. In time these too were abolished and County and City Councils administered education everywhere in Britain.

The Scottish Act of 1918 was further significant in that it dealt with the historic anomaly of the position of Catholic schools in Scotland. From the Reformation to the mid- to late-nineteenth century there were relatively few Catholics in Scotland. Immigration from Ireland increased their numbers and generated a need for many more specifically Catholic schools. At much the same time as Scottish education was being reorganised in the 1870s the legal restrictions on the full operation of the Catholic church were lifted and it became possible for the newly restored hierarchy (the church's bishops) to make extensive plans for the education of Catholic children in explicitly Catholic schools. It was always open to the Catholic church to have its schools 'nationalised' as were those of the Free Church and the Church of Scotland in 1872 but, in common with the small Scottish Episcopal church, it long chose to decline this possibility. The Catholic bishops were concerned that there were insufficient safeguards of their power to insist on and provide overtly Catholic teaching for Catholic children.

The 1872 Act was generally secular but it remained in the power of each Board to enforce the teaching of religious doctrine and dogma in schools in its particular area. Where there were too few Catholic rate-payers to make up a majority or even a significant minority in School Board electorates (and, given widespread Catholic poverty, this was more or less everywhere) it followed that Protestant-dominated Boards would be able to set a tone and content to the religious teaching in their schools which could sway Catholic children in those schools from Catholic belief. Reasoning in this manner, the Catholic bishops preferred, at the pain of considerable cost to church funds, to maintain their own school system.

By the end of the First World War this system was in danger of breaking down and the general poverty of Catholic schools was well known. Fortunately the tenor of Scottish national life was by then less markedly sectarian than it had often been in the past and the time was ripe for more liberal legislation of a sort which would satisfy the demands of the hierarchy. From 1918 on, Catholic (and Episcopalian) schools operated alongside the existing schools of Scotland and on an equal footing and a truly national system existed as had been the case in England and Wales since 1902. (Groups such as the British and Foreign and National Societies having lapsed where religious schools existed they were now run directly by churches, especially the Church of England). Both school systems were now so structured as to allow churches the possibility of running their own schools while having those schools funded as if they were run along secular lines. To summarise the position of Britain's two school systems in 1918: both were run by locally elected authorities for which education was only one responsibility among many. Both had full provision for the equal financing of schooling for those parents who wanted to see their children in largely secular or specifically religious schools. One had, and the other soon would, put an end to half-time schooling. Both offered elementary education free to all pupils (they had been obliged to continue the long-standing practice of charging fees in 1870 to top up local and state finance for some time after 1870). Payment by results was ended everywhere and, as we shall shortly see, both were moving to replace elementary education with recognisable primary schools and to ensure widespread progression from primary to secondary education.

The great struggles and achievements of the nineteenth century had been largely concerned with elementary education. In the twentieth century attention turned elsewhere. From at least 1918 there was, as Herbert Albert Laurens Fisher, architect of the English and Welsh Act of that year said, 'a growing sense … [of all people being] … entitled to be considered … as citizens and as fit subjects for any form of education … [of] which they are capable' (Maclure 1973: 173). It was not until 1945 that secondary education throughout the whole of Britain was finally to be freely available to all. However, between 1918 and 1945 there was an ever-growing erosion of the expectation that secondary schooling would generally be purchased and that its limitation to a select minority was both necessary and desirable. From 1918 education authorities in England and Wales and in Scotland began to run fully-fledged secondary schools of their own and thus there was at last a state school system in existence in Britain and these authorities came increasingly to be the dominant providers of secondary as of primary education.

Generalising secondary schooling

Leaving 1918 behind we can again jump ahead, this time to the years around 1941 when the government set up a Commission under the chairmanship of Cyril Norwood to plan for secondary schooling when the war would be finally won. The Commission reported in 1943 with its *Report of the Secondary Schools Examination Council on Curriculum and Examinations in Secondary Schools* which played a vital part in post-war school reorganisation (Gosden 1976: 368). It was to attain considerable significance by having its recommendations adopted more or less in their entirety by the Labour government which managed the post-war reconstruction of 1945 to 1951. The investigation they had conducted led Norwood and his fellow committee members to reach the simple but profoundly significant conclusion that if there were to be secondary schools for all, there would have to be distinct types of school for distinct types of pupil – 'a curriculum … suited to some is … unsuited to others' they said (Maclure 1973: 201). On the basis of psychological generalisations which can tend to seem more speculative than sound, more artfully crafted than scientifically based, it was concluded that 'three broad groups of pupils … [required] three broad types of secondary education'. First, those 'interested in learning for its own sake' were to be sent to the grammar schools. Next, those who 'may have much ability, but … [only] in the realm of facts… [and who are] interested only in the moment' were to be sent to institutions which were to be styled secondary modern schools. Finally, 'boys and girls…[interested in] taking up certain crafts – engineering, agriculture and the like' were bound for the technical schools (Maclure 1973: 201–2).

The Norwood Report led to the 1944 Education Act for England and Wales and the broadly similar 1945 Education Act for Scotland. These parallel Acts gave full and unequivocal access to secondary and primary education for all. Their development was directly influenced by the experiences of war – the shared suffering of all classes and types of people and the sense that war must be waged *for* some good, not simply *against* some evil. Invigorated with the conviction that the war had been waged for the sake of Britain's children and to secure their future liberty from tyranny, parents, politicians, teachers and others set about a programme of educational expansion which would not simply reconstruct whatever had been damaged or destroyed in the war but which would expand and develop that which had existed before almost beyond recognition (Gosden 1976). Funds were voted; teachers were recruited and trained under emergency schemes – often fresh from service in the armed forces, budding teachers were rushed through courses of qualification – and in a perhaps typically British 'sealing wax and string' solution to the accommodation crisis ex-military huts were pressed into service under the arrangement known as HORSA – Hutting Operation for the Raising of the School [Leaving] Age which was raised to 15 in 1947.

Although it is easy to see the Norwood Report retrospectively as doing nothing but reflecting crude social stereotypes, it was adopted enthusiastically and its adoption ushered into being the age of the tripartite system in England and Wales and the bipartite system in Scotland which remained dominant until the 1960s. At the centre of its system was the testing of all pupils at the completion of their course of primary education to determine to which type of secondary school they would be assigned – the so called 11 plus (in Scotland, the equivalent examination, *The Qualifier*, was at 12 plus, given the longer period spent in primary school). However, it was quickly apparent that the 'parity of esteem' of all types of school which the Norwood Report had hoped for had not materialised. Perhaps more importantly there was also not the envisaged 'parity … [of] amenities and conditions' (Maclure 1973: 203). In general, grammar schools might have what they wanted; other schools would take what they could get and the secondary were widely seen as reserved for those who simply were not able.

The growth of the comprehensive principle

Despite its earlier enthusiasm for Norwood it was the Labour party which initiated the next significant round of changes in British schools, a round which completely reversed its position of 1945–51. In this it operated under such influences as the Newsom Report. If Norwood's report had been a blast from the past in many respects, with its clinging to the traditional values of selection and exclusivity, the Newsom Report (published in 1963 taking its name from John Hubert Newsom) was more like the herald of the future. Its very title, *Half our Future*, indicated its intention to be forward looking and thinking. The essence of its concern was with provision for those average and below pupils (as measured by such standards as the 11 plus) who seemed to be thoroughly neglected as matters stood. The specifics of Newsom's recommendations matter less for present purposes than its general implication that no school system which did not take full account of all its pupils could be considered worthy of a modern, free society. In particular it was insisted that, 'unrealised talent' was no longer to be allowed to go to waste. So it was that in 1965 a Labour government began the process of dismantling the 11 plus selection system and replacing it with something different. Experiments in what came to be known as comprehensive schooling were not entirely new (Bell and Grant 1977). Anglesey had established such a school in 1949, Leicestershire set a precedent in England and dispensed with the 11 plus in the late 1950s but the crucial change came in 1965 in Circular 10/65 issued by the Department of Education and Science under the Labour Education Secretary Anthony Crosland (matched by the Scottish Education Department's Circular 600) with its 'declared objective to end selection…and to eliminate separatism' (Maclure 1973: 302).

The comprehensive school can be understood as that which takes on the task of teaching (more or less) all things to (more or less) all pupils. It is certainly not socially selective and it is not academically selective – except perhaps at the extreme of excluding pupils with certain kinds of very debilitating educational difficulties. From around 1965, with the exception of generally small pockets of resistance (Northern Ireland is a larger pocket than most in this respect (Bell and Grant 1977)) entry to state secondary schools in Britain was not by academic selection and it became generally the case that all pupils would learn something about all manner of subjects until at least such time as they were able to make meaningful choices as to what they might study for themselves. No more prior assumptions were to be made to the effect that only some needed certain sorts of knowledge or that only some were fitted for certain sorts of learning.

Many of the central dilemmas for British education from the mid-1960s to the present can be understood either as repeats of the debate over the introduction of the comprehensive system or as being concerned with its refinement. What are to be the limits of the comprehensive principle – everything to everyone? If there is not to be selection for entry to schools, ought there to be selection for certain purposes within schools? How hard ought teachers to work to ensure that all subjects are truly available to all pupils, irrespective of gender, social background, ethnicity or any such consideration so that the school is comprehensive in deed as in name? Does the comprehensive school require particular styles of teaching, management or staff–pupil relations – how much effort and effort of what kind will be required if all pupils are to understand all that they are taught? At what point, if any, does a disability become a truly insurmountable impediment to inclusion in the 'mainstream' comprehensive school? As democracy must surely be concerned with more than the matter of how people choose governments, so comprehensive schooling must be concerned with more than the matter of how schools choose (or do not choose) their pupils. Being comprehensive can be a way of life.

Towards the Education Reform Act

Another jump now and another turning point. We jump, in relative terms, almost to the present and land in 1976, fully a century on from our nominal starting point. In many respects little had changed in the intervening period. Comprehensive schools were far from universally popular with parents, politicians, the press or even with all the pupils who attended them, but there seemed to be something inevitable about them. Circular 10/70 of 1970 (Maclure 1973), issued at the behest of then Secretary of State for Education, later Prime Minister, Margaret Thatcher withdrew Circular 10/65 and allowed local authorities discretion as to whether or not they would proceed with creating all and only comprehensive schools thereafter, but this was a use of the brake, not a switch to reverse gear. Rightly or wrongly, for good or ill, the comprehensive principle had arrived and looked set to stay. If there was to be a U-turn on the comprehensive principle in some or all of Britain after Thatcher's spell in office, Circular 10/70 was the signal rather than the manoeuvre. Incidentally, it is worth noting that primary schools have rarely been selective by academic ability at any time or in any place, so that effectively they might be said to have always been comprehensive. This presumably strikes us quite correct because it seems almost impossibly difficult to make very significant generalisations as to the intellectual abilities of very young children. Thus Britain's primaries did not participate in the debates over the possibility or desirability of comprehensivisation which touched its secondaries in the 1960s. They did however undergo their own correspondingly significant change associated with the Plowden Report and the methods which it advocated but this is a theme which is discussed in Chapter 2.

However, it remained possible to wonder how schools might better be organised, how pupils might better be taught, how teachers might better conduct themselves and much else besides. This is precisely what Prime Minister James Callaghan set himself to wondering in an influential speech given at Ruskin College (a specialist adult education institution long supported by many trades unions). Of central concern to Callaghan was the claim that schools were failing because they were (apparently) not educating in ways which were economically significant. The so-called Great Debate which followed his speech, with its implicit attacks on schools and the teachers in them for being unable or unwilling to furnish young men and women who were themselves willing and able, in his tautology, 'to do a job of work', has continued in one form or another ever since and if it was Callaghan who proposed debate then his motion was vigorously seconded – in England and Wales at least – by his successor, Margaret Thatcher. The three years of desperate and often rather unseemly political struggle inside and outside parliament which marked the decline of the Callaghan Labour government left little time or energy to be devoted to large-scale educational change, but the incoming government of 1979, with its seemingly impregnable parliamentary majority, had apparently all the time and scope for change it needed and it certainly lacked neither energy nor enthusiasm for change.

An era of change: 1988 and after

The erstwhile Secretary of State for Education in the government of Edward Heath was ever the practical politician and such were her other priorities that widespread change in the nature and operation of the primary and secondary schools of England and Wales was not instant – she had older scores to settle first as, for example, with the trades unions and the nationalised industries – but the reforms associated with the 1988 Education Reform Act were ambitious at the very least. The obvious abbreviation of the Act's title – ERA – has launched a thousand puns, or launched a thousand uses of the one pun, but although the changes were not necessarily swift they were sure when they came and something like a new era did indeed seem to have begun. As they applied in England and Wales, the changes associated with the ERA can be summarised thus: there was an increased role in school management for parents, especially as school governors; through the legal device known as an Order, an appendix of sorts, a National Curriculum was introduced for pupils in the primary and early secondary years mandating in some detail what they were to be taught and how they were to be assessed and certain schools were permitted to leave local authority control (opt-out) and become self-managing (although subject now to direct central government authority).

Meanwhile, in another part of the kingdom, there was also change but in a rather less hurried way and less obviously dogged by the often bitter dispute which accompanied the ERA in England and Wales in England. But change there has been in Scotland in the same period. Provision was made there for opting out and for parental involvement with schools as members of school boards (not to be confused with the School Boards of time past, members elected to these new boards concerned themselves only with their particular school). There has also been change in the primary and secondary curricula, not least with the attempt to engineer a seamless transition from the one to the other, taking pupils through a programme of work and study harmonised from the ages of 5 to 14. Amongst Scottish intellectuals and its middle classes the package of social and economic reforms lumped together as Thatcherism were always less overtly popular than in England (and much the same might be said of Wales as of Scotland) and while this difference can be overstated, it certainly played a part in making Scotland less amenable to educational change such as was wrought in England and Wales (the Welsh position in the Union has always been rather less autonomous than the Scottish so that comparable sentiment there could not be translated into anything concrete). Thus, for example, when erstwhile prime minister Thatcher addressed the members of the General Assembly of the Church of Scotland (for long the closest thing that Scotland had to a parliament with its elected representatives from congregations across the country) she was derided as having delivered the 'Sermon on the Mound' (a reference best appreciated if one reads the biblical Sermon on the Mount then studies the map of Edinburgh to see that the General Assembly meets in that part of the city known as the Mound).

In this sermon she claimed that Christian values were fundamentally Conservative and Conservative values fundamentally Christian. Be this as it may or may not, she was certainly preaching to the unconverted and the unconvertible as most Assembly members were rather more persuaded by a vision of what might be called the 'social gospel' which sets Christianity against the values of capitalism and the variety of authoritarian and uncaring social conservatism which she seemed to them to represent. Scotland's ministers of religion do not set policy in education, or anything else for that matter, and they can ultimately be dismissed by ministers of the crown if the latter so please, but ministers of religion can and do both reflect and shape the general tone of public opinion and debate. It is thus that the story of schools and schooling in Scotland has been markedly different to that in England and Wales in the years since the Great Debate.

Conclusion

Education is arguably central to the essence of humanity. Attending school (or its equivalent) is now the expected norm (Faure *et al.* 1972). In the period from the 1870s to the 1990s more and more children have been more and more subject to formal schooling in Britain for longer and longer. The expectation of progression from primary schooling to secondary has become the norm. The expectation of considerable state funding for an involvement in schooling has also become the norm and this latter trend has certainly indicated ever increased and increasing social interest and concern where schooling is concerned. With their faults and failings, those who run Britain's schools may reveal themselves to be all too human but insofar as we have put more and more into our schools and got more and more out of them we have perhaps all become a little more human.

Suggested further reading

The best way to understand any historical period or subject is always to become familiar with relevant primary documents. A selection of relevant documents covering most of the period under consideration here (although for England and Wales only) is available in J. Stuart Maclure (1973). It is also always necessary to ground any historical understanding in as wide ranging an international context as possible. For this purpose the third volume of James Bowen's (1981) monumental work – the volume concerned with the modern western world – is essential. There is no comprehensive history of Scottish education currently available in print but the second volume of James Scotland's (1969) two-volume work which covers the period from 1872 to the late 1960s is well worth consulting. More up-to-date material is in Margaret Clark and Pamela Munn (1997). Three easily available recent histories of education in England and Wales are Richard Aldrich (1996) and two works by Roy Lowe (1988 and 1997). For a history of the comprehensive school in the UK (but set in an international context) the seminal work is Benn and Chitty (1996).

Notes

1   This relates to the Medieval notion of placing at the foundation of Medieval teaching the learning of Latin (and sometimes Greek) language.

References

Aldrich, R. (1996) *Education for the Nation*. London: Cassell.

Bell, R. and Grant, N. (1977) *Patterns of Education in the British Isles*. London: Unwin Education Books.

Benn, C. and Chitty, C. (1996) *Thirty Years On: Is Comprehensive School Alive and Kicking or Struggling to Survive?* London: David Fulton Publishers/Harmondsworth: Penguin.

Bowen, J. (1981) *A History of Western Education*. London: Methuen.

Central Advisory Council for Education (ACE) (1963) *Half our Future (The Newsom Report)*. London: HMSO.

Clark, M. and Munn, P. (eds) (1997) *Education in Scotland: Policy and Practice from Preschool to Secondary*. London: Routledge.

Corner, T. (1984) 'Multiculturalism in the British Isles', in T. Corner (ed.) *Education in Multicultural Societies*. Beckenham: Croom Helm.

Faure, E. *et al.* (1972) *Learning to Be*. Paris: UNESCO.

Gosden, P. H. J. H. (1976) *Education in the Second World War*. London: Methuen.

Lowe, R. (1988) *Education in the Post War Years*. London: Routledge.

Lowe, R. (1997) *Schooling and Social Change: 1964–1990*. London: Routledge.

Maclure, J. S. (1973) *Educational Documents England and Wales 1816 to the Present Day*. London: Methuen.

Scotland, J. (1969) *The History of Scottish Education*. London: University of London Press.

Chapter 4

Pre-school education in the UK

J. Eric Wilkinson

It should be noted that children at play are not playing about; their games should be seen as their more serious-minded activity.

Montaigne 1533–1592

Introduction

The origins of pre-school education go back nearly 200 years to the time of the social reformer Robert Owen. As part of his model village in New Lanark, Scotland, he established the very first nursery, reputably in the world, for young children with working parents. The emphasis was on a stimulating child-centred curriculum based on play, exploration, singing and dancing. Unfortunately, after Owen left, in 1825, to establish New Harmony in America, the nursery was discontinued, largely as a result of the greed for profit generated by the industrialisation of Britain in the nineteeth century.

More recently, much attention has been given to pre-school education throughout the UK. There are three main reasons for this. Firstly, research has demonstrated the all-round psychological and social benefits to the child that high quality pre-school education offers. Secondly, it has been shown that a good pre-school experience has positive effects on subsequent educational achievement, and thirdly, early childhood services contribute to meeting the objectives of a healthy and prosperous society by promoting an effective and sufficient labour supply.

The findings of research on the effects of pre-school education on children's development are now well established. Studying the effects of childcare on language development, McCartney (1984) identified that the degree of verbal responsiveness of staff in nurseries affected the language development of children in their care. One of the seminal studies that highlighted the significance of childcare quality on the social development of children was reported by Phillips *et al.* in 1987. The ability to establish cooperative relationships was significantly effected by a good nursery experience. In reviewing the literature Clarke-Stewart (1991) identified several indicators that impinge on children's development. These are: a well-organised and stimulating physical environment, a responsive and trained care-giver, a balanced curriculum, relatively small groups of children and relatively generous adult–child ratios.

Turning to the impact of pre-school education on subsequent educational achievement, a review of literature was undertaken by Sylva and Wiltshire (1994). They concluded:

> When pre-school education is of high quality it leads to lasting enhancement of educational performance and later employment. It does this through encouraging high aspirations, motivation to learn and feelings of task efficacy, especially for children from disadvantaged backgrounds. (Sylva and Wiltshire 1994: 47).

This finding was also echoed by Ball in the report of the Royal Society of Arts: *Start Right: The Importance of Early Learning* (1994).

As far as the impact of pre-school education and care on wider social issues is concerned, it is now recognised that nursery provision counteracts poverty by facilitating parental economic activity, it provides the main care-giver (usually the mother) with temporary relief from constant vigilance and can provide employers with continuity in valued personnel if provision for very young children is readily accessible.

Given the convincing evidence in support of pre-school education, writers such as David (1990), Scarr and Eisenberg (1993) and Moss and Penn (1996) have consistently argued that quality pre-school education should be made universally available to families with young children. Only very recently has government responded robustly to the arguments by introducing pre-school places for all four-year-olds whose parents wish it from September 1998 and for all three-year-olds in the very near future.

Early childhood services in the UK

There are three main categories of provision for children under 5 years of age in the UK:

- publicly funded services through local authorities
- voluntary services
- private services.

As far as local authority provision is concerned, this consists of two sub-divisions – *education*-based services and *social (work)* services. Of the specifically educational provision there are three types – nursery schools, nursery classes attached to primary schools and (in England and Wales only) reception classes in primary schools. These types of provision are staffed by both nursery teachers and nursery nurses. Of the social (work) services there are day nurseries, family centres and children's centres staffed largely by nursery nurses. With the exception of reception classes, the differentiation between these two types of nursery is being eroded, largely as a result of the pioneering work on integration in Strathclyde Region in Scotland in the late 1980s (Penn 1992; Wilkinson 1995).

In the voluntary sector playgroups – run by local mothers, assisted by a playgroup leader – are the most common, although most of the places in these groups are for one or two short sessions each week. Less prevalent are mother-and-toddler groups and creches.

In the private sector provision varies widely from childminders (who look after children in their own homes) through private nurseries (very similar to local authority nursery schools) to nursery classes in fully independent schools. Childminders and private day nurseries are the only services available to meet the needs of working parents. Estimates vary, but the percentage of women with children under five in the labour force was estimated in 1989 (Labour Force Survey 1993–4) to be 52 per cent, and for those with children aged 5 to 8, 69 per cent. Those that cannot afford these services tend to work irregular or part-time hours or night shifts, or rely on the help of relatives, and generally see their childcare arrangements as unsatisfactory.

Moss and Penn (1996) have undertaken an extensive and useful comparison of the different types of provision and clearly demonstrated substantial shortcomings in the current system. There is wide variation in uptake, cost, access, staffing and opening times of early childhood services in the UK, resulting in a complex piece-meal system (see Table 4.1).

Until very recently, provision for the education of pre-school children has been woefully inadequate in three main respects: in extent, aspects of its organisation and in ideology.

As far as organisation is concerned the vast majority of places are part-time, attendance being for half a day, either mornings or afternoons. In 1987–8, of those three- and four-year-olds attending nursery schools and classes, 93 per cent did so on a part-time basis. Most nursery schools and classes close for school holidays. In addition, there is a professional distinction between nursery nurses and nursery teachers' resulting in differentiation of status, remuneration and promotion prospects.

In ideological terms there is still a strongly entrenched view among parents and some professionals in Britain that very young children (i.e. under three years) will be seriously disadvantaged unless they are reared by their mothers; mothering is best for young children and is a full-time occupation. This means that in the UK there is very little educational provision for under-threes, despite convincing psychological evidence that young children are able to form multiple attachments successfully and comparative evidence that many other European countries provide extensive and successful facilities for under-threes.

As far as availability of pre-school education is concerned, it has long been recognised that the provision in the UK is insufficient (Wilkinson and Brady 1990; David 1990; Moss and Penn 1996). The case for a large expansion in nursery education was addressed in the Plowden Report (DES 1967) although it was

Table 4.1 Differences between education and care for young children

	Daycare	Education
Main aims	• various: supporting parents, promoting equality, caring for children, providing stable and safe environment	• promoting children's learning • preparation for primary school
Curriculum	• of peripheral concern: basic play materials, rough groupings of material	• central: extremely sophisticated: eight basic areas, subdivided into many parts each with many ideas about practice
School	• little contact with primary school	• dovetailed with National Curriculum
Staff	• two-year vocational training in nursery nursing • multi-role job description	• staff formally qualified to teach in primary school sector following four-year BEd course • Main task to teach, any other tasks a distraction from teaching
Children	• focused on children aged 0–5 • view of child's paramount need to feel safe and secure	• focused on children aged 3–5 • view of children's paramount need • to learn and master basic linguistic and numerical tasks
Style of learning	• meaningful learning, diffuse, occurs throughout day, in many situations	• meaningful learning, intense, concentrated into short periods in educational setting
Staff accountability	• through staff support, supervision and managerial oversight	• through written development planning, individual or team-based
Effectiveness	• mainly measured by child/parent satisfaction	• mainly measured by children's developmental outcomes

(Penn and Wilkinson 1995)

recommended that such expansion should be part-time rather than full-time 'because young children should not be separated for long from their mothers' (DES 1967: 121). The recommendations of the Plowden Report were incorporated into the White Paper (*Education: A Framework for Expansion*, DES 1972). Unfortunately the intentions contained in the White Paper were never fully realised.

In terms of the overall proportion of children under 5 attending one or more of the types of provision listed in Table 4.1, no accurate definitive national figure is available, largely due to the plurality and diversity of the system. Prior to September 1998, it is estimated that between 50 and 60 per cent of 0–5-year-olds have experienced some form or other of early childhood service before starting formal school.

Table 4.2 shows the number of places available based on official statistics in 1993. However, these data do not reflect an accurate picture in the late 1990s. The previous government's policy of expanding provision through its voucher scheme had the effect of increasing the number of places in nursery classes in primary schools (Stephen *et al.* 1998). For example, within a year of the voucher scheme being introduced one local authority increased its nursery places from 767 to 1337 entirely by setting up 12 new nursery classes (Stephen *et al.* 1998: 12).

Table 4.2 Preschool places for children under 5 in England and Wales in 1993

Type of provision	No of places
Nursery schools	46,534
Nursery classes	187,090
Reception classes	337,735
Day nurseries, etc.	26,670
Private nurseries	123,960
Playgroups	464,830
Childminders	338,590
Independent schools' nurseries	39,600

In Scotland, the pattern of provision is somewhat different from that in England and Wales. There is no equivalent of the Reception Class. Where available, parents choose to send their children to a nursery – nursery school, nursery class, day nursery, playgroup and/or private nursery.

In terms of uptake of provision, the most recent official statistics (SO 1995; 1996) would indicate that just less than 50 per cent of 0–5-year-olds in Scotland will have attended one or more types of pre-school provision by the time they start formal schooling at 5 years of age. The breakdown for 0–5-year-olds is as follows: nursery school or class (15 per cent), day nursery, etc. (2 per cent); playgroups (13 per cent); childminders (10 per cent), private nurseries (4 per cent), nurseries in independent schools (0.5 per cent). If one further examines the statistics for three- and four-year-olds only, the proportion of such children attending nursery school or class in Scotland rises to about 40 per cent, although this may have increased a little due to the voucher scheme piloted in four local authorities in Scotland (Brown *et al.* 1998).

In comparison to provision in other countries – particularly Europe – commentators (e.g. Moss 1990; David 1993) have consistently argued that the UK is a relatively low provider. Countries such as France, Belgium, Denmark and Italy are high providers with over 80 per cent of children under school age having pre-school provision. Countries such as Portugal and The Netherlands are relatively low providers.

In an attempt to improve the situation in the UK, the present government is committed to providing a Pre-school place for all four-year-old children whose parents wish it, from September 1998. It is also committed to extending provision for three-year-olds, albeit on a part-time basis.

Theoretical perspectives

The theoretical backdrop to pre-school provision is both complex and extensive. It is complex not only because it is intricately interwoven with several academic disciplines but because the different types of provision give different emphasis to different theories. It is extensive because the field has received much research attention from a wide variety of domains and individuals. The design, restructuring and revision of institutional systems for the education and care of young children is inherently based on an understanding, whether implicit or explicit, of this theoretical backdrop.

The principle theoretical strands that inform and shape provision for families with children under five are:

- *ideology* of childcare
- *psychology* of child development
- *education* and care of children.

Childcare is inextricably bound up with the relief of disadvantage and the realisation of equal opportunities. As such it is immersed in ideology and is a matter of public responsibility. 'Childcare makes a contribution to the relief of disadvantage and the promotion of equality' (Cohen and Fraser 1991: p.ii).

How childcare affects children and families is a critical feature of developmental psychology:

> Far from disrupting the family by taking over some of its childcare functions, day care services ought to be seen as providing experiences that complement those obtained at home, with corresponding advantages for child development. (Schaffer 1990: 153).

Equally, the kind of learning experiences, activities, knowledge and values children are expected to engage with as part of their upbringing and induction into the world are also critical. 'But what do we mean by education for under-fives, what form should it take, what methods should be employed, and what role do adults need to adopt?' (David 1990: 5).

The extent to which these three theoretical strands interact on a practical level can be seen in the work of Gilkes (1987) who, as a nursery head teacher, played a significant part in moving nursery education forward in the 1980s.

The pre-school curriculum

Since the first nursery in New Lanark, 'play' has been a central feature of nursery activities. However, it was not until after the Second World War that governments began to take an interest in the activities inside the nursery. In Scotland, the 1950 Primary Memorandum (SOED 1950) defined the aim of nursery education:

> The aim of nursery school education is to provide the right conditions for growth, and so to ensure the harmonising of the whole personality of the child. Whenever reference is made to aspects of development, whether physical, mental, emotional, spiritual, or social, it must not be forgotten that these are all inter-dependent aspects of a unity. (SOED 1950: 127)

The Memorandum goes on to state:

> The value of the physical aspect is perhaps the most obvious. In general, the term covers medical care, adequate rest and sleep, balanced diet, play within doors and in the open air, suitable clothing, and training in hygienic habits. (SOED 1950: 127)

In other words, it was the 'health care' aspect of nurseries that was stressed by central government. This stress on health was the dominant influence in nurseries for some 30 years, many nurseries being under the direct supervision of the Ministry of Health (DES 1967). In day nurseries, health care was paramount; children had to be protected from disease and squalor. It was not until the 1970s that a change took place when attention was paid to children's intellectual needs. In *Before Five* (SOED 1973), the aim of nursery education was broadened into activities aimed at child development:

> The ideal educational environment in these years will afford opportunities for the child to develop his physical, intellectual, social and emotional capacities. (SOED 1973: 1)

For the first time, priority was to be given to a child's broad developmental needs. More recently (SCAA 1996; SO 1997) central government has taken steps to define the curriculum appropriate for pre-school children in response to the National Curriculum in primary schools (in Scotland, National Curricular Guidelines). In England and Wales, the report *Desirable Outcomes for Children's Learning on Entering Compulsory Education* (SCAA 1996) identified six areas of learning:

- personal and social development
- language and literacy
- mathematics
- knowledge and understanding of the world
- physical development
- creative development

Taken together, the six areas of learning also provide opportunities to address important aspects of children's spiritual, moral, social and cultural development. (SCAA 1997: 4)

In Scotland, the Scottish Office Report *A Curriculum Framework for Children in their Pre-school Year* (SO 1997) redefined the aims of nursery education as to:

- provide a safe and stimulating environment, in which children could feel happy and secure;
- encourage the emotional, social, physical, creative and intellectual development of children;
- promote the welfare of children;
- encourage positive attitudes to self and others and develop confidence and self-esteem;
- create opportunities for play;
- encourage children to explore, appreciate and respect their environment;
- provide opportunities to stimulate interest and imagination;
- extend the children's abilities to communicate ideas and feelings in a variety of ways.

To help achieve these aims, the Her Majesty's Inspectorate (HMI) in Scotland (SO 1997) outlined the nursery curriculum in terms of planned learning experiences based on different aspects of children's development and learning.

Thus, for the first time in the 200-year history of nursery education in the UK, government has specified the parameters of children's learning. The prime motivation for this policy is one of raising standards of educational achievement in the compulsory school years. Reports such as *World's Apart* (OFSTED 1996), which compares educational achievement internationally, have had a major impact on successive government policy, despite evidence to show that performance in external examinations such as 'A' levels and Highers has been rising for several years (e.g. SO 1998a). Nevertheless the government's emphasis on nursery education, which forms a key element of its current childcare strategy (DfEE 1998a; SO 1998b), is to be warmly welcomed.

Although definition of the curriculum by central government agencies is generally accepted among early childhood professionals (Curtis 1986), its delivery and impact on children's general well-being is more controversial. With the influx of young children into reception classes in England and Wales, which have inferior child–teacher ratios compared to nurseries, formalisation of the pedagogy for such children has taken place. Four-year-olds in reception classes no longer enjoy a spontaneous, play-based, caring and stimulating environment associated with good nurseries. Instead they are subject to school pressures to conform and engage with formal, highly structured learning. While there is much to be said for stimulating children intellectually from an early age, excessive rigidity can have undesirable psychological consequences.

The informality of the nursery must be preserved – it is just as important for children to develop socially, emotionally and physically as it is to understand the world. (Wilkinson 1992: 8)

Quality of the nursery experience

Defining quality

Of paramount importance in pre-school education is the pursuit of quality, partly motivated by 'value for money' in public sector services, but also motivated by the now well-established relationship between quality and children's progress. The importance of quality in early childhood services was raised in the Rumbold Report (DES 1990). Since then, various organisations (e.g. ECN 1991; 1996) and several local authorities have recognised that quality matters. However, defining quality in early childhood services is not straightforward. The complex problems of definition have been discussed at length (Elfer and Wedge 1992; Watt 1994; Moss and Pence 1994; Abbott 1994). To reach a universal definition of quality is not feasible – definitions vary according to the perspective of a particular stakeholder group.

As claimed by Moss and Pence (1994) it is more fruitful to examine the different meanings attributed to quality by the various influential stakeholders. Moss (1994) identifies two categories of meaning – one descriptive and relative, the other evaluative and quasi-objective. In the former category of meaning referred to by Pence and Moss as the 'inclusionary paradigm', the process of reaching a common understanding between the various immediate stakeholders is central. The primary purpose in this paradigm is to deliver a service to children and families that both professional educators/carers and parents mutually agree as worthwhile. Clearly such an approach contributes to the development of a dynamic nursery. Unfortunately it ignores the political realities associated with funding and accountability – features with which recent government papers (SO 1998b and DfEE 1998a) are concerned. Both these White Papers recognise the need to pay attention to promoting quality in early childhood services.

In the second category of the meaning attributable to quality, that is, the evaluative meaning, the primary purpose is to assess how well a service performs and/or meets its aims and objectives. In order to do this a benchmark of quality is usually stipulated in advance against which judgements can be made. Very often this is the paradigm used by researchers in this field (e.g. Harms and Clifford 1980). While the strength of this approach affords some degree of comparative analysis (see, for example, Stephen and Wilkinson 1995), the weakness is that context, culture and choice are ignored.

In moving the debate forward it seems not unreasonable to explore the possibility of combining the two paradigms into a unified process of quality definition and quality assessment. Such an arrangement would initially draw on the evaluative tradition by establishing a broad quality framework through mutual agreement between a number of stakeholders. The framework would then be used in such a way as to give individual nurseries the opportunity to describe their practice and generate supportive evidence which would be available for external scrutiny (Wilkinson and Brady 1990). In their work with the Scottish Independent Nurseries Association (SINA) Wilkinson and Stephen (1998) specified such a framework based on defined standards in six key areas:

- the learning environment
- partnerships
- management
- the social experience
- staff
- accommodation and resources

These areas interact to generate what is now regarded as a quality early childhood service (see Figure 4.1).

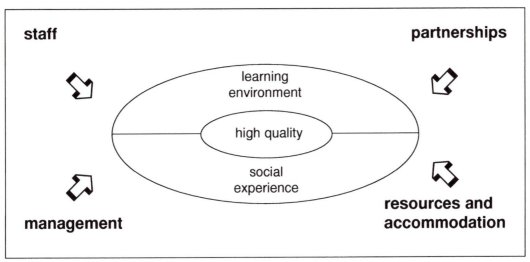

Figure 4.1 Quality factors in preschool provision

Drawing on a range of literature, Wilkinson and Stephen (1998) identified a wide range of performance indicators for each of the six key areas. In the case of key area 1 (The Learning Environment) the indicators covered:

- curriculum
- record-keeping/assessment
- planning
- promoting learning
- special needs
- equal opportunities.

Quality assessment

Two approaches to the assessment of quality can be identified in practice (Wilkinson and Stephen 1994). The qualitative approach relies on the professional judgement of teachers, nursery nurses and others, while the quantitative approach is based on 'objective' measurement often using pre-specified scales. The former approach, which characterises inspections by HMI, has the advantage of being more comprehensive and detailed but is open to potential bias and possible dispute. It is also only feasible to undertake intensive inspections at lengthy intervals of time (in the case of HMI inspections, every two to three years). The latter is potentially more rigorous and quasi-objective but necessarily depends on a rigid definition of 'quality'.

Quality improvement

All professionals who work in education strive to make improvements. Nursery workers, whether nursery nurses, teachers or playleaders are no exception. Increasingly, different types of nurseries are involved in formal inspections by OFSTED, HMI and others. However, it is now considered insufficient to leave quality improvement as a bonus of quality assessment. Most nurseries now accept the need for on-going development planning and have been supported in this process by recent documents (for example, *Using Performance Indicators in Nursery School/Class/Pre-Five Unit Self Evaluation* (SOED 1995). The recent *Consultation Paper on the Regulation of Early Education and Daycare in England and Wales* (DfEE 1998b) has identified the need for nurseries to prepare action plans following inspection in order to address specific weaknesses and improve standards. The *Self-Appraisal Schedule* (DfEE 1996) is intended as a start in this direction.

Assessment and record-keeping

Assessment is an essential element in the educational process. It is essential because it is an integral part of that process. We progress educationally by acquiring a facility for assessing our own learning achievements and thus our own learning needs. The role of the teacher in this process is to assist in the acquisition of that facility. And it will be clear that such assistance is especially important in the early years of education. (Blenkin and Kelly 1992: viii)

Until very recently, the assessment of the educational progress of young children has been overwhelmingly concerned with the teaching and learning process either to help in pedagogical planning (Wolfendale 1993) or in screening children for special educational needs (Lindsay and Pearson 1981). Blenkin and Kelly (1992) make out a strong case for the primacy of the pedagogical purpose in assessment:

We have throughout this book advocated those forms (of assessment) we consider most conducive to the promotion of educational growth in pupils – those which are formative, holistic, emphasising strengths rather than weaknesses, judgemental rather than weaknesses, judgmental rather than metric. (Blenkin and Kelly 1992: 165)

Since the introduction of national testing by the last government, a sea change has taken place in the purpose of assessment (Blatchford and Cline 1994; Burgess-Macey 1994). Information from assessment is now required to evaluate the effectiveness of different educational institutions, principally schools.

No longer is it accepted that all schools are doing a good job. Recent events in Hackney, where the present government has taken direct action in the management of schools in Hackney LEA, are testament to the government's concern that schools should be taking greater responsibility to improve national standards. Further, accountability and new management practices have heralded the concept of 'value-added'. Head teachers, Directors of Education and HMIs are all interested, for different reasons, in evaluating the effectiveness of particular schools.

> Schools feel the need to prove that they are teaching children effectively and that the learning that a child can demonstrate by the age of the Key Stage 1 tests of assessment has in fact been facilitated by the school. Without baseline assessment on entry to school the value-added component of a child's later performance cannot be calculated. (Burgess-Macey 1994: 48)

Inventing the concept of value-added was in recognition of the fact that different schools have to conduct their business with pupils from different socio-economic groups. It has long been recognised that a relationship – albeit complex – exists between educational attainment and social class. It is therefore unreasonable to expect all schools to educate their pupils to the same level of achievement.

However, it is not only the 'value-added' requirements that have prompted the use of assessments for evaluative purposes. The present government's policy of raising education standards (DfEE 1997) partly through its programme of early intervention also plays an important role. In order to assist the process of raising standards, considerable investment is now taking place in the early stages of a child's education. Various schemes are being put in place to identify children 'at risk' and to offset any possible subsequent learning difficulties. Evaluative questions are being asked about the effectiveness of such intervention. Answers to these questions are increasingly being located in the assessment of children's progress.

Lindsay (1997) identified seven purposes of assessment in two main categories: those which are child-focused and those which are school-focused. In the child-focused category he includes such matters as screening, monitoring and pedagogy while in the school-focused category he locates resource planning and accountability.

There is considerable debate in the literature (Drummond 1993; Lindsay 1997) as to whether any one scheme for assessing four- and five-year-old children – now referred to as Baseline Assessment – can adequately address each of the purposes. Wolfendale (1993) identified a number of concerns and dilemmas which are 'an amalgam of technical, educational and socio-political issues'. Despite what Wolfendale refers to as 'a long list of objections to Baseline Assessment – at every level – theoretical, ideological, practical and financial' she concludes:

> Paradoxically in fact there does appear to be a consensus, based on reality principles, that a form, or forms of on-entry to school assessment is a viable idea. (Wolfendale 1993: 33)

However, considerable concern has been expressed about the purpose and practice:

> Early years educators need to treat the issue of assessment very carefully. We need to be clear about which purposes of assessment we are working towards, and which models of the early years curriculum and of children's learning underpin our models of assessment. We cannot uncritically adopt a model handed down from the National Curriculum and assessment procedures. (Burgess-Macey 1994: 48).

Similarly Lindsay, in a recent paper concludes: 'Baseline assessment is potentially a very useful addition to the education system – but only if developed and used wisely' (Lindsay 1997: 26).

Pre-school education and national childcare strategies

In 1998, the government published its Childcare Strategy for the UK (SO 1998b; DfEE 1998a). The key element of the government's approach is that early childhood services should be planned in each local authority through an Early Years Development Plan drawn up by the local authority in full cooperation with a body which represents all the relevant early years interests in the area, and known as the Early Years Development Partnership. A concept of 'partnership' is central to the national strategy. Subsequent to publication of the strategy, the DfEE published Planning Guidance for 1999–2000 (DfEE 1998c). The new Partnerships between the local authorities, the private and voluntary sectors should:

- ensure that the Plan enhances the care, play and educational experience of young children and the care and play experience of children up to age 4, including those with special educational needs and those with disabilities;
- bring together the maintained, private and voluntary sectors in a spirit of co-operation and genuine partnership, based on existing good practice;
- be directed by the diverse needs and aspirations of children locally, and of their parents, and pay attention to the support of families;
- be further directed by the requirements of the local labour market and the needs of local employers, seeking advice from the local Training and Enterprise Council as appropriate;
- generate genuine partnership and debate between all providers and others, and seek agreement about how needs can best be met;
- recognise that the private and voluntary sectors have particular strengths;
- recognise that these sectors often give support to, and in turn are supported by, parents;
- understand the reality of the constraints on the local authority, both financial and other; and
- pay regard to value for money, taking both cost and quality into account, including recognition that the majority of childcare provision normally will be, or will become, financially viable within a short period.

Partnership with parents

While the government's policy of promoting partnerships between the different providers of pre-school education and local authorities is welcome, the partnership that individual nurseries have with parents is crucial. Attending a nursery is often the first step to independence for most children. Parents must have confidence that by sending their child to a nursery their child will be well cared-for and be helped to learn. It must not be forgotten that the home environment in general is richly educative (Tizard and Hughes 1984).

In their relationship with parents, different nurseries operate different models of partnership. In the independent sector (where parents often have full-time employment) partnership depends on effective and efficient communication, whereas in the voluntary sector, parents take an active involvement in the delivery of a caring and stimulating environment.

Most nurseries now recognise the importance of continuity between home and nursery, often interpreting their role as helping parents to provide complementary experiences at home to those in nursery, for example, reading stories and responding to questions. Many nursery teachers and nursery nurses now regard it as part of their job to communicate with parents about the progress of individual children.

Conclusion

Pre-school education has come a long way since the days of Robert Owen. Although much of the original informality has been retained, there is a more formal definition of children's pre-school experience. It is now considered to be one of the most important sectors of education. Rapid expansion of provision is taking place which throws into sharp focus the debate about the nature of experiences most beneficial to young children.

In most nurseries, the concept of 'good practice' is better understood by both parents and professionals alike. However, for children in reception classes the traditions of good pre-school education have been lost. For such children, exposure to a formal pedagogy can have detrimental effects on their subsequent education. In many European countries – particularly in Scandinavia – formal school does not begin until children are over seven years old. Children's experiences prior to this are firmly rooted in experiential learning – exploration, play, music and social activities. In Scotland much of this spontaneity is also in evidence. However, in England and Wales the situation is far from ideal. Urgent action is now required to ensure that all children whose parents wish it can have the benefit of a play-based, high quality pre-school experience.

An all-rounded, quality nursery experience has untold benefits for children and parents. It is fundamental not only to the subsequent schooling process but to the promotion of a more humane society.

Bibliography

Abbott, M. (1994) 'Introduction: The search for quality in the early years', in Abbott, L. and Rodger, R. (eds) *Quality Education in the Early Years*. Buckingham: Open University Press.

Ball, C. (1994) *Start Right: The Importance of Early Learning*. London: Royal Society of Arts.

Blatchford, P. and Cline, T. (1994) 'Baseline assessment: selecting a method of assessing children on school entry', *Education*, **3**(13), 10–15.

Blenkin, G. M. and Kelly, A. V. (1992) *Assessment in Early Childhood Education*. London: Paul Chapman.

Brown, S., Stephen, C., Low, L. (1998) 'A research analysis of pre-school provision in the market place', *Scottish Educational Review*, **30**(1), 4–14.

Burgess-Macey, C. (1994) 'Assessing young children's learning' in Keel, P. (ed.) *Assessment in the Multi-ethnic Primary Classroom*. Stoke-on-Trent: Trentham Books.

Clarke-Stewart, A. (1991) 'Day care in the USA' in Moss, P. and Melhuish, E. (eds), *Current Issues in Day Care for Young Children*. London: HMSO.

Cohen, B. and Fraser, N. (1991) *Childcare in a Modern Welfare System*. London: IPPR.

Curtis, A. (1986) *A Curriculum for the Pre-school Child*. Slough: NFER/Nelson.

David, T. (1990) *Under Five – Under Educated?* Buckingham: Open University Press.

David, T. (1993) *Educational Provision for our Youngest Children – European Perspectives*. London: Paul Chapman.

Department of Education and Science (DES) (1967) *Children and their Primary Schools (The Plowden Report)*. London: HMSO.

Department of Education and Science (DES) (1972) *Education: a Framework for Expansion*. Education White Paper, Cmnd 5174. London: HMSO.

Department of Education and Science (DES) (1990) *Starting with Quality. The Report of the Committee of Inquiry into the Quality of Educational Experience Offered to three- and four-year-old Children (The Rumbold Report)*. London: HMSO.

Department for Education and Employment (DfEE) (1996a) *Nursery Education: Self-Appraisal Schedule*. London: DfEE.

Department for Education and Employment (DfEE) (1996b) *Excellence in Schools*. London: HMSO.

Department for Education and Employment (DfEE) (1998a) *Meeting the Childcare Strategy*. London: HMSO.

Department for Education and Employment (DfEE) (1998b) *Consultation Paper on the Regulation of Early Education and Daycare in England and Wales*. Sudbury: DfEE Publications.

Department for Education and Employment (DfEE) (1998c) *Early Years Development and Childcare Partnerships – Planning Guidance 1999–2000*. Sudbury: DfEE Publications.

Drummond, M. J. (1993) *Assessing Children's Learning*. London: David Fulton Publishers.

Elfer, P. and Wedge, D. (1992) 'Defining, measuring and supporting quality', in Pugh, C. (ed.) *Contemporary Issues in the Early Years: Working Collaboratively for children*. London: Paul Chapman and National Children's Bureau.

European Childcare Network (ECN) (1991) *Quality in Services for Young Children*. Brussels: Commission of the European Communities.

European Childcare Network (ECN) (1996) *Quality Targets in Services for Young Children*. Brussels: Commission of the European Communities.

Gilkes, J. (1987) *Developing Nursery Education*. Milton Keynes: Open University Press.

Harms, T. and Clifford, R. M. (1980) *Early Childhood Environment Rating Scale*. New York: Teachers College Press.

Lindsay, G. A. (1997) *Baseline Assessment: A Positive or Malign Initiative?* Coventry: Institute of Education, University of Warwick.

Lindsay, G. A. and Pearson, L. (1981) *Identification and Intervention: School Based Approaches*. Oxford: TRC.

McCartney, K. (1984) 'Effect of quality day care environment on children's language development', *Developmental Psychology.* **20**(2).

Moss, P. (1990) *Childcare in European Communities 1985–1990.* Brussels: Commission of the European Communities.

Moss, P. (1994) 'Defining quality: values, stakeholders and processes', in Moss, P. and Pence, A. (eds) *Valuing Quality in Early Childhood Services.* London: Paul Chapman.

Moss, P. and Pence, A. (1994) *Valuing Quality in Early Childcare Services.* London: Paul Chapman.

Moss, P. and Penn, H. (1996) *Transforming Nursery Education.* London: Paul Chapman.

OFSTED (1996) *World's Apart. A Review of International Surveys of Educational Achievement Involving England.* London: HMSO.

Penn, H. (1992) *Under Fives – The View from Strathclyde.* Edinburgh: Scottish Academic Press.

Penn, H. and Wilkinson, J. E. (1995) 'The future of pre-five services in the UK', *Early Child Development and Care* **108**, 147–160.

Phillips, D. *et al.* (1987) 'Child care quality and children's social development', *Developmental Psychology* **23**(4).

Scarr, S. and Eisenberg, M. (1993) 'Child care research: issues and results', *Annual Review of Psychology* **44**.

Schaffer, H. R. (1990) *Making Decisions about Children.* Oxford: Basil Blackwell.

School Curriculum and Assessment Authority (SCAA) (1996) *Desirable Outcomes for Children's Learning on Entering Compulsory Education.* London: SCAA.

School Curriculum and Assessment Authority (SCAA) (1997) *Looking at Children's Learning.* Hayes: SCAA Publications.

The Scottish Office (SO) (1995) *Statistical Bulletin – Education Series* Edn/A2/1995/16. Edinburgh: The Scottish Office Statistical Services.

The Scottish Office (SO) (1996) *Statistical Bulletin – Social Work Series* Swk/DC1/1996. Edinburgh: The Scottish Office Statistical Service.

The Scottish Office (SO) (1997) *A Curriculum Framework for Children in their Pre-school Year.* Edinburgh: HMI.

The Scottish Office (SO) (1998a) *Statistical Bulletin – Education Series,* Edn/E2/1998/6. Edinburgh: The Scottish Office Statistical Service.

The Scottish Office (SO) (1998b) *Meeting the Childcare Challenge – A Childcare Strategy for Scotland.* Edinburgh: The Stationery Office.

The Scottish Office Education Department (SOED) (1950) *The Primary School in Scotland.* Edinburgh: HMSO.

Scottish Office Education Department (SOED) (1973) *Before Five.* Edinburgh: HMSO.

Scottish Office Education Department (SOED) (1995) *Using Performance Indicators in Nursery School/Class/Pre-Five Unit Self-Evaluation.* Edinburgh: Scottish Office Education and Industry Department.

Stephen, C. *et al.* (1998) *Pre-school Education Voucher Initiative: National Evaluation of the Pilot Year.* Stirling: University of Stirling.

Stephen, C. and Wilkinson, J. E. (1995) 'Assessing the quality of provision in community nurseries', *Early Child Development and Care* **108**, 99–114.

Sylva, K. and Wiltshire, J. (1994) 'The impact of early learning on children's later development', *Education Section Review* **18**(2), 47.

Tizard, B. and Hughes (1984) *Young Children Learning.* London: Fontana.

Watt, J. (1994) *Early Education – The Current Debate.* Edinburgh: Scottish Academic Press.

Wilkinson, J. E. (1992) 'Young children thinking', in *Reflections on Curriculum Issues – Early Education.* Dundee: SCCC.

Wilkinson, J. E. (1995) 'Community nurseries: integrated provision for pre-fives', *Early Child Development and Care* **108**, 1–160.

Wilkinson, J. E. and Brady, J. (1990) 'Pre-five evaluation research in strathclyde', *The School and its Community*. Edinburgh: SCRE.

Wilkinson, J. E. and Stephen, C. (1994) 'The assessment of quality in early education', in Watt, J. (ed.) *Early Education: The Quality Debate*. Edinburgh: Scottish Academic Press.

Wilkinson, J. E. and Stephen, C. (1998) 'Collaboration in pre-school provision', *Early Years* **19**(1), 29–38.

Wolfendale, S. (1993) *Baseline Assessment: A Review of Current Practice, Issues and Strategies for Effective Implementation*. Stoke-on-Trent: Trentham Books.

Chapter 5

Children's rights and adult responsibilities
Richard Rose

The word 'education' comes from the root *e* from *ex*, out and *duco*, I lead. It means a leading out. To me education is a leading out of what is already there in the pupil's soul. To Miss Mackay it is a putting in of something that is not there, and that is not what I call education.

Muriel Spark (1961) *The Prime of Miss Jean Brodie*

In November 1989 the United Nations General Assembly unanimously adopted *The Convention on the Rights of the Child* (UN 1989). This document, with its 54 articles can be seen to provide a comprehensive instrument, which, in recognising the civil, social, political, and economic needs of all children, attempts to afford protection to a potentially vulnerable section of society. The key principles of the convention have been summarised in terms of four broad categories, these being described as:

- survival rights – to basic needs such as food, shelter and health care;
- development rights – to education, freedom of thought, conscience and religion;
- protection rights – to be protected from abuse, neglect and exploitation;
- participation rights – to free expression, and to play a full part in community and national life.

To many people, and particularly those working within the 'caring' professions, it may appear that the contents of the convention are little more than an affirmation of those conditions, which are generally taken for granted within a modern society. There is, however, sufficient evidence to suggest that any assumptions, which are made about the overall ability of society to offer adequate protection to children, may be naïve. It also presupposes that the nature of childhood, and the expectations placed upon children, and those who care for or educate them, is a well-defined state. In truth, the changing expectations and demands of society are such that a failure to continually reappraise the conventional wisdom of the ways in which we work with children could result in a generation which is ill-equipped to deal with an ever increasing and complex set of demands.

The period of childhood has often been termed the 'formative years'. This implies a time during which children develop, not only physically and cognitively, but also in their adoption of a set of attitudes, morals, and principles, which they will take forward with them into adulthood. The very term 'formative' infers that during this period children may be moulded and directed by those influences with which they come into contact. A related term, describing children as being of an 'impressionable age' identifies similar implications, and suggests that this is a time when the influence of environment, and experiences may have long-term consequences for the development of the individual. It is true to say that the attitudes, behaviours and beliefs of others with whom we come in to contact will continue to influence us throughout our lives. However, there is a significant body of evidence (Rutter 1972; Vallender and Fogelman 1987) which suggests that many of the influences to which we are subjected in childhood years will remain with us well into adulthood. This being the case, we should consider that childhood is not only an impressionable time, but equally one of vulnerability. A time when the child is dependent upon adults for all basic human, social and economic needs, and therefore requiring more care, attention and affection than at any other stage of life. It is in recognition that such conditions cannot be taken for granted that the United Nations Convention on the Rights of the Child assumes such an important status.

An equally significant piece of legislation, The Children Act (1989), has asserted the right of the child to be heard and to be involved in processes which determine their needs, treatment and care. This has had a particularly profound effect upon the working practices of many professionals, in particular those who are working with children in care. Due regard must now be given to the opinions and wishes of children and their ability to have some control over their own destiny has been recognised in statute.

If the fortunes of childhood are to favour the development of well-adjusted, confident and secure adults, the role which can be played by teachers in securing a positive future must be seen to be critical. Teachers must be encouraged to assume a responsibility which goes well beyond the provision of subject knowledge, and must embrace the well-being and development of the whole child. Those aspects of school life which have been regarded as pastoral in nature, and have often played a minor role in the development of the curriculum, may be required to adopt a higher profile in schools which assume a more holistic view of the teaching process. The notion of pastoral care within schools has its etymological roots within the Christian church, and emphasises a responsibility on the part of teachers to have regard for the spiritual and moral welfare of children.

Yet in an age when the influence of the church has lessened, and many people would regard schools as bearing a major responsibility for the moral guidance of children, we arguably see an education system which measures, compares, and values academic achievement, and gives little attention to matters of pastoral care. Such a situation inevitably influences the way in which the role of the teacher is interpreted. A school system which values collective academic achievement, above the development of the individual child, may achieve positive results in league tables, but is in danger of losing the respect of its pupils, and alienating itself from the most vulnerable members of its community.

It is true that through the current arrangements for the inspection of schools in England and Wales, OFSTED (the Office for Standards in Education) inspectors are required to report on the spiritual, social, moral and cultural education of pupils, and that they do make reference to the 'ethos of the school' (OFSTED 1995). However, the lack of prominence of this section within the majority of inspection reports can be seen as an indicator of the low significance with which it is generally regarded within the educational establishment.

Marland (1995) suggests that during periods of our educational history when pastoral care has appeared to be divorced from the curriculum, the 'content of the latter appeared almost irrelevant to the achievements of the former'. In promoting the view that education should embrace the needs of the whole child, Marland reminds us that while many schools in England and Wales regard their curriculum largely in National Curriculum terms, there exists a statutory requirement to build pastoral care into every school's curriculum programme. Indeed *Curriculum Guidance 3* (National Curriculum Council (NCC) 1990) recognises the need for achieving a curriculum balance which recognises pupil individuality, and celebrates diversity through the teaching of citizenship, personal and social education, equal opportunities, and life in a multicultural society.

While the National Curriculum may afford many opportunities to address these issues through subject content, the teacher and pupil relationship may be considered equally important in providing a firm foundation upon which to build an understanding of the positive roles which children can ultimately learn to play within society. However, if we accept the premise of childhood vulnerability, and juxtapose this with the established authority figure of the teacher, it is clear that the nature of this relationship is likely not only to be influential, but possibly critical in the development of the child. Furthermore, the ways in which teachers perform their role can have a profound effect upon the self-esteem and the future adjustment of their pupils. Pupils who are confident, secure and happy in their relationships at school would seem more likely to achieve good results than those who feel pressured or who regard their interests as disenfranchised by a system which fails to recognise their individuality. Recent government-inspired advertising campaigns through the media would have us believe that most adults can remember a good teacher. This is probably true. It is also a fact that too many adults can recall a teacher who, for a whole range of reasons, may be remembered in less than endearing terms. Time spent on ensuring the development of positive teacher and child relationships may ultimately prove to be as invaluable as that focused upon other aspects of school development.

The nature of teacher and child relationships

It is in recognition of the shortcomings of a traditionally established role for teachers, and the relatively brief history of formal state education, that educationalists have questioned whether the patterns of teacher and child relationships, and indeed the nature of the teaching process itself, are now in need of review. In particular the perception of the teacher as a figure of control, and power, is one which seems to fit less easily within a liberalised system of education. While the figure of the teacher as a person of authority persists, a perception of teaching as a facilitation of learning, recognising the individuality of children, and appreciating the diversity of their needs, means that the nature of that authority needs to be carefully considered.

Foucault (1977), in addressing the nature of control, suggests that the organisation of individuals according to a strict regime, managed by routines and institutional disciplines, is likely to result in the repression of creativity, and is more allied to the ergonomics of function than to the development of individuality. In similar vein, Fromm (1978) recognises the need for discipline and clear guidance, but calls for a 'rational authority' based upon experience and competence, and which is used in order to enable the individual to grow. 'Irrational authority', he claims, is based solely upon position and power, and serves only to exploit the individual who is subjected to it. No one individual has a right to a position of authority, but each person should strive to earn the respect of others through his actions, and the responsible way in which he behaves towards others.

Neither of these writers would suggest that the position of the teacher should be in any way undermined by removing their position of authority from the classroom. Both would rather suggest that teachers may become more effective by considering how their role, and the authority vested in them as teachers, can be developed to encourage and support children in their development as effective learners. Any understanding of children's rights and teacher responsibilities must be based upon an assumption of respect for the individual by both parties. Humanist writers, such as Foucault and Fromm, can provide us with sound philosophical arguments for developing systems of mutual respect and tolerance. Similarly, the legislation passed by national government and august bodies such as the United Nations can make demands upon the ways in which we behave. Ultimately it is left to teachers working in schools to develop the systems which will enable rights to be upheld and responsibilities to be met.

Developing mutual respect

In many school staffrooms across the country today a regular topic of conversation centres upon the behaviour of children. Some schools have invested considerable sums in the deployment of behaviour management schemes and techniques in a bid to arrest anti-social and disruptive behaviours in schools. In the manual for one such scheme, known as 'assertive discipline', the author has written:

> In the not-so-distant past, teachers were empowered with instant authority due to the simple fact that they were 'the teacher'. Society reinforced this authority by the high esteem in which it held educators. Parents reinforced this authority by stressing the importance of education and the importance of listening to the teacher. (Canter and Canter 1992: 6)

Canter and Canter, in referring back to this not-so-distant past, reflect upon some of the changes in society which have impacted upon the classroom. A few lines later they write:

> Things are much different today. Today a teacher has to deal with society's lack of respect for teachers and the education process in general. Today a teacher does not automatically have the respect of students and their parents. (Canter and Canter 1992: 7)

In considering the language adopted here by Canter and Canter, attention must be drawn to terms such as 'authority', 'respect', and 'empowerment', and the implication that these have been automatically the possession of teachers in a bygone age. By contrast, Canter and Canter suggest that in today's classroom such notions are less likely, and that both students and parents are often less than deferential to the post of teacher. This is not an isolated belief and we can, of course, speculate about the role of the teacher in the past, when often they would be one of the few individuals within some communities, possibly alongside the doctor and the priest, to have received a formal higher education. This in some instances would have been seen as sufficient in itself to qualify for a degree of respect. That there has been a shift in the status of teachers can be in little doubt. More interesting, however, is the suggestion implicit in Canter and Canter's statement that the very title of teacher should qualify for immediate respect.

Any discussion of the authority of the teacher should not be divorced from an understanding of the learning process, and the various roles which a teacher may play in this. The fictitious character of Jean Brodie, quoted at the outset of this chapter, drew a distinction between an educational process, which provides the pupil with an opportunity to learn, and contrasts this with one which identifies the teacher as the expert provider of wisdom. This latter concept is a common one and needs to be taken seriously. Indeed, the teacher who is not possessed of wisdom appropriate to the content to be taught is hardly likely to be successful. However, to regard wisdom in simplistic terms, as a store of knowledge, provides only the narrowest of definitions. Knowledge alone is of very little value unless the teacher has the skills, the understanding, the ability and the desire to impart information in an interesting manner. Similarly, wisdom implies an ability which goes beyond subject content and embraces an understanding of the needs of the individual learner which enables appropriate teaching methods to be used in order to promote effective learning. The teacher who cannot inspire and interest his/her pupils has only a limited value in the classroom. Similarly, the teacher who has only a narrow band of strategies is likely to be unable to provide for a broad range of needs and abilities. It is quite possible, for example, that such a teacher may succeed in providing a good learning experience for the majority of the class, but fail to reach the most and least able.

The teacher and pupil relationship is at the hub of any successful learning process, and is dependent upon the ability to provide pupils with the freedom to learn. The creation of a learning climate which is supportive to the learner, is as critical a function of the teacher as are those elements of lesson planning and classroom management which are at the core of teacher training competencies. In using the word 'freedom' in association with learning, one should be in little doubt about the complexities inherent within it. If we return to the writings of 'liberal' educators, such as Illich (1971) and Fromm (1978) we will see that 'freedom does not mean freedom from all guiding principles', it rather means the freedom to grow which is achieved when a teacher wins the confidence of a pupil and mobilises his abilities to engage in purposeful activity, to think critically, and to gain in creativity and understanding.

Freire (1972) has described the 'fundamentally narrative' nature of the teacher and pupil relationship. At its worst, this relationship views the pupil as a vessel to be filled by the teacher, and teaching as an act of depositing. This is what Freire describes as the 'banking concept of education'. Warnock (1977) has expressed similar concerns, describing this as a false picture of education which will lead to bad practice. In her questioning of the teacher role, Warnock asks

> Should teachers adopt a godlike role, or even the role of pedlar of his wares? Should they not rather allow the pupils to lead in the very definition of the wares themselves? If the ideal of education as a kind of growth (rather than as the receiving of stuff to be consumed) is to be realized, then perhaps we ought to be looking in a rather different direction. For it might be that a condition of growth is self-determination. To be a mere receiver or consumer might be actually stunting. (Warnock 1977: 57)

Freire calls for a reconsideration of this relationship and calls for learning as a process of sharing based upon problem solving and a quest for understanding. In such an approach the teacher continues to play a leading role, based upon experience and understanding, but rather than providing solutions, the teacher now becomes a catalyst for the pupil's thinking, a poser of questions which challenge, and a guide through approaches to learning. Such definitions of the teacher and pupil relationship, built upon mutual trust and a shared approach to learning, inevitably takes us some distance from the nostalgic longing for the teacher as a figure of authority. However, this is not to suggest that the role of the teacher can be defined in terms which are *laissez-faire*. Indeed, the teacher who is prepared to move in this direction must take on new responsibilities for planning and preparation which anticipate a greater range of demands from pupils. Neither does this approach provide for an easy life for pupils. They will be encouraged to accept greater responsibility for their own learning, and to develop working practices which enable them to become self-sufficient in their studies. Teachers who develop such a relationship with their pupils will be equally concerned to adopt those teaching strategies which have traditionally proved effective in all classrooms. They are more likely to look beyond the simplistic range of approaches which are evident in some classrooms, in an effort to address the needs of all pupils in ways which are best suited to their individual learning needs.

Joyce *et al.* (1997) describe three elements of learning experiences, these being content, process and social climate. A concentration upon any one of these elements, without due attention to the others, is likely to lead to an impoverished education system. While much of the focus in recent years has inevitably been upon content, driven largely in England and Wales by the National Curriculum, the processes of learning have been to some extent marginalised, and the consideration of social climate forgotten. A climate of mutual respect should be regarded as an equally important element of this triumvirate of learning needs for all schools, which desire to measure their successes in terms which are wider than are results at the end of a particular stage of schooling. This demands a reappraisal of the traditional teacher and pupil roles in order to extend the rights and responsibilities of both parties within the learning process.

Implications for classroom practice

For the teacher who wishes to promote opportunities for pupils to become more autonomous learners, there are many positive strategies which can be adopted. Traditionally, as pupils have gained in maturity, and particularly through secondary schooling, teachers have begun to encourage independent study skills. Yet the pursuit of independence in learning can begin much earlier. Lawrence (1988) has shown a high correlation between positive self-image and effective learning, and he, along with other writers (Purkey 1970; Bernstein 1992), indicates that the development of confidence through being trusted and given responsibility at an early age can enhance academic performance. These writers suggest that pupils who are respected and encouraged to make decisions from the outset of schooling are likely to develop positive attitudes to learning and a desire to succeed. Scott (1996), in reviewing approaches to education in the early years, emphasises that research in the area of pupil rights indicates that children who are given choices, when this is coupled with an encouragement to take responsibility for their actions, are more likely to use adults as a 'resource for learning', rather than simply seeking approval for their actions. She also suggests that pupils presented with a degree of autonomy from early in their schooling are likely to develop the positive learning traits of perseverance and determination when confronted by a challenge.

Griffiths and Davies (1995) reviewed the teacher and pupil relationship in a Nottinghamshire primary school, and introduced strategies which enabled pupils to play a leading role in decision-making. Pupils were encouraged to identify their own learning needs, building upon their strengths, and considering the ways in which they might address their weaknesses. The pupils in their study were fully involved in target setting to address their own learning needs, and teachers invested time in listening to pupil opinions, and assisting them in planning their own learning programmes. In their work, Griffiths and Davies recognised that for many pupils, high levels of autonomy would only be achieved after skills of negotiation and reasoning had been taught. They introduced a system of contracts into the school, accompanied by a series of key questions which enabled pupils to focus upon their personal learning needs and to gain confidence in their own abilities. These researchers reported that after a short period of encouraging pupil decision-making, which recognised their right to be involved in all aspects of planning and recording, they witnessed pupils who had heightened self-esteem, were more task-focused, and had a positive and mature attitude to work. They also write of the excellent teacher and pupil relationships which they observed, with no lessening of respect for the teacher by the pupils, and the creation of an effective learning environment.

Those who would counter the view that pupils should be involved in decisions about their own education from an early age often cite two particular arguments for maintaining the *status quo* in schools. Firstly, they will claim that children cannot have rights until they have learned how to take responsibility for their own actions. Lansdown (1996), in his lucid review of the United Nations Convention on the Rights of the Child, addresses this argument by suggesting that the very process of being consulted from an early age about decisions which affect their lives heightens children's awareness of their own place within the community. Pupils who are consulted begin to develop an understanding of the implications of the decision-making process, to see other points of view, and to acquire a respect for opinions, and a concept of negotiation. A second argument, which suggests that children are not competent to be entrusted with decision-making, is similarly questioned by Lansdown. Decision-making requires skills which must be taught. Unless an early commitment to the promotion of learning opportunities is provided, the child is unlikely to rehearse these skills and will be a long time in gaining the understanding which promotes effective decision-making. As Lansdown states, there is a need to distinguish between participation and full autonomy at the beginning of this process. As has already been suggested, the move towards greater pupil involvement as a means of developing independence is not about handing over control. In the early years, pupils will need to be encouraged to participate as part of the process of learning how to become independent decision-makers.

Bennathan (1996) conducted empirical research in primary and comprehensive schools in order to ascertain if, and how, pupils were being consulted about their own learning needs. In some of the schools visited, Bennathan discovered anxieties on the part of teachers that, if they reduced their directive approach to teaching pupils, they would be in danger of losing control of their classes. She discusses the creation of an ethos which is conducive to the encouragement of pupil participation, which begins from a listening culture. Listening to and respecting the views and ideas expressed by pupils is a critical starting point in the establishment of any school wishing to protect pupil rights. Bennathan recognised that those schools within her study which had moved furthest towards full pupil participation were the ones in which staff morale was high, and teachers were confident in responding to pupil opinions.

A particular advantage of recognising children's rights, and of pupil involvement cited by Bennathan is that of improved behaviour. This theme is one which occurs regularly throughout the literature in this area. Cooper (1993), in his consideration of underlying factors which contribute to problems of disaffected school children, cites the lack of attention provided by schools to the individuality of pupils. In particular, Cooper is concerned to address those pupils who, as a result of poor behaviour management on the part of teachers, have become disillusioned and see themselves as disenfranchised by the education system. Many pupils who exhibit poor patterns of behaviour are seen by Cooper as having been managed through a culture of conflict, which arises largely from a desire on the part of some teachers to impose control. Often, this is the beginning of a spiral of confrontation between the teacher and the pupil. This approach is contrasted to that which encourages both teachers and pupils to view each other in terms of their positive qualities. Cooper is concerned that in schools where behaviour is poor, in a desire to get through each day, the emphasis of management is placed upon survival and control. His research indicates that the school which moves away from this model to one which emphasises cooperation and consultation, is more likely to reduced stress, and to improve both social and academic performance. Clearly within such a climate, the concerns expressed by Canter and Canter (1992) with regards to respect for the teacher are more likely to be addressed. Respect must be earned, and the teacher who generates consideration for his or her pupils, is more likely to find this reciprocated.

Cooper's concern was largely for those pupils who may be described as having emotional and behavioural difficulties, and it is in this area of special educational needs that much of the groundwork in respecting the rights of pupils and recognising the responsibilities of adults has been conducted. Practical examples of the steps taken by teachers working in the field of special educational needs to encourage full pupil participation have been well documented (Rushton and Hardwick 1994; Garner 1996). These and other writers have endeavoured to show how, for example, pupils with severe learning difficulties and communication disorders can be enabled to make choices and decisions through the use of information communications technology or the use of signs and symbols. They have further demonstrated how pupils can develop skills of advocacy and express their own wishes during procedures established to review their progress. Increased confidence on the part of the individual pupils, and greater respect shown towards them by professional adults, have been recorded as a major triumph for such levels of pupil participation. It has been further argued (Rose *et al.* 1996; Lindsay 1997, Rose 1998) that the successful inclusion of pupils with learning difficulties into mainstream schools may well be dependent upon these schools adopting some of the pupil-involvement strategies adapted in segregated provision. Schools for pupils with special educational needs which have recognised pupil rights to participation in decision-making processes have ensured that pupils have played a full role in:

- setting targets to address their individual needs;
- reviewing the results of assessments;
- discussing of individual performance;
- discussing of plans for work to be undertaken over a period of time;
- discussing of the intended advantageous outcomes which a course of action should bring;
- discussing of preferred learning approaches which enable teachers to plan more effectively.

This has demanded a radical reappraisal of educational priorities, and in many instances a shift in teacher perceptions with regards to their role. However, as we have seen from the literature and research conducted into this area, teachers who respect pupil rights and promote greater involvement can see many benefits, which include:

- improved pupil self-esteem
- greater levels of motivation
- mature attitudes to learning
- improved behaviour
- acceptance of responsibility
- greater independence in study skills.

These qualities alone should be sufficient to warrant a greater consideration for the ways in which we conduct classroom practice.

There is much that an individual teacher can do to both promote and protect the rights of the child, and this is most likely to reap benefits if it begins in the classroom. Many will find this change of approach difficult to accept, but, as Charlton (1996) has stated:

> These involvements by pupils are not about either handing over control to pupils or allowing their wishes to predominate; it is about recognition, about participation, about consultation and about fulfilling responsibilities associated with pupils' rights. It is as much about pupils having opportunities for their views to be expressed as it is about pupils becoming involved in decision making, processes which provide recognition that pupils have rights and that, for good reasons, those rights are being respected, valued, heeded and exercised. (Charlton 1996: 41)

Suggested further reading

For discussion on various approaches to the rights of children and responsibilities of adults, see Illich (1971) and Charlton (1996). Freire (1972) is more concerned with learners rather than with just children, but much of his critique of education in general applies to school in particular. For implications for practice and the articulation of policy with practice, see the work of Rose and his associates.

Bibliography

Bagley, J. J. and Bagley, A. J. (1969) *The State and Education in England and Wales, 1833–1968*. London: Macmillan.

Bennathan, M. (1996) 'Listening to children in schools: an empirical study', in Davie, R. and Galloway, D. *Listening to Children in Education*. London: David Fulton Publishers.

Bernstein, B. (1992) *The Structuring of Pedagogic Discourse. Vol. IV: Class, Codes, and Control*. London: Routledge.

Canter, L. and Canter, M. (1992) *Assertive Discipline*. Santa Monica: Canter and Associates.

Charlton, T. (1996) 'Where is control located?' in Jones, K. and Charlton, T. *Overcoming Learning and Behaviour Difficulties*. London: Routledge.

Cooper, P. (1993) *Effective Schools for Disaffected Students*. London: Routledge.

Cunningham, H. (1991) *The Children of the Poor. Representations of Childhood Since the Seventeenth Century*. Oxford: Blackwells.

Foucault, M. (1977) *Discipline and Punish*. London: Allen Lane.

Freire, P. (1972) *Pedagogy of the Oppressed*. Berkhamstead: Penguin.

Fromm, E. (1978) *To Have or To Be?* London: Jonathan Cape.

Garner, P. (1996) 'Involving pupils in policy development', in Jones, K. and Charlton, T. *Overcoming Learning and Behaviour Difficulties*. London: Routledge.

Griffiths, M. and Davies, C. (1995) *In Fairness to Children*. London: David Fulton Publishers.

Illich, I. (1971) *Deschooling Society*. New York: Harper Row.

Joyce, B., Calhoun, E., Hopkins, D. (1997) *Models of Learning – Tools for Teaching*. Milton Keynes: Open University Press.

King, M. (1997) *A Better World for Children*. London: Routledge.

Lansdown, G. (1996) 'The United Nations Convention on the Rights of the Child – Progress in the United Kingdom', in Nutbrown, C. *Children's Rights and Early Education*. London: Paul Chapman.

Lawrence, D. (1988) *Enhancing Self-esteem in the Classroom*. London: Paul Chapman.

Lindsay, G. (1997) 'Values, rights and dilemmas', *British Journal of Special Education* **24**(2), 55–59.

Marland, M. (1995) 'The whole curriculum', in Best, R., Lang, P., *et al. Pastoral Care and Personal–Social Education*. London: Cassell.

National Curriculum Council (NCC) (1990) *The Whole Curriculum*. (Curriculum Guidance 3) York: NCC.

Office for Standards in Education (OFSTED) (1995) *Framework for the Inspection of Schools*. London: HMSO.

Purkey, W. (1970) *Self-concept and School Achievement*. London: Paul Chapman.

Rose, R., McNamara, S., O'Neil, J. (1996) 'Promoting the greater involvement of pupils with special needs in the management of their own learning and assessment processes', *British Journal of Special Education* **23**(4), 166–171.

Rose, R. (1998) 'Including pupils: developing a partnership in learning', in Tilstone, C., Florian, L., Rose, R. *Promoting Inclusive Practice*. London: Routledge.

Rushton, P., and Hardwick, J. (1994) 'Pupil participation in their own Records of Achievement', in Rose, R., Fergusson, A., Coles, C., Byers, R., Banes, D. *Implementing the Whole Curriculum for Pupils with Learning Difficulties*. London: David Fulton Publishers.

Rutter, M. (1972) *Maternal Deprivation Reassessed*. Harmondsworth: Penguin.

Scott, W. (1996) 'Choices in learning', in Nutbrown, C. *Children's Rights and Early Education*. London: Paul Chapman.

Spark, M. (1961) *The Prime of Miss Jean Brodie*. London: Macmillan.

United Nations (1989) *The Convention on the Rights of the Child*. Brussels: United Nations General Assembly.

Vallender, I. and Fogelman, K. (1987) *Putting Children First*. Lewes: Falmer Press.

Warnock, M. (1977) *Schools of Thought*. London: Faber and Faber.

Chapter 6

'Race' and education

Ian Grosvenor

How do we recognise the shackles that tradition has placed upon us? For if we can recognise them, we are also able to break them.

Franz Boas

Thinking about concepts

Britain is a racialised society. That is, in Britain, as in other Western economies, as migrant labour has been incorporated into the economy so social relations have become racialised and subordination has been produced and reproduced. In order to fully explain the meaning of these two statements certain theoretical concepts which underpin them need to be explained, namely, the concept of 'race' and the related concepts of 'race relations', racialisation and racism.

The concept of 'race' is widely used in everyday discourse. It is used to categorise or classify populations into distinct, biologically-defined collectivities. The criteria employed to designate 'race' boundaries can vary. The House of Lords, for instance, ruled that a 'racial group' could be defined by reference to:

- colour,
- nationality,
- ethnicity,
- a long shared history,
- a cultural tradition of its own,
- a common geographical origin,
- descent from a small number of common ancestors,
- a common language,
- a common literature,
- a common religion, or
- by being either a minority or a majority within a larger community (CRE 1989: 29).

Through 'race' categorisation individuals can be located as social subjects with a given and fixed identity. This identity is fixed by virtue of individuals being born into a designated 'racial group', they inherit a 'race identity'. When individuals or collectivities so identified as being members of different 'race' groups come in to contact they are said to be involved in 'race relations'. Nevertheless, 'races' do not exist in reality.

After the Second World War a meeting of scientists was organised in Paris by the United Nations Educational Scientific and Cultural Organisation (UNESCO) to objectively discuss Hitler's 'final solution' to the 'Jewish question'. A collective statement was issued in 1950 which concluded that:

> The scientific material available to us at present does not justify the conclusions that inherited genetic differences are a major factor in producing the differences between cultures and cultural achievements of different peoples or groups ... For all practical purposes 'race' is not so much a biological phenomenon as a social myth. The myth of 'race' has created an enormous amount of human and social damage. In recent years it has taken a heavy toll in human lives and caused untold suffering. It still prevents the normal development of millions of human beings and deprives civilization of the effective co-operation of productive minds...

This position was reaffirmed at further UNESCO meetings in 1951 and 1964. In 1967 UNESCO convened a fourth panel of experts which included sociologists, lawyers, social psychologists, ethnographers, historians and geneticists. Again they reaffirmed the 1950 declaration, but the tone of their document was much more uncompromising and expressed in terms chosen to convey a sense of urgency:

> Racism continues to haunt the world. As a major social phenomenon it requires the attention of all students of the sciences of man...[it] stultifies the development of those who suffer it, perverts those who apply it...The human problems arising from so-called 'race' relations are social in origin rather than biological...Racism falsely claims that there is a scientific basis for arranging groups hierarchically in terms of psychological and cultural characteristics that are immutable and innate...In order to undermine racism it is not sufficient that biologists should expose its fallacies. It is also necessary that psychologists and sociologists should demonstrate its causes. (UNESCO 1979: 24–26, 41–43)

'Race' is a social construct, it exists in the imagination and it is the product of what Green and Carter (1988) have called 'race thinking'. 'Race-thinking', whether it be in everyday thought or in academic research, produces the object of its own knowledge. 'Races' are not naturally occurring populations, a 'race' is an imagined collectivity. It follows, therefore, that without 'races' there can be no 'race relations'. What does exist are racialised relations, racism and its effects (Miles 1993).

Some social scientists have argued that despite the constructed character of 'race' categories, 'races' are still valid ways of classifying populations for social scientific and historical analysis since the concepts have meaning within popular culture (Rex 1983; Cashmore and Troyna 1990; Solomos and Back 1995). Certainly, it is important to re-present commonsense ideas as those held by historical subjects, to give full recognition to the importance of the concept in the meaning systems of the past. However, it does not follow that the concept 'race' should be reproduced in our analyses of those systems, or that we neglect to question how the concept developed as such a powerful and seductive idea. The use of the term 'race' has also been defended by the claim that all concepts are 'constructs', all 'social facts' discourse-dependent such that 'common sense' constructs such as 'race' are as descriptively and analytically useful as, say, gender and social class. This position seems to suggest that we can make no judgement of a concept's suitability for analysis. But, just such judgements are essential since the concept 'race' is so problematic. Claims, for example, that Britain has a 'race' problem elicit a knowing nod, but to what are we assenting? Is 'the problem' that of racist beliefs, or discriminatory practices, or identities deemed 'racial', or the unequal distribution of resources related to colour, language, religion, nationality, or, perhaps, that there are just too many of 'them'? When a concept serves so many ends, usually unspecified, questions must be asked about its theoretical integrity.

The ideological process by which 'race' identities are constructed has been termed 'racialisation' (Miles 1982). Racialisation involves 'a dialectical process of signification', in that it defines and recognises difference between the Self and the Other. Racialisation is not a recent process since earlier in the twentieth century migrants from Eastern Europe and Ireland, for example, were perceived and treated as members of 'race' groups. Since the Second World War, however, it is colour around which race-making has largely cohered and Irishness, for example, has been ethnicised. Several social scientists have documented aspects of post-war racialisation in Britain in, for example, their work on the state. They have shown that from the 1940s onwards, the concept of 'race' has been an organising principle of immigration and nationality law. Wedded to this principle were notions of 'blood' and 'stock', notions which carried messages about some innate capacity for assimilation into the nation (Joshi and Carter 1984; Carter *et al.* 1987; Carter and Grosvenor 1992). Cultural differences associated with 'race' groups were conceived, and perceived, in opposition to an indigenous culturally connected identity. These differences constituted boundary lines between those who were 'of' the nation and those who were 'outside'. Cultural differences were mobilised and manipulated by politicians in debates over immigration legislation to provide a sense of solidarity, to demonstrate that 'race' identities were a barrier to assimilation and to express opposition to the settlement of those who threatened the indigenous unified cultural community.

Through the racialisation process a sense of historical descent and identity are made public. This sense of identity is dependent upon the maintenance of racialised boundaries. Once a group has been racialised it is possible to justify discriminatory behaviour towards its members on the grounds of 'racial difference'. Thus, racialisation is a process through which exploitation and exclusion, physical and verbal abuse, and discrimination can become manifest (Miles 1989: 75, 79, 84). This brings this opening discussion to the final related concept of racism.

Racism is an ideology, that is, a way of viewing and understanding the world. The distinguishing content of racism as an ideology is first 'its signification of some biological characteristic[s] as the criterion by which a collectivity may be identified'. In this way, the collectivity is represented as having 'a natural unchanging origin and status, and therefore as being inherently different'. Secondly, the collectivity so identified is attributed with additional 'negatively evaluated characteristics' and/or is represented as 'inducing negative consequences' for other collectives. These characteristics may be either biological or cultural. Finally, the group that is identified as the object of racism, the biological features which are signified, and the characteristics which are attributed to the group and negatively evaluated are all historically variable (Miles 1989: 79, 84).

What, then, of ethnic thinking and categorisation? In 1970s and 1980s Britain there was a shift in the racialised language of political discourse. 'Ethnic' replaced 'race' as a term of reference signifying identity: essentialist individual and collective attributes were attached to 'ethnic' identities as opposed to the earlier signification of essentialist individual and collective attributes to 'race'. Ethnic-thinking entailed immersion in a discourse at the heart of which is a belief that 'ethnics' are discrete human groups whose consciousness and conduct can be identified and evaluated in ways deemed 'ethnic'. Associated with this belief is another: that the social relations which exist among these alleged groups are to be primarily comprehended as 'ethnic relations'. Both beliefs essentialise the social with the effect that fluid socio-politically-generated perceptions become fixed, frozen relations and identities. Or, to put it another way, people once perceived through the prism of 'race' identities were reconstructed as 'ethnics'. Ethnicity and 'race' are ideologically linked. So, in the parliamentary debates on immigration and nationality since the 1970s, while 'ethnic' emerged among politicians as the preferred descriptor, its usage was always in the context of a discussion focusing on the improvement of 'race relations' (Grosvenor 1997: 40–45; Green and Grosvenor 1997: 884–90).

This opening discussion of concepts has been included for several reasons. First, it clarifies the ideological position adopted by the author; secondly, it seeks to provoke in the reader a recognition that writing about 'race' and/or 'ethnicity' is an area of critical academic debate and that 'race' and/or 'ethnic' categorisation do not have to be accepted as given; and finally, it provides an introductory frame-work for a discussion of the debates which currently engage researchers focusing on racism and education.

Researching racism and education

There are, as Paul Connolly has observed, 'not many areas within the social sciences than can equal research on 'race' and ethnicity in terms of the heated methodological debates and controversies that have been generated' (Connolly and Troyna 1998: 2). Educational research before the 1980s tended to produce studies which offered stereotypical and pathological accounts of minority communities. Children, whose families had their origins in South Asia, were presented as being 'caught between two cultures' and consequently faced by a crisis of identity, while Afro-Caribbean youth were portrayed as aggressive as a consequence of loose family structures within the black communities (Green and Grosvenor 1997). Such research was increasingly criticised as being value-laden, both reflecting and reinforcing the race thinking of society, and researchers were challenged to consider the implications of their work. This concern led to a call for an explicitly antiracist research agenda which focused not on 'ethnic communities' but on white racism (Bourne 1980; Lawrence 1981).

Since the mid-1980s there has been a distinctive shift towards qualitative research on racism and schooling. A series of ethnographic studies have appeared – Wright (1986, 1992); Mac an Ghaill (1988); Gillborn (1990); Troyna and Hatcher (1992); Mirza (1992); Connolly (1994, 1998) – which have employed observational and interview data and documentary evidence to uncover and analyse how racism operated within schools and shaped minority students' experiences of schooling. These in-depth studies of particular schools and groups of students and teachers within them have themselves generated further academic debate and controversy. Indeed, there is now a 'project of methodological criticism', to use Gillborn's phrase (Gillborn 1998a: 52), which calls into question whether such studies offer 'convincing evidence' that school-based processes actually disadvantage minority groups (Foster *et al.* 1996; Hammersley and Gomm 1996; Hammersley 1998). In particular, ethnographic studies which have pointed to teacher racism as playing a significant part in the schooling of minority youngsters, have been singled out for criticism and researchers accused of political bias:

> Recently, especially under the influence of feminism and anti-racism, there has been increasing pressure to make educational research serve political ends. The result, in many cases, it seems to us, has been a distortion in the process of enquiry. (Hammersley and Gomm 1996: 20)

Inevitably, this critique has, in turn, generated further debate over how 'racism' is to be defined, the type of data required to constitute proof of its manifestation in schools and the 'myth' of neutrality in educational research (Connolly and Troyna 1998).

What is undeniable is that racism has shaped and continues to shape the school experiences of minority youngsters in Britain:

> When I first started infant school, you know, this was in 1955. I was the only coloured boy there in the school ... [and was] always an object of ridicule or ... some form of comical jest more or less to the other pupils in the class ... (Humphry and John 1971: 94)

> I don't like this school because children hit me and call me names. They call me 'second hand', 'toilet paper', 'bloody Asian'...Sometimes I tell my teacher. She

tells them off…then they go to the Head and he is also angry with them…now they don't fight in the school, they fight when we are coming home. (*Times Educational Supplement* 1986)

I'm coloured. They call me nigger and black bitch. I just want to be respected. (The *Guardian* 1996)

One way of exploring and trying to understand the various dimensions of this experience is to document how racism in education has the effect of excluding people in British society.

Racism and exclusion

In 1993 the Department for Education (DfE) published figures which revealed that African–Caribbean children made up 8 per cent of all children permanently excluded from school in England and Wales, but comprised only 2 per cent of the total school population (DfE 1993). Throughout England and Wales, as Table 6.1 demonstrates, there is a pattern of high exclusion rates of black children from school.

Table 6.1 The exclusion of black pupils from school

Location	Date	Exclusions %	School population %
Sheffield	1990	6.7	2.0
Brent	1991	85.0	17.0
Birmingham	1990–91	31.0	9.0
Birmingham	1993–94	33.0	9.0
Leicestershire	1994–95	7.1	1.4

Exclusion is not limited to the secondary years. In the London Borough of Lewisham between the summer of 1990 and the spring of 1991 61 per cent of children excluded from primary school were black, but black children represented only 14 per cent of the school population. These patterns of exclusion are not new. For example, the CRE carried out a formal investigation into the suspension of pupils from Birmingham schools in a period which pre-dates the above. The CRE found that between 1974 and 1980 black children were almost four times more likely to be suspended than white pupils. Black children represented 10 per cent of Birmingham's school population and 40 per cent of excluded children (Bourne *et al.* 1994). Indeed, we can go back further in time to the 1960s where black children – especially of African–Caribbean background – were regularly excluded from mainstream schooling and placed in schools for the educationally sub-normal (Coard 1971). It should be stated at this juncture that it was evidence of inequality in schooling in the 1960s onwards which was a critical factor in the mobilising of black and Asian community groups to challenge racism in education and in the development of supplementary schooling (Carter 1986: 83–7;Grosvenor 1997: Chapter 4).

The number of *all* students permanently excluded from school has risen dramatically in the 1990s. The annual increase has slowed in recent years, but the overall numbers have continued to rise with more than 12,000 young people excluded in 1998 (DfEE 1998). Black young people are disproportionately represented among those excluded from full-time mainstream education. Statistics published by the DfEE have been used by David Gillborn to calculate 'a head-count' quantifying in human terms the meanings of the percentages in inequalities. Based on figures for the whole of England in 1995–96 he found that compared with the rate for white and 'Asian' students each year, around 1,000 extra young black people are permanently excluded from school. Further, depending on the timescale and categories used, local data on exclusions suggest that black young people are anywhere from two, four and six times more likely to be excluded from school than their white peers (Gillborn 1998b). Indeed, the most recent data available for England and Wales suggests that black children are up to 15 times more likely to be excluded in some areas than their white counterparts (*Times Educational Supplement* 11 December 1998). Does this mean that black students are six or even 15 times more unmanageable than their white counterparts, or is there something at fault with the system?

This disproportionate number of black exclusions from school has been directly related to the Conservative restructuring of the education system through the Education Reform Act 1988 and the Education Acts of 1992 and 1993 (Bourne *et al.* 1994; Bridges 1994). It has been argued that a system has been created where white parents can, and have, exploited the 'market' for school places and avoided schools with significant numbers of black pupils. A parent's right to choose has become predominant over 'race relations' legislation and any commitment to equality of opportunity. Opting out and open enrolment provide the mechanisms through which racist parental choice can express its demands for 'Christian', all-white schools. Schools, operating under the new market philosophy where they compete with one another for pupils, for money and for reputation among parents 'stirred up to exercise choice', have been expelling those pupils who are seen as 'troublesome, too expensive, different' (Bridges 1994: 34). Children who are identified as having the potential to drive school examination results or attendance records down on the league tables are not wanted, and cannot be afforded, by schools. In this climate teacher prejudices – seeing black children as 'underachievers' or 'problems' – are resurfacing in the classroom, but instead of finding themselves redirected to educationally sub-normal schools (ESNs), as happened in the 1960s, black children are being forced out of school into the education wilderness, where a lack of qualifications (in a qualifications-driven society) is their learning reality. Nationally, only 15 per cent of *all* permanently excluded pupils are successfully reintegrated into mainstream education (*Times Educational Supplement* 25 September 1998).

In August 1997 the Labour Government launched the Social Exclusion Unit (SEU) with an initial remit to report to Prime Minister Blair on how to 'make a step change in the scale of truancy and exclusions from school, and to find better solutions for those who have to be excluded' (SEU 1998: np). Almost a year later the SEU presented its report which included a survey of current research regarding truancy and exclusion. It acknowledged 'race' inequalities and attention was drawn to the over-representation of black students among those excluded. It committed the Government to a range of measures and recommended a target that 'by 2002 there will be a one third reduction in the numbers of both permanent and fixed-term exclusions from their current levels' (SEU 1998: 29). However, the report failed to make a reduction in the number of black exclusions a specific target – an action which the CRE had strongly endorsed (*Carf* 1998). Consequently, exclusion is set to continue as the 'educational experience' of many black youngsters.

Exclusion from school is also paralleled by exclusion within school. Minority youngsters are excluded from the curriculum. As the National Union of Teachers (NUT) commented during the consultation exercise about the Education Reform Act (ERA):

> The act does not address the needs of the multi-ethnic and multicultural community which Britain has become. This again is a pointer to the conformist thrust of a national curriculum approach. Where in a syllabus of minimum content is there space for that which is not English, white and Christian. (Haviland 1988: 22)

Curriculum reforms, new campaigns focusing on standards, literacy and numeracy have offered no improvement; the mainstream school curriculum remains essentially 'English, white and Christian'. This formal curriculum, coupled with a school's hidden curriculum – its rules, procedures, ethos – can create, according to some commentators, an environment where minority pupils are more likely to underachieve and fail (Mac an Ghaill 1988; Gillborn 1990; Hatcher 1997). In *Black Masculinities and Schooling* (1997) Tony Sewell asked a group of African–Caribbean secondary pupils to devise a model of a school which deliberately excluded them. They were readily able to identify ten factors, in order of importance:

1. teachers who were afraid of children and couldn't control their classes;
2. teachers and head teachers who were not consistent;
3. boring lessons;
4. teachers who would pick on black kids because of their hairstyle;
5. intelligent children being called 'boffins' and getting beaten up;
6. teachers not explaining their lessons clearly;
7. teachers not showing black kids respect;
8. no heating in classrooms;
9. no black history;
10. ancillary staff being racist (Sewell 1997:217–18).

Kamala Nehaul, in a parallel study based on primary schools, identified factors central for minority pupil achievement: academic and behavioural expectations 'of this group of pupils equalling those of other pupils'; an academic environment which is 'inspiring and stimulating'; a curriculum 'permeated with a high-profile antiracist ethos'; and 'trust between parents and teachers' (Nehaul 1996: 114, 187).

It follows, therefore, that ineffective schools can produce pupil under-achievement and failure, which in turn can create pupil alienation from schooling and thereby may constitute a contributory factor to high exclusion rates. There is also, the other possibility – that teachers expect minority youngsters to fail. Teachers, as Williams and Carter observed, 'do not accept stereotypes as a result of indoctrination but because in certain circumstances, and in various ways, they make "sense" in explaining their day to day experiences' (Williams and Carter 1985: 7). Professional knowledge is not only experiential (encompassing first-hand experiences of student learning), but is shaped by beliefs about teaching, students and the community of which the school is a part. Such knowledge is value-laden and orientated towards practice. In a society where identities deemed 'race-ial' and ethnic are conceived as the primary determinants of attitudes and behaviour, a child's perceived learning difficulties, it can be argued, are best understood as a function of their 'race'/ethnic identity rather than as a product of pedagogical assumptions of the curriculum or the school environment. In other words, by positing a 'race' or ethnic base for learning problems, the responsibility for failure is removed from the teacher/school/education system and is placed squarely on the minority child and family. Failure is a product of 'their' culture, it is not the fault of schools.

Another form of exclusion which minority pupils encounter is exclusion from the right to safety on the way to, from, and at school. It has been estimated by the British Crime Survey that only 10 per cent of 'racist' incidents are reported to the police (CRE 1997). In other words, the majority of incidents are not reported. Children feature in many of these incidents. A ChildLine study *Children and Racism* (1996) found that of a sample of 1,616 callers to the charity's helpline one in four said that they had experienced racist bullying, half of them for more than a year before seeking help, 56 callers had suffered racist street violence and 14 callers spoke about racist experiences inside school. The callers came from a variety of backgrounds including African, Afro-Caribbean, Asian, Jewish and Irish and most of them described themselves as British. The charity concluded that 'many black and ethnic minority children in Britain endure blatant, unrelenting racist harassment and bullying on a daily basis' (ChildLine 1996), a view echoed on the reports publication by Herman Ouseley, chairman of the CRE, 'For too many young people growing up in Britain today means facing racially motivated violence and persistent racial discrimination' (The *Guardian* 23 July 1996).

The ChildLine researchers reported that many callers were afraid to discuss racist bullying with their teachers or families. This finding was graphically illustrated a year later in the case of Vijay Singh of Stretford, Manchester. On 12 October 1997, his family came home to find that the 13-year-old boy had tied a scarf around the bannister and hanged himself. After Vijay's death his mother found a diary containing vivid accounts of daily racist abuse:

I shall remember this for eternity and will never forget.
Monday: My money was taken.
Tuesday: Names called.
Wednesday: My uniform torn.
Thursday: My body pouring with blood.
Friday: It's ended.
Saturday: Freedom.

A few days before his death Vijay had been awarded a merit by his English teacher for a poem on bullying he had written. Neither his mother nor his teachers knew about the bullying he had suffered at the hands of white boys (Klein 1997: 16). Such bullying, as one NSPCC officer observed, 'only comes to light when a young person is harmed or commits suicide. We are not waiting for a crisis to happen. We have to act more preventively' (Francis 1998: 6).

Despite the experience of racism and discrimination in schooling, minority pupils remain ambitious in their educational aspirations and achieve academic success. However, research shows that many students find a continuance of racist and discriminatory practices, covert and overt in higher education (HE). For example, the CRE in its submission to the National Commission on Education in 1992 concluded that:

- some ethnic minority students have a different and inferior experience of HE than their white peers;
- there was a 'lack of understanding' and progress in HE institutions with regard to the development and implementation of equal opportunities policies;
- most common interpretations of equal opportunities focused upon staff employment procedures, or upon the recruitment of students with disabilities;
- issues such as black student recruitment, discrimination and harassment, staff development, curriculum reviews, the overall institutional ethos and links with community groups were the concern of only a very small minority of HE institutions.

These failings, coupled with minority students feeling isolated and victimised were, the CRE concluded, 'fed back into the communities, making higher education a less attractive option'. (CRE 1992). In other words, minority students were and are being excluded from achieving success in HE. A postscript to this form of exclusion is provided by the research of Chris McManus of University College, London, who reported in October 1998 that two-thirds of the 27 medical schools who recruited students in 1996–97 'discriminated against ethnic minority applicants' (The *Guardian* 16 October 1998).

Finally, those students who do come through the system can find themselves excluded from success in employment. There is, for example, a large (and growing) literature, relating to the experience of minority students who choose teaching as their career: Gibbes (1980); Grosvenor (1990); Henry (1991); Ghuman (1995); Osler (1997). The following four examples are representative of the life histories of many minority teachers:

> For my first teaching post (in 1969) I was inevitably appointed to a reception class [newly arrived 'immigrant' pupils] in a secondary school. I say inevitably because as an 'immigrant teacher' I was regarded as having nothing to offer except a 'race-cast' role teaching English as a second language to immigrant pupils'. (Mukherjee 1988)

> I think it is a great struggle to get promotion if you are black. I have applied for other jobs in other schools. The heads seem to think about the image of the school and not your ability. To them the image of the school means that if a black person is seen about the school white parents will not send their children to the school. (Gibbes 1980)

> I have often been mistaken for the cleaner or the dinner lady, anything but a teacher. (Minhas 1992)

> The education system has changed rapidly in recent years...And yet, sadly, so much remains the same. Our life histories reveal that racial and sexual struggles inside the education system [*sic*] in the UK still remain unchanged. (Rakhit 1998)

These experiences, again fed back into the communities, have been a critical factor in the rejection of teaching as a career by many minority students. In this context, it useful to point to the employment figures for the largest LEA in England: minority pupils currently represent 35 per cent of the school population in Birmingham (and rising) but only 4 per cent of the teaching force is from a minority community.

In the very early days of Channel 4 Salman Rushdie appeared on the series *Opinions* and described 'The New Empire Within Britain'. His purpose was simple, to tell the white majority how life in Britain all too often felt to members of minority groups. Britain, he said, consisted of 'two entirely different worlds' and 'the one you inhabit is determined by the colour of your skin' (Rushdie 1991: 134). Rushdie, in articulating a grievance, hoped to 'build bridges of understanding' (Rushdie 1991: 4). It is clear that debates over research methodology, over the where, why and how of school-based processes, over the value systems of the researcher and the credibility of politically engaged writing will continue to be central features of academic discourse about racism and education. At the same time, it is also clear that the consequences of racism in education for minority children, for their parents and for their families are very real, and they will continue to be experienced. Ignorance is a barrier to action; everyone involved in education has a responsibility to confront the layers of data which describe the contemporary reality of living 'in the new Empire' if there is to be any possibility of understanding, of embracing rather than excluding.

Suggested further reading

The three Open University readers for the course *'Race', Education and Society* provide the best introduction to the issues tackled in this chapter: Gill *et al.* (1992); Donald and Rattansi (1992) and Braham *et al.* (1992). Gillborn and Gipps (1996) provides a review of research on the educational achievements of minority children; Grosvenor (1997) offers an historical analysis of national education policy-making; and the collection edited by Connolly and Troyna (1998) offers a comprehensive overview and assessment of the debates associated with research into racism and education. Two case studies of schooling which come to very different conclusions about the incidence and impact of teacher racism can be found in Gillborn (1990) and Foster (1990). For accounts of black resistance to racism see Sivanandan (1982) and Carter (1986). Gaine and George (1999) provides an excellent introduction to the interaction of 'race', gender and class in shaping school inequalities. The journals *Carf, Multicultural Teaching, Race and Class, and Race, Ethnicity and Education* (new in 1998) provide valuable insights and up-to-date research and data.

References

Bourne, J. (1980) 'Cheerleaders and ombudsmen: the sociology of race relations in Britain', *Race and Class* **XXI**(4), 331–5.

Bourne, J., Bridges, L., Searle, C. (1994) *Outcast England. How Schools Exclude Black Children.* London: Institute of Race Relations.

Braham, P., Rattansi, A., Skellington, R. (eds) (1992) *Racism and Antiracism.* London: Sage Publications.

Bridges, L. (1994) 'Tory education: exclusion and the black child', *Race and Class* **36**(1), 33–48.

Carf, August/September 1998 'Is Labour failing black children?'

Carter, B. and Grosvenor, I. (1992) *The Apostles of Purity. Black Immigration and Education Policy in Post-War Britain.* Birmingham: AFFOR.

Carter, B., Joshi, S., Harris, C. (1987) 'The 1951–55 Conservative government and the racialisation of black immigration', *Immigrants and Minorities* **6**(3), 335–47.

Carter, T. (1986) *Shattering Illusions. West Indians in British Politics.* London: Lawrence & Wishart.

Cashmore, E. and Troyna, B. (1990) *Introduction to Race Relations.* London: Routledge.

ChildLine (1996) *Children and Racism* [www document] URL http://www.childline.org.uk/

Coard, B. (1971) *How the West Indian Child is Made Educationally Subnormal in the British Education System.* London: Beacon Books

Commission for Racial Equality (CRE) (1989) *Code of Practice for the Elimination of Racial Discrimination in Education.* London: CRE.

Commission for Racial Equality (CRE) (1992) *Submission to the National Commission on Education.* London: CRE.

Commission for Racial Equality (CRE) (1997) *Racial Attacks and Harassment.* London: CRE.

Connolly, P. (1994) 'All lads together? Racism, masculinity and multicultural/anti-racist strategies in a primary school', *International Studies in Sociology of Education* **4**(2), 191–211.

Connolly, P. (1998) *Racism, Gender Identities and Young Children.* London: Routledge.

Connolly, P. and Troyna, B. (eds) (1998) *Researching Racism in Education.* Buckingham: Open University Press.

Department for Education (DfE) (1993) 'A new deal for out-of-school pupils', *DfE News.* 126/93, 23 April.

Department for Education and Employment (DfEE) (1998) *Statistics of Schools in England.* London: DfEE.

Donald, J. and Rattansi, A. (1992) *'Race', Culture and Difference.* London: Sage.

Foster, P. (1990) *Policy and Practice in Multicultural and Anti-Racist Education.* London: Routledge.

Foster, P., Gomm, R., Hammersley, M. (1996) *Constructing Educational Inequality: An Assessment of Research on School Processes.* London: Falmer Press.

Francis, J. (1998) 'Study in harmony', the *Guardian*, 11 March, 6–7.

Gaine, C. and George, R. (1999) *Gender 'Race' and Class in Schooling. A New Introduction*. London: Falmer Press.

Gill, D., Mayor, B., Blair, M. (eds) (1992) *Racism and Education*. London: Sage.

Ghuman, P. (1995) *Asian Teachers in British Schools: A Study of Two Generations*. Clevedon: Multilingual Matters.

Gibbes, N. (1980) *West Indian Teachers Speak Out*. London: Caribbean Teachers' Association and Lewisham Council for Community Relations.

Gillborn, D. (1990) *'Race', Ethnicity and Education*. London: Unwin Hyman.

Gillborn, D.(1998a) 'Racism and the politics of qualitative research: learning from controversy and critique', in Connolly, P. and Troyna, B. (eds) (1998) *Researching Racism in Education*. Buckingham: Open University Press.

Gillborn, D. (1998b) 'Race, nation and education: New Labour and the new racism', in Demaine, J. (ed.) *Education Policy and Contemporary Politics*. London: Macmillan.

Gillborn, D. and Gipps, C. (1996) *Recent Research on the Achievements of Ethnic Minority Pupils*. London: HMSO.

Green, M. and Carter, B. (1988) '"Race" and "race-makers": the politics of racialization', *Sage Race Relations Abstracts* **13**(2), 4–30.

Green, M. and Grosvenor, I. (1997) 'Making subjects: historians, education and "race" categorisation', *Paedagogica Historica* **XXXIII**(3), 883–908.

Grosvenor, I. (1990) 'Education, racism and the employment of black teachers', *Multicultural Teaching* **8**(2), 9–13.

Grosvenor, I. (1997) *Assimilating Identities: Racism and Education Policy in Post-1945 Britain*. London: Lawrence & Wishart.

The *Guardian* (1996) 'Ethnic minority children "still suffer racism daily"'. 23 July.

Hammersley, M. (1998) 'Partisanship and credibility: the case of antiracist educational research', in Connolly, P. and Troyna, B. (eds) (1998) *Researching Racism in Education*. Buckingham: Open University Press.

Hammersley, M. and Gomm, R. (1996) 'Exploiting sociology for equality?' *Network: Newsletter of the British Sociological Association* **65** 19–20.

Hatcher, R. (1997) 'New Labour, school improvement and racial inequality', *Multicultural Teaching* **15**(3), 8–13.

Haviland, J. (ed.) (1988) *Take Care Mr Baker!* London: Fourth Estate.

Henry, D. (1991) *Thirty Blacks in British Education. Hopes, Frustrations, Achievements*. Crawley: Rabbit Press.

Humphry, D. and John, G. (1971) *Because They're Black*. Harmondsworth: Penguin.

Joshi, S. and Carter, B. (1984) 'The role of Labour in the creation of a racist Britain', *Race and Class* **XXV**, 53–70.

Klein, R. (1997) 'Rescuing the Lost Boys of racism', *Times Education Supplement*. November 14.

Lawrence, E. (1981) 'White sociology, black struggle', *Multiracial Education* **9**(3), 3–17.

Mac an Ghaill, M. (1988) *Young Gifted and Black: Student-teacher Relations in the Schooling of Black Youth*. Buckingham: Open University Press.

Miles, R. (1982) *Racism and Migrant Labour*. London: Routledge.

Miles, R. (1989) *Racism*. London: Routledge.

Miles, R. (1993) *Racism After 'Race Relations'*. London: Routledge.

Minhas, R. (1992) 'The impact of the National Curriculum on teacher education', in Arora, R. (ed.) *Teacher Education and Ethnic Minorities*. Bradford: Race Relations Unit.

Mirza, H. S. (1992) *Young, Female and Black*. London: Routledge.

Mukherjee, T. (1988) 'The journey back', in Cohen, P. and Bains, H. S. (eds) *Multi-Racist Britain*. London: Macmillan.

Nehaul, K. (1996) *The Schooling of Children of Caribbean Heritage*. Stoke-on-Trent: Trentham Books.

Osler, A. (1997) *The Education and Careers of Black Teachers.* Buckingham: Open University Press.

Rakhit, A. (1998) 'Silenced voices: life history as an approach to the study of South Asian women teachers', in Connolly, P. and Troyna, B. (eds) (1998) *Researching Racism in Education.* Buckingham: Open University Press.

Rex, J. (1983) *Race Relations in Sociological Theory.* London: Routledge Kegan Paul.

Rushdie, S. (1991) *Imaginary Homelands.* London: Granta.

Sewell, T. (1997) *Black Masculinities and Schooling.* Stoke-on-Trent: Trentham Books.

Sivanandan, A. (1982) *A Different Hunger.* London: Pluto Press.

Social Exclusion Unit (SEU) (1998) *Truancy and School Exclusion. Report by the Social Exclusion Unit.* Cm 3957. London: HMSO.

Solomos, J. and Back, L. (1995) *Race, Politics and Social Change.* London: Routledge.

Times Educational Supplement (1986) ' "They call me blacky" – a story of everyday racism', 19 September.

Times Educational Supplement (1998) 'Racism fears as exclusions rise', 25 September.

Troyna, B and Hatcher, R. (1992) *Racism in Children's Lives: A Study of Mainly White Primary Schools.* London: Routledge.

UNESCO (1979) *Declaration on Race and Racial Prejudice.* Paris: UNESCO.

Williams, J. and Carter, B. (1985) ' "Institutional racism": new orthodoxy, old ideas', *Multiracial Education* **13**(1), 3–8.

Wright, C. (1986) 'School processes: an ethnographic study', in Eggleston, J., Dunn, D., Anjali, M. (eds) *Education for Some: The Educational and Vocational Experiences of 15–18 Year-Old Members of Minority Ethnic Groups.* Stoke-on-Trent: Trentham Books.

Chapter 7

Social class and education
Dave Hill

The history of all hitherto existing society is the history of class struggles...Our epoch...has simplified the class antagonisms...into two great hostile camps, into two great classes directly facing each other: Bourgeoisie and Proletariat.

Marx [1848] 1978: 35–36

Introduction

In this chapter I discuss the relationship between social class, society and education. The perspective adopted is Marxist. In Part One, I discuss social class and how it is measured. In Part Two, I present some of the main concepts of Marxist social class analysis. In Part Three, I relate these concepts to education, referring to the work of Bourdieu, Althusser, Bowles and Gintis, and recent work by Duffield and her associates. In Part Four, I differentiate between two types of Marxist analysis – Structuralist neo-Marxism and Culturalist neo-Marxism.

Part One: What is social class and how is it measured?

What is Social Class?

What social class are you? What social class were the people you went to school with, or work or study with? All people can be categorised, or classified in different ways – for example by religion, ethnicity, sex, sexuality, height, age, reading ability. One classification, social class, is generally recognised as having particular significance. Social class is generally recognised as *both reflecting and causing* major social, economic, and cultural differences in, for example, income, wealth, status, education, and lifestyle (see, for example, Ahmad 1997; Boseley 1998; Rowntree Foundation 1995). Income (pay packet, salary, and dividends) and wealth (what we own, such as housing, shares, money in the bank, and possessions) *reflect* our social class position. However, not only does social class reflect such social differences, it also *causes* them. Our social background, social class, social class-related ways in which we present ourselves tend to affect the ways in which we are treated by teachers, by the police, by friends, by employers, by sexual partners, and by many others in society. As with racism and sexism, this can take the form of *personal discrimination* – positive or negative stereotyping, labelling and expectation. It can also take the form of *structural discrimination* – taking place on a systematic, repetitive, embedded nature within particular social structures such as schooling, housing, employment, credit agencies, police, armed forces.

In the education system there are different social class-related:

• patterns of educational attainment (such as reading age, SATs scores, number of GCSE passes, entry into higher education);
• patterns of teaching methods (or pedagogy) used by teachers for different social classes;
• 'hidden curricula';
• formal (subject) curricula (to an extent, despite the existence of a National Curriculum in schools);
• job destinations.

Of course these statements are generalisations. Not all sons and daughters of the upper class go into higher education and subsequently take up jobs with high social status, a high degree of power over others, and a high income. And not all the children of semi-skilled or unskilled workers leave school or further education at the age of 16 or 18, and work in low-status and low-paid jobs. But most do.

Official measurement of social class

The Registrar-General's classification of occupations Tables 7.1 (used for official government purposes) has been the most commonly used system of classifying people between 1911 and 1998. It is based on Weberian[1] notions of the status value of different occupations that have been grouped into a number of broad categories. In the Registrar-General's scheme unskilled, semi-skilled and skilled manual workers were denoted 'working class'. The 'working class' was differentiated from 'the lower middle class' – employees such as those in 'routine', low-paid white-collar jobs. These, in turn, were differentiated from other, better paid, more highly educated, and higher status sections of the middle class. These official classes (Classes I, II, IIINM, IIIM, IV and V) have also been also used as the basis for the A, B, C1, C2, D and E social class/consumption group indicators used by sociological research, market research bureaux, opinion pollsters and advertisers. They are also, incidentally, based on the occupational status of the male head of household, where there is a male 'head of household'.

In November 1998 the Registrar-General's classification was amended to take into account some recent changes in the occupational structure of the labour force. The new classifications shown in Table 7.2, will be used for the census in the year 2001.

Table 7.1 The Registrar-General's Classification of Occupations 1911–1998
Social class distribution, economically active persons, 1991

Class I (Class A)	Professional	accountant; architect, clergyman [sic], doctor, lawyer, university teacher	5%
Class II (Class B)	Managerial/Technical Intermediate	aircraft pilot; chiropodist; MP; nurse; police officer; teacher	28%
Class IIINM (Class C1)	Skilled non-manual	clerical worker; draughtsman [sic]; secretary	23%
Class IIIM (Class C2)	Skilled manual	driver; butcher; bricklayer; cook	21%
Class IV (Class D)	Semi-skilled	bus conductor; postman [sic]; telephone operator	15%
Class V (Class E)	Unskilled	labourer; messenger; cleaner; porter	6%

Figures adapted from 1991 Census, HMSO

Table 7.2 The Office for National Statistics Classification of Occupations (1998)

Class 1	*Professionals; Employers, Administrators and Managers employing 25 or more people* (e.g. doctor, lawyer, scientist, company director)
Class 2	*Associate Professionals; Employers, Administrators and Managers employing fewer than 25 people* (e.g. supervisor, nurse, sales manager, laboratory technician)
Class 3	*Intermediate Occupations in Administrative, Clerical, Sales and Service Work* (e.g. secretary, nursery nurse, salesman [sic], computer operator)
Class 4	*Self-Employed Non-Professionals* (e.g. plumber, driving instructor)
Class 5	*Other Supervisors, Craft and Related Workers* (e.g. factory foreman [sic], joiner)
Class 6	*Routine Occupations in Manufacturing and Services* (e.g. Lorry driver, traffic warden, assembly line worker).
Class 7	*Elementary Occupations* (e.g. fast-food waiter [sic], supermarket cashier, cleaner, labourer)
Class 8	*Never Worked, Unemployed, Long-term Sick*

These types of classification are clearly useful. Positions within this wealth/income/status hierarchy clearly do have important correlation, with for example, health, diet, conditions at work, age of death, and educational attainment. However, in Part Three I critique such classifications.

Part Two: Marxist analysis of social class

There have been many theorists and activists over the centuries who wrote about, and acted upon, the belief that societies contained antagonistic classes. However, it was Karl Marx (1818–1883) more than anyone else who developed a comprehensive theory about the relationship between social class and social structures, in particular the relationship between social classes in capitalist society. In a capitalist economy the *means of production* (raw materials, machinery and so on) and *the means of distribution* (such as transport) and *exchange* (such as finance companies and banks) are concentrated into a few hands. This capitalist world order is based on a few owning the means of production, and the vast majority being forced to sell their labour power in order to survive. Workers are paid only a proportion of the value they create in productive labour. Therefore, the capitalist mode of production is a system of exploitation of one class (the working class) by another (the capitalist class).

For Marx this class exploitation and domination are reflected in the *social relations of production*. These are how people relate to each other – for example relationships between 'bosses' and senior management, supervisors/foremen/women/middle management and, for example, shopfloor workers in factories, finance companies, telesales centres, offices and schools.

A condensed definition of social class is that,

> Classes are large groups of people differing from each other by the place they occupy in a historically determined system of social production, by their relation (in most cases fixed and formulated by law) to the means of production, by their role in the social organisation of labour, by the dimensions of the share of the social wealth of which they dispose and their mode of acquiring it. (Lenin 1965: 421)

Marx, as evidenced by the introductory quote to this chapter, believed that the proletariat and bourgeoisie (workers and capitalists respectively) are in *objective* conflict with each other: the former are materially exploited by the latter whether they *subjectively* know it or not, or whether they like it or not.

Furthermore, during most periods of history, the state acts, to a major degree, in the interests of the ruling capitalist class. Politics is about the allocation of scarce resources in society. It is about who gets what and who doesn't, who wins and who loses, who is empowered and who is disempowered, 'who gets the gravy' and who has to make it. It is also about how this system is organised, legitimated and resisted. And it is about how, to refer to Althusser's concepts, *ideological state apparatuses* (such as the education system and the mass media) and the *repressive state apparatuses* (such as the police, the law, the army) seek to ensure the continuation and enforcement of the current system.

Class consciousness

Marxists believe that the point is not simply to describe the world but to change it. Class consciousness does not follow automatically or inevitably from the objective fact of economic class position. Marx's *The Poverty of Philosophy* [1847] distinguishes between a 'class-in-itself' (an objective determination relating to *class position*) and a 'class-for-itself' (a subjective appreciation of *class consciousness*). *The Communist Manifesto* [1848] (1978b) explicitly identifies '[the] formation of the proletariat into a class' as *the* key political task facing the communists. In *The Eighteenth Brumaire of Louis Napoleon* [1852] Marx observes,

> In so far as millions of families live under economic conditions of existence that divide their mode of life, their interests and their cultural formation from those of the other classes and bring them into conflict with those classes, they form a class. In so far as these small peasant proprietors are merely connected on a local basis, and the identity of their interests fails to produce a feeling of community, national links, or a political organisation, they do not form a class. (Marx [1852] 1974: 239)

The process (and conceptual category) which links economic and social class is that of 'class consciousness'. The class conflict arising from class consciousness and class struggle is fundamental to understanding economic, political and educational change. It is also fundamental in understanding why some social classes of children and students do, on average, so very much better than others.

The changing composition of social classes

In the introductory quotation to this chapter Marx refers to two mutually antagonistic classes in capitalist society, the proletariat (working class) and the bourgeoisie (the capitalist class). However, social class, for Marx, is not simply monolithic nor static. Under capitalist economic laws of motion the working class is constantly decomposed and reconstituted due to changes in the forces of production, technological changes in the type of work. New occupations, such as telesales and computing have come into existence, others, such as coal mining, manufacturing and other manual working class occupations, decline.

Class as internally differentiated

There are manifestly different layers, or strata among the working classes. Skilled workers, (if in work, and particularly in full-time, long-term work), in general have a higher standard of living than semi-skilled or unskilled, or unemployed workers. Their income and wealth are likely to be considerably higher. They are more likely, for example, to have equity on an owner-occupied home. In contrast, families in poorer sections of the working class, may have no wealth whatsoever, and are far more likely to live in private rented accommodation or in council housing. Whatever their stratum, or 'layer' in the working class, however, Marxists assert that there is a common identity of interest between these strata.

Intermediate class locations – the 'new middle class'

Another economic change is the growth of a professional and managerial stratum, such as social workers, teachers, lecturers in further and higher education, probation officers, employment service workers, local government workers. These are 'between capital and labour' in the sense that while being entirely dependent on capital, often in the shape of the national or local state, they exercise *supervisory functions* over the working class (Walker 1979: 5). Teachers or supervisors or office managers are not capitalists – they do not themselves take profit from the surplus value extracted from working-class labour. Nor are they working class in the sense that they have surplus value directly extracted from their own labour. For many Marxists they are defined as working class. For others they are a 'new middle class', while for yet others they occupy a contradictory class location (see Edgell 1993 and German 1996 for discussion).

Many of them have a consciousness of status in which they place themselves above other, especially manual, sectors of the working class. However, on the other hand, their conditions of work and pay have resulted in a degree of *proletarianisation* – loss of autonomy, loss of status, loss of pay and also loss of jobs. Once secure professions are now, since the Thatcher governments, subject to loss of job security, privatisation, and redundancy. Many of 'the new middle class' identify with the aims and values of the working class.

Criticisms of Marxist social class analysis

There are a number of objections to Marxist social class analysis put forward by rival sociological theories such as Weberian analysis, Functionalism and Postmodernism.[2]

1. Social class and individualism

First, some say 'we are all individuals, why can't we treat people simply as individuals?' A Marxist objection to this criticism is that this ignores or denies the well substantiated patterns of treatment, lifestyle, and ways in which we relate to others in the employment and educational processes. It ignores the social relationships we have with our employers/employees, our teachers. It also ignores the different relationships we have to 'the means of production'. Do we own the bakery or the factory, or the school, or the bank, or the insurance company or fashion house or football club – either as outright owner, senior manager, or major shareholder – or are we employed by the owner(s)?

2. Social class and post-Fordism/Post-Modernism

Secondly, perhaps the most frequent 'common-sense' rejection of class is that it is an anachronistic, outdated category which is no longer relevant in the context of a (postmodern) society which has become 'classless' – as, for example, claimed by the former Conservative British Prime Minister, John Major.[3] A similar claim – that the old establishment is being replaced by a new, larger, more meritocratic middle class...that will include millions of people who traditionally see themselves as working class but whose ambitions are far broader than those of their parents and grandparents' has been made, more recently (in January 1999) by Tony Blair

(White 1999). Since the consumer boom of the 1950s, they claim, and since social mobility – moving from one class to another – has been made easier by the expansion of higher education since 1960s, people are less imprisoned (or liberated) by their class – 'anybody can become anything they want'.

For the most part these theories agree that class has only disappeared relatively recently from the historical stage (i.e. in the post-war period and for many not until the political changes of the 1980s – the virtual demise of Soviet style 'communism'). They also argue that the disappearance of class has resulted from cultural changes occurring as a result of economic changes such as the transition from a mass production ('Fordist')[i] to a specialist production ('post-Fordist') economy. Their claim is that relations of production have been superseded in political, educational and social importance by relations of consumption; that we live in a postmodern and post-Fordist society and economy – there is no mass production assembly line culture, no longer mass production and no mass consumption any more. Instead there are myriad ways of working, types of work, types of product, types of consumption, brand names, niches in the market. The social and cultural order organised around class has been replaced, they allege, by a 'new order' based on individual rights, social mobility, job mobility, geographical mobility, consumer choice, lifestyle choice, choice over sexual identity and type of sexuality. Sanders *et al.* (1999), however, point out that such post-Fordist changes are limited to certain labour market and production sectors, in certain areas of the globe, and that these changes are cosmetic. Whether individuals work in computer- and consumer-driven niche production, their relationship to the means of production is essentially the same.

3. Social class and identity

Postmodernists and others (see German 1996) then proceed to say that people no longer *identify* themselves by their social class, or of they do, it is one, not a hugely important, self-identifier. Subjectivities, the ways we define ourselves are complex, and we define ourselves according to many aspects of our person and our behaviour – what we do, where we get our entertainment, how we dress, for example. They suggest that class identity and affiliation are outdated concepts.

Postmodernist accounts of identity, of a fragmented, de-centred subjectivity are currently intellectually dominant. Postmodernists have objected to the Marxist project of class struggle on the grounds that it denies or suppresses the facts of 'social difference'. David Harvey summarises this critique:

> Concentration on class alone is seen to hide, marginalise, disempower, repress and perhaps even oppress all kinds of 'others' precisely because it cannot and does not acknowledge explicitly the existence of heterogeneities and differences based on, for example, race, gender, age, ability, culture, locality, ethnicity, religion, community, consumer preferences, group affiliation, and the like. (Harvey 1993: 101)

At times in the history of the socialist project the white, male, heterosexual worker was represented as the exclusive (or at least the most significant) model of worker. However, current academic neo-Marxism, and Radical Left political activity have significantly departed from this exclusivity, and recognised the importance of non-social class movements.

Nomenclature

In Britain, official classifications of social class are based, not only on income, but on Weberian notions of status and associated consumption patterns and lifestyles. Thus, for Weberian sociologists, some classes are 'higher' and some `lower' than others. Issues of *nomenclature* – what we call people – are crucial in understanding the nature of social class. For example, the use of the terms 'upper class' and 'lower class' can imply a justification for the existence of differentiated social classes and says nothing about the relationship between these classes. For Marxists, the terms 'ruling' and/or 'capitalist class', on the one hand, and 'working class', on the other, however, implies a specific relationship between them.

Hiding the ruling capitalist class and its solidarity

Such classifications need to be criticised on a number of grounds. First, they ignore, indeed hide, the existence of the capitalist class – that class which dominates society economically and politically. This class owns the means of production (and the means of distribution and exchange). These consumption-based patterns mask the existence of the super-rich and the super-powerful – the ruling class.[5] In the Registrar-General's classification, the mega-rich John Paul Getty, Richard Branson and the Duke of Westminster are placed in the same class as, for example, university lecturers, journalists and solicitors.

Hiding working class unity and its solidarity

A related criticism of consumption based classifications is that, by segmenting the working class, they both (a) hide the existence of the working class and (b) serve a purpose of 'dividing and ruling' the working class. They segment different groups of (for example white-collar and blue-collar) workers. Such classifications hide and work to inhibit or disguise the common interests of these different groups. They serve, in some way, to inhibit the development of a common (class) consciousness against the exploiting capitalist class. In a similar way, Marxists note that the promotion of ethnic or 'racial' *divisions* between black and white workers, between women and men and between heterosexuals and homosexuals also serves to weaken the solidarity and 'muscle' of the working class.

Marxists note that sex or 'race' exploitation[6] is very widespread. However, in contrast to the exploitation of women and particular minority ethnic groups, Marxists go on to note the fundamental nature of class exploitation in capitalist economy. Social class exploitation is seen as basic and necessary to the continuation of capitalism. Capitalism can (and may) survive with sex and 'race' equality – indeed, for neo-liberals[7] these are desirable attributes of an economy and education/training system – but to conceive of equality between different social classes in a capitalist economy and society is impossible. Capitalism is defined as the exploitation of one class by another.

This is not to trivialise the issue of identity and of identity politics, either in the micro-sphere of day-to-day personal existence, delight and dismissal, or in the macro-sphere of structural forms of positive and negative discrimination. Social class is clearly only one of a range of possible identifications and one which is sometimes less immediately 'obvious' than, for example, those of gender or `race' or religion or fashion. However, for millions, the duality 'worker/boss' is not at all abstract. Despite political and academic claims that 'class is dead', it should be noted that the proportion of [British] voters believing there is a 'class struggle' in Britain rose from around 60 per cent in the early 1960s to 81 per cent in the mid-1990s, according to Gallup (Deer 1996). Similarly a *New York Times* poll in 1996 'found that 55 per cent of Americans now defined themselves as working class' (Leys and Panitch 1998: 20–21).

4. Social class, class conflict and political strategy

A range of sociologists, politicians and political theorists and postmodernist social theorists have challenged socialist and Marxist analysis and socialist solidaristic, egalitarian educational and political programmes. In addition to postmodernist academics, there are a number of political tendencies seeking to bury Marxism and socialism and egalitarianism. These include Radical Right-wing Conservative Thatcherites/Reaganites and their neo-liberal/ neo-conservative successors. They also include 'Third Way' politicians such as Bill Clinton and Tony Blair.[8]

The *political* argument related to the above is that 'the class struggle is over', that we live in a free and democratic society which is not characterised any more by such old-fashioned struggles as those of workers against bosses, or of the working class against the ruling capitalist class. Instead, for postmodernists, there are just local, particularistic struggles around a myriad of political issues and aspects of identity.

Such arguments, together with status- and consumption-based classifications of social class, gloss over and hide the fundamentally antagonistic relationship between the two main classes in society, the working class and the capitalist class. In Marxist analysis, the working class includes not only manual workers but also millions of white-collar workers – such as bank clerks and supermarket checkout operators, as well, whose conditions of work are, in many ways, similar to those of manual workers. They are exploited in fundamentally the same way as are the manual working classes (German 1996). While it may be of sociological interest to be informed of, for example, the different leisure pursuits of different occupational groups, research based on occupational hierarchies tells us little, if anything about the *relationship* between social classes, which, Marxists argue, is based fundamentally on conflict. This conflict is not just 'class war from below', workers on strike, for example. Class war takes place from above as well as below, with the ruling capitalist class holding and using the levers of power, using, by and large, the ideological and repressive apparatuses of the state.

Part Three: Marxist theory and education

With respect to schooling and education, what are the detailed explanations for working class under-achievement in schools and in education that follow from the above four analyses? Who is to blame? What, therefore, should be the locus and the focus of policy?

- Should the blame be attached to the *individual* child, as lazy or individually unintelligent?
- Should the blame be spread more widely, attached to the *working class* itself – (its 'defective culture' and child-rearing patterns, its supposed attitude to life such as the demand for 'immediate gratification', or its 'defective genetic pool')?
- Should the blame be attached to individual *schools* and individual 'ineffective' teachers? Will the problem of differential social class achievement be sorted out by naming and shaming and improving ineffective schools and going along with the Effective Schools' Movement, improving school management and performance.[9]

Or is the problem a larger one, that of (capitalist) *society* itself – that schools' formal curriculum and the hidden curriculum are deliberately geared to failing most working-class children, and to elevating, middle- and upper-class children above them? In other words, is the problem with the way society is organised, organised around the exploitation of the working classes by the ruling capitalist class with the assistance – willing or unwilling – of teachers?.

Marxists would accept the final one of the above explanations. I now explore Marxist analyses of education. In particular, I refer to some of the concepts of Althusser, Bourdieu, and Bowles and Gintis, and contemporary work of Jill Duffield and her colleagues.

The National Curriculum is clearly a political and ideological creation, as indeed is the creation of any education or schooling system, or school or college curriculum. The aims of the Conservative governments' National Curriculum were clearly 'culturally restorationist', an attempt to purge the existing school curricula of their anti-Conservative content. A clear aim was to remove oppositional liberal progressive and socialist ideas from schools and from the minds of future citizens, to create and perpetuate a Conservative hegemony in ideas.[10]

Reproduction theorists (who were *Structuralist neo-Marxist*, looking at the power of the capitalist economic structure to heavily affect education and social structures) and analysts agree that this is, largely, what schools do. However, unlike Functionalists, rather than welcoming this ideological hegemonising, this use of schools by the ruling capitalist class to reproduce society culturally, economically and ideologically, Marxists critique it and regard it as immoral and in need of radical change.

Below, I give examples of Structuralist neo-Marxist theorists, or theorists working broadly within this tradition, and seek to explain a number of their key concepts.

- Bourdieu and his theory of *Schooling as Cultural Reproduction*, and his concepts of *Habitus* and of *Cultural Capital*, whereby schools recognise and reward middle-class knowledge, language, body language.

- These theories can incorporate Bernstein and his theory of class specific *Language Codes*, whereby schools reward middle-class 'Elaborated Language' and devalue working-class 'Restricted Language'.
- Bowles and Gintis' theory of *Schooling as Economic Reproduction*, whereby the *Correspondence Principle* explains the way in which the hidden curriculum of schools reproduces the social (and economic) class structure of society within the school, training school students for different economic and social futures on the basis of their social and economic pasts – their parental background.
- Althusser and his theory of *Schooling as Ideological Reproduction*, whereby schooling as an *Ideological State Apparatus* (ISA) works to persuade children that the *status quo* is fair and legitimate.

Schooling as cultural reproduction[11]

The concepts of *culture* and *cultural capital* are central to Bourdieu's analysis of how the mechanisms of cultural reproduction functions within schools. For Bourdieu the education system is *not* meritocratic. Its major function is to maintain and legitimate a class-divided society. In his view schools are middle-class institutions run by and for the middle class. Cultural reproduction works in three ways.

Cultural capital – knowing that

Firstly, it works through the formal curriculum and its assessment. The curriculum and examinations serve to confirm the advantages of the middle-class while having the appearance of being a free and fair competition. They clearly privilege and validate particular types of 'cultural capital', the type of élite knowledge that comes naturally to middle- and, in particular, upper-class children, but which is not 'natural' or familiar to non-élite children and school students. Therefore, at the same time, and as a consequence, it disconfirms, rejects, invalidates the cultures of other groups. Individuals in classrooms and school corridors bring with them and exhibit different sets of linguistic and cultural competencies. *Knowledge that* is presented, and rewarded, (or disregarded and penalised) for being part of, or not part of, the formal curriculum.

Cultural capital – knowing how

Secondly, cultural reproduction works through the hidden curriculum. This second type of cultural capital is '*knowing how*', how to speak to teachers, not only knowing *about* books, but also knowing *how* to talk about them. It is knowing *how* to talk with the teacher, with what body language, accent, colloquialisms, register of voice, grammatical exactitude in terms of the 'elaborated code' of language and its associated *habitus*, or way of behaving.

> In a number of social universes, one of the privileges of the dominant, who move in their world as a fish in water, resides in the fact that they need not engage in rational computation in order to reach the goals that best suit their interests. All they have to do is follow their dispositions which, being adjusted to their

positions, 'naturally' generate practices adjusted to the situation. (Bourdieu 1990: 109, quoted in Hatcher 1998a)

For Bourdieu, children and teenagers bring their social class backgrounds into school with them (as well as, of course, other aspects of their subjectivities). Some ways of being and behaving, language, clothing, body language, and attitudes and values are not viewed quite as tolerantly or supportively by teachers as are others. 'Loud-mouthed' (i.e. assertive) girls/young women, or large African–Caribbean, or shell-suited cropped headed working-class white young men/boys tend to be regarded as regrettable, 'nasty', alien and/or threatening – indeed, suitable subjects for exclusion, if not from school itself then from academic success. Teenagers attending The Ridings Secondary School in Halifax tend to have different expectations, labelling and stereotyped work futures than those attending the selective London Oratory School or the most prestigious of private schools, Benenden or Eton.

Cultural reproduction through separate schooling

Thirdly, cultural reproduction works, in Britain, through the separate system of schooling for the upper and upper middle classes, nearly all of whom send their children to private (independent) schools. Adonis and Pollard show how Britain is still a deeply divided society, characterised by class distinctions. In particular, they focus on the system of secondary education, which is rigidly separated into a flourishing, lavishly-funded private sector, as compared to demoralised, under-financed public sector. They point out that those who benefit from private education are almost invariably from privileged backgrounds: the fact that they attend 'the best schools' and/or the highest status schools in the country merely entrenches their privileges and enhances their prospects still further (Adonis and Pollard 1997).

Schooling as ideological reproduction

Althusser's analysis of schooling was concerned with a specific aspect of cultural reproduction, namely, ideological reproduction. He suggested that schools are concerned with the reproduction, the recycling of what is regarded as 'common sense' – in particular, with an acceptance of current capitalist, individualistic, inegalitarian, consumerist society and economy.

How does the school function as an ISA? Althusser suggests that what children learn at school is 'know-how'. But besides these techniques and knowledges, and in learning them, children at school also learn the 'rules' of good behaviour, rules of respect for the socio-technical division of labour and ultimately the rules of the order established by class domination. The school takes children from every class at infant-school age, and then for years in which the child is most 'vulnerable', squeezed between the family state apparatus and the educational state apparatus, it drums into them, whether it uses new or old methods, a certain amount of 'know-how' wrapped in the ruling ideology in its pure state (Althusser 1971).

Schooling as economic reproduction

Schools play a major role in reproducing educational, social, cultural and economic inequality. For Bowles and Gintis (1976), it is the 'hidden curriculum' of the school/further/higher education system which is crucially important in providing capitalism with a workforce which has the personality, attitudes and values which are most useful. Thus the educational system helps integrate youth into the economic system through a structural correspondence between its social relations and those of production. The structure of social relations in education develops the types of personal demeanour, modes of self-presentation, self-image, and social-class identifications which are the crucial ingredients of job adequacy. Specifically, the social relationships of education – the relationships between administrators and teachers, teachers and students, students and students, and students and their work – replicate the hierarchical division of labour (Bowles and Gintis 1976).

They suggest that different levels of education feed workers into different levels within the occupational structure. Furthermore, at each level of the certification process, they showed that, regardless of similar qualifications, job destination was class-related.

In the classroom: the contemporary work of Jill Duffield and her colleagues

As part of this social class-based differentiation between schools via 'the hidden curriculum', there is ample evidence that the pedagogies – the teaching and learning methods used by teachers and pupils – vary according to the pupils' social class. Sally Brown, Sheila Riddell and Jill Duffield's research in the second half of the 1990s involved following two classes in each of four Scottish schools through their first two years of secondary education, observing 204 lessons. Their findings were that children in the two working-class schools spent between 3 and 6 per cent of their time in English class discussion compared with 17 to 25 per cent in the middle-class schools. They observed that pupils in predominantly working-class secondary schools appear to be given many more time-consuming reading and writing tasks than children in middle-class schools and have less opportunity for classroom discussions. Their study demonstrated that teachers of English in the two middle-class schools were more likely to give a reading or writing assignment as homework leaving time in class for feedback and redrafting written work The long writing tasks were very much associated with control and the lack of discussion was, the writers suggested, also to do with teachers thinking that the children could not really manage to discuss things among themselves.

According to this research, children at the middle-class schools were positive about the individual help they received. This was in contrast to a typical response from a pupil in a working-class school which was: 'I'd rather get right into it, get on and let them mark it and if there is something wrong, do it again.' Brown *et al.* concluded that although social class had been pushed off the *research* agenda by the focus on school effectiveness and improvement, this particular study indicated that it still needed to be investigated. It seems in many ways to replicate the findings of Bowles and Gintis' (1976) *Schooling in Capitalist America* referred to above, concerning the social class based reproductive nature of the curriculum of schools (Brown *et al.* 1995, 1997; Duffield 1998a, b, c).

Part Four: Two types of Marxist analysis

Culturalist or *Humanist neo-Marxist* theorists of the 1980s and 1990s have paid more attention to the possibility of successful *resistance* by non-dominant subcultures and groups, and more attention to the 'clash of ideologies' than did Structuralist neo-Marxist theorists. They see rather more space for resistance to the dominant politics and culture, and to many of the messages within the National Curriculum (and pedagogy) than did theorists within the more deterministic *Structuralist neo-Marxism* of the 1970s such as Althusser, Bourdieu, and Bowles and Gintis. Culturalist neo-Marxists criticise the Structuralist neo-Marxist for focusing on the way in which the capitalist economic structures 'determine' state policy, with the capitalist state 'inevitably' reproducing the capitalist system within and through education.

Culturalist neo-Marxist writers suggest that teachers and schools *can make a difference*, that they can work to, and have some degree of success in promoting, an ideology, understanding of, and commitment to, for example, antiracism and anti-sexism. As such they refute what they see as the pessimism and determinism and fatalism of the Structuralist neo-Marxists, and stress the power of human *agency*, the power of people to intervene and to change history.

Sarup (1983) sets out the contribution of Antonio Gramsci (1891–1937) in the Culturalist neo-Marxist understanding of the concept of ideological *hegemony*, or dominance. For Gramsci, hegemony is the ability of a class to assume a moral and intellectual leadership over other classes without resorting to coercion. In this sense the battle of ideologies, or 'culture wars' between different versions of 'common sense' (for example, between Conservatism, Liberalism, 'New Labourism' and Socialism/Marxism) leaves more space for 'resistance' to ruling ideas than does Structuralist neo-Marxist analysis. For Gramsci, the state, and state institutions such as schools, rather than being the servant of the interests of capitalism and the ruling class, were, instead, an arena of class conflict and a site where hegemony has to be continually striven for. Thus schools and other education institutions such as universities are seen as *relatively autonomous* apparatuses, providing space for oppositional behaviour. They are *sites of cultural contestation*, where the central messages of schooling and education are often refused and rejected.

Having recognised validity in the above Culturalist Gramscian analysis, I do consider that the particular concepts of Althusser, Bourdieu, and Bowles and Gintis are valid and illuminating. In particular this seems to be the case with respect to the National Curriculum and to restructuring of other education state apparatuses, such as Initial Teacher Education and to the restructuring of education in general. Some neo-Marxists, such as Cole and Hill in the late 1990s, consider the neo-Marxist pendulum has swung too far in the Culturalist direction and too far away from Structuralist neo-Marxist reproduction analysis. However, while I do think that Culturalist neo-Marxists are too starry-eyed about the possibility of major change, I also recognise the debilitating and counter-productive effects of unmitigated deterministic Structuralist analysis.

With 'human agency', with human resistance, and with collective class consciousness and action, Marxists would argue, then, although there are major difficulties, people can successfully struggle to change events and systems – at micro-levels and at societal levels. In this struggle for social justice the ideological state apparatuses of education can play a crucial role.

Conclusion

Postmodernists explain contemporary developments in society and the restructuring of schooling and education systems, such as that brought about by the 1988 Education Reform Act in England and Wales, as reflecting the increased diversity of society, the increased position and self-perception of people as consumers. They see, for example, the end of mass provision in schooling (such as the comprehensive school) and the emergence of educational niche-marketing with a variety of types of school as both welcome and inevitable – reflecting economic and social changes.

Marxist interpretation, whether Culturalist neo-Marxist or Structuralist neo-Marxist, is very different. These changes are seen as rendering the schooling and education systems as more locked into and more supportive of the current requirements of capitalism. The Conservative 'reforms', continued in essence by 'New Labour', are seen as reinforcing economic, ideological and cultural reproduction in support of the *status quo* of social class exploitation.

While it is not essentially the intention to demarcate and intensify gender and racial differentiation more rigidly, it is, through a use of the various Marxist concepts outlined in this chapter, possible to see that the essential *intention* and the *effect* of Conservative government policy has been to *increase social class differentiation*, that is, to increase differences *between and within* the social classes. The rich *have* got richer while the poor have got poorer, in income, wealth – and in education.

Suggested further reading

For readers wishing to develop or find out about policy that flows from the analysis in this chapter, then the following should be useful: Cole *et al.* (eds) (1997) *Promoting Equality in Primary Schools*; Hill and Cole (eds.) (1999a) *Schooling and Equality: Factual and Conceptual Issues*; Hill and Cole (eds) (1999b) *Promoting Equality in Secondary Schools*; and Cole (ed.) (1999) *Education, Human Rights and Equality*. Edgell (1993) *Class* and German (1996) *A Question of Class* discuss class *per se*.

For a wider discussion of education policy, see the two Hillcole Group books, (1991 and 1997) *Changing the Future: Redprint for Education*, and *Rethinking Education and Democracy: Education for the Twenty First Century*. The education magazines *Forum (for Comprehensive Education)*, *Education for Today and Tomorrow*, and the journal *Education and Social Justice* include highly relevant articles.

Notes

1   The sociological analysis of Max Weber (1864–1920), like that of Karl Marx, stressed the *conflict* between different groups in society. However, unlike Marx, he considered that this conflict was between different status groups as much as between different social classes.

2   Functionalists, following Emile Durkheim (1858–1917) justify inequality and stratification as being necessary for economic efficiency, profitability and social stability. Talcott Parsons and Davis and Moore are leading functionalist writers. For them, the primary function of schooling and education is fitting people into society. Post-modernism is described in Section 3 below. Its major theorists are Lyotard, Baudrillard, Foucault and Derrida. Sarup (1993) and Boyne and Rattansi (1990) are accessible summaries of postmodernism. Butler (1990) and Lather (1991) are prominent postmodern feminists.

3   By 'classless' John Major (Conservative Prime Minister 1990–97) presumably meant 'socially mobile' and meritocratic.

4   Fordist refers to assembly line mass production and, historically, its associated limited consumer choice. When the Ford Motor Company first started mass production of cars for a mass market, it was said that you could buy any colour you wanted as long as it was black.

5   This class and its occupational, familial, educational and other interconnections has been well documented, for example by Adonis and Pollard (1997), and might be described as the 'overclass'.

6   In the light of this it is interesting to note the renewed interest in class analysis within British Feminism see, for example, Beverly Skeggs', *Formations of Class and Gender* (1997), and the first of a proposed new series on 'Women and Social Class', *Class Matters* (1997) edited by Pat Mahony and Christine Zmroczek. Of course, for socialist feminists such as Jane Kelly (1999) the class basis of womens' oppression has remained their key ideological analysis. The class-based analysis can be applied to oppression and exploitation of some minority ethnic groups such as the African–Caribbean descended, Pakistani-descended and Bangladeshi-descended population. While there is 'Paki-bashing', widespread sexism, and, indeed homophobia, social class position is, for Marxists, the primary form of exploitation and oppression. In a nutshell, rich women and bourgeois blacks have, in important respects, an easier life than working-class populations, whatever their ethnicity, sex, sexuality.

7   Neo-liberals are one particular type of Radical Right conservatives, probably the dominant type/group. They believe in the primacy of profit, that the national and local state should be 'rolled back', that state-controlled industries and utilities should be privatised, that 'competition', diversity of product, 'choice' should characterise services such as schooling, pensions, health, welfare benefits. As such, the Conservative Education Reform Act of 1988, except for the state-determined National Curriculum, are neo-liberal measures.

8   For expositions of 'The Third Way' in politics, 'beyond socialism and capitalism' see Blair 1998, Giddens 1998. For critical commentaries, see Cole 1998; Hobsbawm 1998; Jacques 1998; Hill, 2000 forthcoming.

9   The Effective Schools Movement, one of the main bases of 'New Labour' government education policy, is based on work by Rutter *et al. Fifteen Thousand Hours* (1979) and Mortimore *et al. School Matters: The Junior Years* (1988). The Movement concentrates on improving a number of mainly management-based factors internal to the school. For criticisms of the School Effectiveness Movement, see Brown *et al.* 1995; Chitty 1997; Hatcher 1998b; Hill 2000 forthcoming. The main criticism is that the School Effectiveness Movement ignores questions of social class intake to a school, and ignores related questions about the nature of the curriculum.

10 Classic texts relating curricula to ideological and political factors in the selection and organisation of knowledge – in other words, in the construction of a curriculum, include Henry Giroux's (1983a) essay in the *Harvard Educational Review*, 'Theories of reproduction and resistance in the new sociology of education', and Geoff Whitty's (1985) *Sociology and School Knowledge: Curriculum Theory, Research and Politics.*

11 See, for example, Bourdieu and Passeron (1977).

References

Adonis, A. and Pollard, S. (1997) *A Class Act, The Myth of Britain's Classless Society.* London: Hamish Hamilton.

Ahmed, K. (1997) 'Privileged few tower over mass of UK poor', *The Guardian*, 28 July.

Althusser, L. (1971) 'Ideology and ideological state apparatuses', in Althusser, L. *Lenin and Philosophy and Other Essays.* London: New Left Books.

Blair, T. (1998) *The Third Way: New Politics for a New Century.* London: The Fabian Society.

Boseley, S. (1998) 'State of children's health linked to their place on the class ladder, survey shows', The *Guardian*, 15 December.

Bourdieu, R. (1976) 'The school as a conservative force in scholastic and cultural inequalities', in, Dale, R. *et al. Schooling and Capitalism.* London: Routledge and Kegan Paul.

Bourdieu, R. (1997) 'The forms of capital', in Halsey, A., Lauder, H., *et al. Education: Culture, Economy, Society.* Oxford: Oxford University Press.

Bourdieu, R. and Passeron, J. (1977) *Reproduction in Education, Society and Culture.* London: Sage Publications.

Bowles, S. and Gintis, H. (1976) *Schooling in Capitalist America.* London: Routledge and Kegan Paul.

Boyne, R. and Rattansi, A. (1990) *Postmodernism and Society.* London: Macmillan.

Brown, S., Duffield, J. and Riddell, S. (1995) 'School Effectiveness Research: The Policy Makers' Tool for School Improvement?', EERA Bulletin, March, pp.6-15.

Brown, S., Riddell, S., Duffield, J. (1997) *Classroom approaches to learning and teaching: the social class dimension.* Paper delivered to the ECER (European Educational Research Association) Annual Conference, Seville, Spain.

Butler, J. (1990) *Gender Trouble: Gender and the Subversion of Identity.* London: Routledge.

Chitty, C. (1997) 'The school effectiveness movement: origins, shortcomings and future possibilities', *The Curriculum Journal* **8**(1), 52–3.

Cole, M. (ed.) (1988) *Bowles and Gintis Revisited: Correspondence and Contradiction in Educational Theory.* Lewes: Falmer Press.

Cole, M. (1998) 'Globalization, modernization and competitiveness: a critique of the New Labour Project in Education', *International Studies in the Sociology of Education* **8**(3), 315–332.

Cole, M. (ed.) (1999) *Equality, Education and Human Rights.* London: Falmer Press.

Cole, M. and Hill, D. (1995) 'Games of despair and rhetorics of resistance: postmodernism, education and reaction', *British Journal of Sociology of Education* **16**(2), 165–82.

Cole, M., Hill, D., Shan, S. (eds) (1997) *Promoting Equality in Primary Schools.* London: Cassell.

Cole, M., Hill, D., Rikowski, G. (1997) 'Between Postmodernism and nowhere: the predicament of the Postmodernist', *British Journal of Education Studies* **45**(2), 187–200.

Deer, B. (1996) 'Still struggling after all these years', *New Statesman*, 23 August.

Duffield, J. (1998a) 'School support for lower achieving pupils', *British Journal of Special Education* **25**(3), 126–34.

Duffield, J. (1998b) *Unequal opportunities or don't mention the (class) war.* Paper to the Scottish Educational Research Association (SERA) Conference, Dundee.

Duffield, J. (1998c) 'Learning experiences, effective schools and social context', *Support for Learning* **13**(1) 3–8.

Durkheim, E. (1968) *The Division of Labour in Society.* New York: Free Press.

Edgell, S. (1993) *Class.* London: Routledge.

Engels, F. (1976) *Ludwig Feuerbach and the End of Classical German Philosophy.* Peking: Foreign Languages Press.

Gaine, C. and George, R. (1999) *Gender, 'Race' and Class in Schooling: a New Introduction.* London: Falmer Press.

German, L. (1996) *A Question of Class.* London: Bookmarks.

Giddens, A. (1998) *The Third Way: The Renewal of Social Democracy.* London: Plity.

Giroux, H. (1983a) 'Theories of reproduction and resistance in the new sociology of education: a critical analysis', *Harvard Education Review* **53**(3), 257–293.

Giroux, H. (1983b) *Theory and Resistance in Education: a Pedagogy for the Opposition.* London: Bergin and Harvey.

Harvey, D. (1993) 'Class relations, social justice and the politics of difference', in Squires, J. (ed.) *Principal Positions.* London: Lawrence & Wishart..

Hatcher, R. (1997) 'New Labour, school improvement and racial equality', *Multicultural Teaching* **15**(3), 8–13.

Hatcher, R. (1998a) 'Class differentiation in education: rational choices?', *British Journal of Sociology of Education* **19**(1), 5–24.

Hatcher, R. (1998b) 'Social justice and the politics of school effectiveness and improvement', *Race, Ethnicity and Education* **1**(2), 267–89.

Hill, D. (1989) *Charge of the Right Brigade: The Radical Right's Attack on Teacher Education.* Brighton: Institute for Education Policy Studies.

Hill, D. (1990) *Something Old, Something New, Something Borrowed, Something Blue: Teacher Education, Schooling and the Radical Right in Britain and the USA.* London: Tufnell Press.

Hill, D. (1994) 'Initial teacher education and ethnic diversity', in Verma, G., and Pumfrey, P. *Cultural Diversity and the Curriculum Vol. 4 Cross Curricular Contexts, Themes and Dimensions in Primary Schools.* London: Falmer Press.

Hill, D. (1997) 'Equality in British schooling: the policy context of the reforms', in Cole, M., Hill, D., Shan, S. (eds), *Promoting Equality in Primary Schools.* London: Cassell.

Hill, D. (1999a) 'The National Curriculum as ideological and cultural reproduction', in Hill, D. and Cole, M. (eds) 1999a.

Hill, D. (1999b) '"New Labour" and the conservative revolution in teacher education', in Hill, D. and Cole, M. (eds) *Equality and Education: Empirical and Conceptual Issues: Factual and Conceptual Issues.* London: Tufnell Press.

Hill, D. (ed.) (2000 forthcoming) *Education, Education, Education: Capitalism, Socialism and the Third Way.* London: Cassell.

Hill, D. and Cole, M. (eds) (1999a) *Schooling and Equality: Social Class, Factual and Conceptual Issues.* London: Tufnell Press.

Hill, D. and Cole, M. (eds) (1999b) *Promoting Equality in Secondary Schools.* London: Cassell.

Hill, D., Cole, M., Rikowski, G. (eds) (1999) *Postmodernism in Education Theory: Education and The Politics of Human Resistance.* London: Tufnell Press.

Hillcole Group (1991) *Changing the Future: Redprint for Education.* London: Tufnell Press.

Hillcole Group (1997) *Rethinking Education and Democracy: Education for the Twenty First Century.* London: Tufnell Press.

Hobsbawm, E. (1998) 'The death of Neo-Liberalism: the present global crisis marks the end of market fundamentalism', *Marxism Today* November/December 1998.

Jacques, M. (1998) 'As we move into a new era, New Labour remains firmly stuck in the old one', *Marxism Today* November/December 1998.

Kelly, J. (1999) 'Postmodernism and feminism: the road to nowhere', in Hill D., McLaren, P., Cole, M., Rikowski, G. (eds) *Postmodern Excess in Educational Theory: Education and the Politics of Human Resistance.* London: Tufnell Press.

Lather, P. (1991) *Getting Smart: Feminist Research and Pedagogy within the Postmodernism.* New York: Routledge.

Lenin, V. I. (1965) 'A great beginning', in *Collected Works*, vol. 29. Moscow: Progress Publishers.

Leys, C. and Panitch, L. (1998) 'The political legacy of the manifesto', in Panitch L. and Leys, C. (eds) *Socialist Register 1998.* Rendlesham: Merlin.

Mahony, P. and Zmroczek, C. (1997) *Class Matters: 'Working-class' Women's Perspectives on Social Class.* London: Taylor & Francis.

Marx, K. (1974) [1852] 'The Eighteenth Brumaire of Louis Bonaparte', in *Surveys from Exile.* New York: Vintage Books.

Marx, K. (1978) [1845] 'Six theses on Feuerbach', in Tucker, R. C. (ed.) *The Marx-Engels Reader.* New York: Norton.

Marx, K. (1978a) [1847] 'The poverty of Philosophy', in Tucker, R. C. (ed.) *The Marx-Engels Reader.* New York: Norton.

Marx, K. (1978b) [1848] The Communist Manifesto, in Tucker, R. C. (ed.) *The Marx-Engels Reader.* New York: Norton.

Mortimore, P. (1997) 'Can effective schools compensate for society?' in Halsey, A. H., Lauder, H. *et al.* (eds) *Education: Culture, Economy, Society.* Oxford: Oxford University Press.

Mortimore, P. *et al.* (1988) *School Matters: The Junior Years.* Wells: Open Books.

Office for Standards in Education (OFSTED) (1993) *Access and Achievement in Urban Education.* London: HMSO.

Office for Standards in Education OFSTED (1994) *Improving Schools.* London: HMSO.

Rikowski, G. (1996) 'Left alone: end time for Marxist educational theory?' *British Journal of Sociology of Education* **17**(4), 415–51.

Rikowski, G. (1997) 'Scorched Earth: prelude to rebuilding Marxist educational theory', *British Journal of Sociology of Education* **18**(4) 551–74.

Rowntree Foundation (1995) *Inquiry into Income and Wealth.* York: Joseph Rowntree Foundation.

Rutter, M. *et al.* (1979) *Fifteen Thousand Hours.* London: Open Books.

Sanders, M., Hill, D., Hankin, T. (1999) 'Social class and the return to class analysis', in Hill, D., McLaren, P., Cole, M. and Rikowski, G. (eds) *Postmodernism in Education Theory: Education and The Politics of Human Resistance.* London: Tufnell Press.

Sarup, M. (1982) *Education, State and Crisis.* London: Routledge and Kegan Paul.

Sarup, M. (1983) *Marxism, Structuralism, Education.* Lewes: Falmer Press.

Sarup, M. (1986) *The Politics of Multiracial Education.* London: Routledge.

Sarup, M. (1993) *Post-structuralism and Postmodernism*, (2nd edn). Hemel Hempstead: Harvester Wheatsheaf.

Skeggs, B. (1997) *Formations of Class and Gender.* London: Sage Publications.

Walker, P. (ed.) (1979) *Between Labour and Capital.* Brighton: Harvester Press.

Weber, M. (1979) *Economy and Society: An Outline of Interpretative Sociology.* Los Angeles: University of California Press.

White, M. (1999) 'Blair hails middle class revolution', The *Guardian*, 1 January.

Chapter 8

Gender in education

Jane Martin

> My deepest concern is with girls whose alternative to staying at home for forty years is not the professions – not even the skilled bench, the high wage packet bringing financial independence, the industrial training which gives her job security, responsibility, and mobility. It is low pay, canteen cleaning, helping with school meals, the typewriter, the unskilled labour market, short-term employment. The cause: a different, often inferior education planned perhaps with no conscious ill-intent by the men who represent 97 per cent of the government of education, but which nevertheless gives no foundation for a later career in either work or government. (Byrne 1978: 15)

Eileen Byrne's book *Women and Education* published in 1978, focused attention on patterns of gender differentiation; as well as the dominance and control of education by men. Stimulated by the Sex Discrimination Act (1975), a growing body of feminist scholarship put forward strategies to equalise the opportunities for girls in school. It is now around 20 years later and there is a great deal of public debate about 'lost boys' and the education and educational attainments of boys and men. Although the gendered division of labour has not broken down, change around men and work is prominent in the construction of the 'crisis' in masculinity in the contemporary UK. Certainly the increased interest in the 'trouble with men' is linked to growing concern with the longer term consequences of under-education, unemployment and social exclusion. These changes throw up a series of questions about gender in education that are considered in this chapter. Firstly, has there been something of a shift in attitudes towards gender equity issues? Secondly, has the gender challenge been reversed? And finally, *is* the future female as some media publications would have us believe?

The chapter is divided into three parts. The first section offers a broad historical account of the position of women in education in the state sector from 1944 to 1975, the year when policy initiatives were first developed to address issues concerning the education of girls. It aims primarily to show the ways deep-rooted social stereotypes and a separated, two-track approach to schooling directed the great majority of girls towards an exclusively domestic role, even at the expense of scholastic ability. The second section looks at examples of gender analyses and projects from the 1970s and 1980s, before moving on to consider relatively recent work on masculinities in education. In the final section the emphasis is on prevalent discourses around gender and education that date from the mid-1990s. Male educational under-achievement has been identified as a cause for concern and the political will to effect change is clearly evident. However, the deluge of publications propagating the notion of 'gender crisis' has served to obliterate the fact that not all boys are under-achieving and not all girls are succeeding in the years of compulsory schooling. Further, patterns of performance change in the post-compulsory stages of education with persistent differences in choice of educational routes and vocational pathways. This chapter is concerned both with the differing qualities culturally attributed to men and women and social expectations of masculine and feminine behaviour. In conclusion, it stresses the need to deconstruct the myths about performance central to the composition of the underachieving boy in order to take account of continuing gender inequality for girls.

Gender in English state education after 1944

The 1944 Education Act encouraged intense speculation about the potential impact of free secondary education for all. Many saw the reform as primarily about the realisation of class equality and the production of a new type of society. However, hopes for broader social transformation and equality did not extend to the sexual division of labour in families, employment and social policy. Examining the education policy context after the 1945 Labour election victory, Dean (1991) discusses the gendered nature of education policies and the impact of those policies on practice. In particular, he develops the argument that the victorious politicians saw the domestic role of women as crucial for the construction and rehabilitation of social harmony and cohesiveness. Women's responsibility for domestic work and childcare was seen as central and permanent and gender divisions were reinforced by government recruitment policies that encouraged married women to re-enter the labour market as part-time workers (Briar 1997). In the secondary modern schools (the main providers of secondary education) domestic subjects formed a significant part of the curriculum for girls. At the same time, new arrangements prompted by the Minister of Labour, George Isaacs, excluded most female school leavers from university education between 1946 and 1949. He was unapologetic for having persuaded vice-chancellors of British universities to give priority to ex-servicemen:

> With regard to girls leaving school, I asked that if their admission would result in excluding men of the priority classes, they should not be admitted except where they are of exceptional promise. I feel this to be an equitable arrangement. (*Hansard*, Vol. 423, col. 534: George Isaacs, cited in Briar 1997: 97)

This was an example of overt discrimination. Other examples of social exclusion were more covert.

Throughout the 1940s and 1950s (when selection through the 11+ examination predominated), girls had to do much better than boys to obtain a place at a grammar or technical school. Yet the writing about selection was all about boys and class comparisons in educational achievements. Sexual inequality was not newsworthy in the cultural landscape of post-war Britain, even though girls frequently obtained higher average scores than boys but then had their scores adjusted downwards. There were no reports of unfairness or inequality because these results prompted some local education authorities (LEAs) to use separate sex norms in selection, while others added new tests in order to avoid a substantially higher proportion of girls than boys 'passing'. Informed by inherited assumptions about the inferiority of women, the rationale was a tendency to attribute boys' failure to 'immaturity' and the illusion of male meritocracy was sustained by the conventional wisdom that late-developing boys catch up later. It was generally understood that technical adjustment was necessary to balance the numbers of successful girls and boys; there was also a historic shortage of girls' grammar school places.

Meanwhile, the prevalent discourses of gender and education accepted and reinforced a set of linked assumptions advocating separate but complementary adult roles for women and men. On the one hand, the female curriculum was discussed in terms of girls' biology and what this meant for their future after school. On the other, the principle of male-as-norm meant the teaching of other subjects was informed by the assumption that boys were future breadwinners and secondarily fathers. Overall the discourse of achievement was male and officials at the Ministry of Education stressed the need to maintain the place of gender categories in the structure and organisation of education. This was made clear when the influential school inspector John Newsom attacked the girls' grammar schools for ignoring domestic skills and placing too much emphasis on public examinations and obtaining professional careers. Significantly, Newsom's critique also suggests that stated aims do not necessarily match with practice. In a study of girls' secondary schooling between 1900 and 1950, Summerfield (1987) found housewifery remained marginal in the curriculum of the more academic schools where university education was the main aim. Here the lessons in femininity could be seen as preparation for middle-class professional destinations:

> First, the ladylike behaviour and decorum taught within the schools by female authority figures could serve independent women taking places within a new female professional class as well as, if not better than, those destined for a dependent married status. Secondly, the ban on contact with boys could be seen not primarily as a way of supplying virgins to the middle-class marriage bed, but as protection against the distraction from academic work presented by boyfriends and the dilution of ambition effected by adolescent marital

aspirations. Stories of 'underachievement' told by those who maintained secret relationships with boys from the 1920s to the 1950s testify to such impediments. (Summerfield 1987: 166)

That being the case, teaching was the favoured career goal of educated middle-class girls but they did not have effective access to the same education and training as their male counterparts post-16. The operation of LEA quotas meant that instead of being offered financial assistance to attend university, women were offered financial assistance to take two-year teacher training courses (Briar 1997: 111). It follows that by 1958 there were 100 teacher training colleges for women, 18 for men and 18 coeducational institutions (Heward 1993: 23–4). Ultimately, the availability of universal student grants attracted women to university in the 1960s, but women's training grants for vocational education remained lower than men's until 1973. Class and gendered concepts of adult destiny were similarly evident in the curriculum recommendations of the 1959 Crowther Report on the education of 15 to 18-year-olds. First, it contained statements that assumed a clear-cut difference between boys and girls and that education should take account of them. Secondly, it differentiated between the educational needs of able and less able adolescent girls. In the secondary modern schools (virtually synonymous with working-class schooling) this report described less able girls thus: 'their needs are much more sharply differentiated than those of boys of the same age than is true of the academically abler groups'. They were 'to study subjects based on direct interest in their personal appearance and problems of human relations, the greater psychological and social maturity of girls makes such subjects acceptable – and socially necessary'. (Crowther Report 34, para. 51; cited in Thom 1987: 133)

In the 1960s, however, the issue of class divisions in state secondary education captured policy-makers' attention. Reassessments of the concept of equal access saw a shift in policy in favour of coeducational, comprehensive schooling, although the focus was on working-class male disadvantage. The subject of girls' educational opportunities was a non-existent issue and those who showed awareness of differences between boys' and girls' experiences of school accepted them with little or no concern.

Full critiques have been elaborated elsewhere (Deem: 1981) but the underlying continuities with the selective system were quickly apparent. Thus, an initial survey of the whole field of comprehensive schools in 1968 and two follow-up sample surveys conducted in the school year 1971–2, revealed that very few schools offered a common curriculum in the early days of the comprehensive reform (Benn and Simon 1972). In many instances, low-status school subjects such as domestic science, typing and childcare were not open to boys, while girls were excluded from woodwork, metalwork and technical drawing. This gendered legacy undermined the potential for comprehensive schools to add to the educational aspirations of girls, particularly the working-class girls who had been largely confined to the modern schools. Nonetheless, girls increasingly participated in public examinations at the secondary stage, notably after the minimum leaving age was raised in 1972 from 15 to 16. Previous to this, early leaving was the first reason for not having any exam results and the 1959 Gurney–Dixon Report commented on the fact that grammar school girls were more likely to leave at the statutory age (Deem 1981). However, there was still evidence that gender was affecting subject choice and the tendency for girls to lean strongly towards the arts constrained their life-chances post-16. The vital significance of this was that they were less likely to have maths and science qualifications (the usual requirements for some kind of apprenticeship or training for a skilled job in industry) and this was particularly pertinent at a time of restricted openings for unskilled or semi-skilled labour, cutbacks in teacher training and fierce competition for university places in the Arts.

It is fair to say that the extract from Eileen Byrne (quoted at the start of the chapter) graphically illustrates the two central emphases of the liberal view of education that dominated feminist thought in the 1970s. The first is the implication that schools are partly responsible for instilling sexist attitudes into children, although they also have the ability to change those attitudes and, by implication, to change society. The second is the concentration on girls, rather than boys. In particular, Byrne directs her attention towards the relation between the experience of schooling and the occupational segregation of men and women which takes place after education is completed. For instance, female school-leavers faced unequal opportunities in planned training such as apprenticeships, as well as low and unequal pay in comparison to their male counterparts. In this situation the emphasis was on female disadvantage and this was crucial to the passing of anti-discrimination legislation in 1975. These events directed attention to wider social practices and encouraged the development of equal opportunities initiatives in schools and in the workplace. They also provided the impetus for a growing body of feminist scholarship within the sociology of education.

The sociology of women's education

Canvassed by feminists as a broad measure to promote women's rights, the Sex Discrimination Act was intimately linked to concepts of fair treatment and equality. Access to education was seen as a basic right and the new legislation

> contained the provision that it was the duty of LEAs, governing bodies and proprietors of schools, colleges and other educational institutions, universities and private educational institutions to provide, for both sexes, facilities of *like quality*, in *like manner and like terms*. (Arnot 1987: 313)

Although the Equal Opportunities Commission (EOC) was empowered to remove discriminatory behaviour through the courts, the potential effectiveness of the British legislation was reduced by its concern with equality of *access* not of *outcomes*. Another weakness is the lack of attention given to the long history of debates over sexual differences in academic achievements and the possible influence of tradition, custom and prejudice.

In the sociology of education literature a growing body of theoretical and empirical work focused specifically on the 'problem' of female education, exploring the processes and outcomes of schooling for girls. There was criticism of gender differentiation across a diversity of areas as studies began to show the ways in which patriarchal relations are deployed and used in schools (Deem 1978). Teaching styles were challenged to avoid a tendency to encourage competition between the sexes in sports, academic learning and examinations; attention also turned to management hierarchies within schools. Most are dominated by male teachers and the proportion of women holding senior posts in secondary schools was highest in such female 'spaces' as home economics and girls' games. Further, although the 'female' atmosphere of primary schooling was seen to undermine the performance of boys, it seems that even here sexual divisions were constantly reinforced. For instance, Clarricoates (1981) has described how primary school teachers readily clustered behaviour into two categories: one for boys, another for girls. Boys were livelier, adventurous, boisterous, self-confident, independent, energetic, couldn't-care-less, loyal and aggressive; girls were obedient, tidy, neat, conscientious, orderly, fussy, catty, bitchy and gossipy. During her observations in the field Clarricoates found that teacher expectations of pupils were influenced by societal myths of stereotypes:

> Michael, much to the concern of his teachers and to the contempt of his peer group, loved to play with dolls. He liked to bake and constantly sought the company of girls, despite their insults. [...] The headteacher, a kind and progressive woman, remarks that Michael is confused between masculine and feminine roles, and she suspects that he has 'feminine genes'. If he is not 'cured' by the time he leaves school, she suggested to me, then the only solution to his 'problem' is that he enter the 'world' of the arts, drama or music, where 'that kind of behaviour' is much more acceptable. (Clarricoates 1980: 36)

As this example graphically illustrates, schools play a key role in the creation and sustenance of gender identity: with implications for girls and boys. It is because Michael fails to conform to particular forms of hegemonic masculinities that his learning and performance (as well as post-school destination) is discussed in terms of derision linked to gender categorisation. In further education, gender divisions were sustained by heavily masculinised classroom environments and higher teacher expectations towards boys (Stanworth 1981). Males dominate space and time at primary, secondary and higher levels of schooling, as well as classroom talk. This is crucial to student–teacher and student–student relations and plays an important role in shaping gendered experiences, choices and expectations.

In relation to fields of study selection, the 1975 Report on curricular differentiation highlighted the areas in which sexism flourished. There were high levels of sex stereotyping in option choices and teachers found themselves being criticised for influencing the preferences of pupils choosing subjects after age 14. Beyond that, evidence of illegal segregation of craft subjects was found in 19 per cent of the schools studied by Her Majesty's Inspectorate (HMI) from 1975 to 1978 (cited in Pascall 1997: 119). The extent of this divergence prompted feminist scholars to focus particularly on specific subject concerns, such as the lower attainment and participation of girls in mathematics, science and technology. Research looked at the preponderance of male teachers, male pupils and masculine imagery in the teaching of the physical sciences and the 1980s witnessed a number of interventions designed to render schooling more 'girl friendly' (Whyte *et al.* 1985). In Manchester, the Girls into Science and Technology Project (GIST) attempted to raise teacher awareness of the subtle messages conveyed by the hidden curriculum in schools. Textbooks and tasks were redrafted to reflect girls' interests and positive female role models were introduced to encourage girls to consider careers in this area. Hence the GIST schools were visited by women working in science and technology, while the EOC declared 1984 to be Women into Science and Engineering Year. To some extent, this intervention rested on a deficit model of female socialisation that was itself potentially problematic, since it assumed that equalising opportunities for girls in schools would result in great equality for women. Essentially, it was limited by a failure to recognise that educational gender differentiation does not occur in a social and political vacuum. The implications of this are also evident in debate over the introduction of the National Curriculum at the time the Education Reform Act (1988) became law.

All students in England and Wales now take mathematics, science, English, a modern foreign language, and technology and information technology (IT) until the age of 16. For some, this was a positive response to the need to afford pupils equal access to the same curriculum. However, it remains the case that the privileging of mathematics, science and technology embodied a persistent tendency to emphasise traditional gender hierarchies (Miles and Middleton 1995). Critics argue, for instance, that the traditional approach to school science education has now been enshrined in a national curriculum (in England and Wales) giving boys a gender-based advantage. Knowledge is not a neutral commodity and the status accorded male-centred forms of knowledge do little to challenge the legacy of a masculine-centred education system. The National Curriculum is posited on a male paradigm and fails to recognise the cultural resources pupils bring to it. Moreover, a system of attainment that measures all schools and pupils against 'objective criteria' serves to reinforce the illusion of neutrality. Equal opportunities recommendations in this area are in effect asking for the masculinisation of the education and training of girls and young women, while no concomitant feminisation is asked of boys and young men. For instance, a section of opinion in the campaign to encourage boys back into learning recommends engaging reluctant male readers through material that legitimates the male macho culture (football books and suchlike). In contrast, there is no equivalent initiative to present traditional female territory (such as childcare) as of equal concern to boys.

By the mid-1990s, the dominant discourses of education in general targeted school effectiveness and improvement (Slee *et al.* 1998). Meanwhile, it was in this political climate that the publication of examination results put the spotlight on male educational under-achievement at GCSE (General Certificate of Secondary Education, introduced in 1988). The reported statistics show that both boys and girls have improved their performance at GCSE level and equivalent, but girls' performance has increased more rapidly than that of boys'. Unlike the 11-plus the present examination system is not weighted in favour of boys, but this does not figure in the dominant reaction to the figures, neither does the significance of ethnicity and social class. Simply put, the phenomenon of girls on top in GCSE league tables generated a media frenzy expressed in terms of threats to male breadwinning, the association of young men and crime, the collapse of family life and the crisis of fatherhood. A tendency to treat boys as an undifferentiated mass was further reinforced when girls' schools headed the league tables of GCSE results for independent schools in the autumn of 1998 (*Independent*, 5 September 1998). Nonetheless, it is important to treat the reported statistics with care.

Lost Boys?

The 1990s have witnessed a growing emphasis on male disadvantage. Change is defined in terms of girls' relative academic success at the school-leaving level and intervention is now just as likely to be associated with improving boys' performance, as it is with girls. In the spring of 1996 this received official legitimation when Christopher Woodhead (Her Majesty's Chief Inspector and Head of the Government's Office for Standards in Education OFSTED) wrote a column in *The Times* entitled 'Boys who learn to be losers: on the white male culture of failure.' In it he asserted that the apparent failure of white working-class boys 'was one of the most disturbing problems we face within the whole education system' (quoted in the *Times Educational Supplement* 26 April 1996). But what is the evidence for the assertion that young men are losing out? What are the terms and implications of the current debates?

In their longitudinal study of England and Wales from 1985–1994, Arnot *et al.* (1996) note changing patterns of entry and performance in public examinations. They use the concept of gender gap to show the difference between the sexes in the period under study. Thus, for example, the GCSE entry gender gap is increasing in favour of male students in chemistry and economics, but there has been a change from boys to girls in history and mathematics. A lower percentage of the male cohort achieved five A–C grades at GCSE, but this reporting hides other differences when both groups are compared. For instance, teachers' perception of girls' maths anxiety does not serve young women well:

> There is evidence that some 1 per cent of students (about 5000) who were entered for the intermediate tier could have achieved a higher grade and that this affects more girls than boys. This 'misclassification' restricts their ability to continue their study of mathematics to A level. (Gipps and Murphy 1994: 224–5)

In other words, the middle tier acts as a 'safety' option that provides the key grade C without the risks associated with the grade-limited top and bottom tiers. As yet, there has been no gender monitoring of the tiered entry system in double-award science but it is significant that more boys study the élite single science subjects. The girls who outperform boys in GCSE physics are a highly select group and close examination of choices within options show the persistence of gender segregation. Within design and technology, for example, graphics or resistant materials is traditional male territory, whereas food technology is traditional female territory (Paechter 1998). Further, the link between gender and subject choice is still marked at A-level. Young women are less likely to study physics or maths in the sixth form (thereby denying themselves career opportunities in scientific and technological professions) whereas the arts and humanities remain female-dominated. For those who take the vocational route, the gap between men and women appears to be widening. So, young women are more likely to gain Royal Society of Arts (RSA) qualifications (largely secretarial and clerical) while more young men gain Business and Technology Education Council or City and Guilds (largely craft-related) awards. Moreover, the most recent figures show that female participation on the Modern Apprenticeship Scheme (initiated in 1995) has improved, but women are over-represented in hairdressing and business administration and under-represented in engineering manufacturing (EOC Research Findings 1998).

Evidently the broad trends in the position of women in education require careful analysis but gender equality varies according to class and ethnicity, as does the value of having or not having educational qualifications. However, several factors have been glossed over in the dominant interpretations of the link between gender and underachievement in current times. First, the improvement in female achievement has not occurred for all girls. Interaction based on socio-economic factors and ethnicity is crucial for all pupils. Secondly, the very highest achievers are still in the main men. At A-level more men than women achieve higher level grades and in higher education more men than women perform at the extremes. In the UK in 1996–7 8.5 per cent of men and 6.9 per cent of women achieved a first-class degree, for example, while 12 per cent of men and 7 per cent of women achieved a third-class or pass degree (EOC Research Findings 1998). It is also the case that the situation differs in individual institutions, with around 16 per cent of men at Oxbridge awarded first-class degrees, compared to about 9 per cent of women (The *Guardian* 13 January 1998). Overall, this represents a continuation of the tendency for boys to score at the extremes (either very high or very low) during compulsory schooling. Moving on to the third point, dominant interpretations of performance differentials show close connections with sexist assumptions about intellectual differences between the sexes. Thus, for example, when it comes to girls' relationship to school science:

More effort has gone into exploring cognitive deficits in girls to explain their poor performance than into asking whether the reliance on tasks and apparatus associated with upper middle-class white males could possibly have something to do with it. (Gipps and Murphy 1994: 33)

In contrast, within a publication focused on improving boys performance, Bleach (1998: 3) urges caution with regard to new information on gender differences in brain function 'for fear of thinking there is nothing that we, as teachers can do about the aspects of boys' behaviour to which it is related'. Further, the phenomenon of underachieving girls at A-level is explained in terms of 'the style of examination and assessment at post-16' that favours the 'flair and confidence and risk-taking demonstrated by some boys' (Bleach 1998: xv). Where girls outperform boys this is put down to compliant hard work rather than intellectual ability, which leads on to a final, and related, point. Contrary to the popular belief that coursework favours girls, it seems that such explanations for why girls have accelerated ahead at GCSE are misplaced. Analysis of the 1997 GCSE data suggests coursework does not contribute disproportionately to the final grade; the more powerful discriminators are the 'more traditionally styled examination papers' (Murphy and Elwood 1998: 17).

Deep connections between knowledge and power mean girls' good performance in a particular subject may affect its status and perceived difficulty, as well as its place in society. There does not seem to be a corollary between the poor achievement of boys in modern languages and under-representation in important positions in industry, for instance, despite the impact of globalisation. In contrast, IT is a central subject of the National Curriculum and use of the new forms of technology will play a major role in the extension of opportunities for employment. However researchers report a tendency for boys to dominate both computer and teacher resources, as well as the longevity of perceptions that girls are technologically more inept than boys (Opie 1998).

Clearly it is important to avoid oversimplified definitions of educational winners and losers. The danger is that the needs of girls will again become sidelined in the prevalent concern with the education of boys. In May 1997 the Professor of Education at Exeter University, Ted Wragg, entered the public debate when he delivered the *Times Educational Supplement*'s Greenwich lecture. In it he put forward a 10-point plan to help the boys. The plan did not extend to girls; neither did it attend to the implications of certain masculine norms (such as aggression and competitiveness) for behaviour and learning in schools. Hence the problem of boys behaving badly was resolved by a recommendation that teachers appeal to boys' interests – humour, adventure and sport (*Times Educational Supplement*, 23 May 1997). This is problematic because a bias towards particular teaching and learning activities may serve to reinforce the hegemonic masculinities that continue to dominate the state education system. If so, it will have implications for boys as well as girls.

It is important to note, as Skelton (1998) does, that many studies carried out in the 1960s and 1970s demonstrated a male bias in their concentration on boys' experiences of education. Much of this work fails to consider the broader implication of male power relations and this neglect is similarly evident in current ways of thinking about the under-achieving boy. More recent academic analyses of masculinities in education consider the wider system of male power and the variety of masculine forms that exist across a spectrum of difference. For example, and very briefly, gender is used to induce conformity to conventional masculine behaviour. Certainly social categorising of activities that carry connotations of 'effeminate' behaviour was evident in Mac an Ghaill's study of masculinity, sexuality and schooling in the early 1990s. He writes:

> In one secondary school that I taught in, a male student, after hearing that he had passed his exams, gave me a bunch of flowers in the school playground. Within a short period of time, the incident was common knowledge in the staffroom and the male teachers responded with heterosexist jokes. At the same time, the student got into a fight defending himself against homophobic abuse. The headteacher asked me to report to his office, where he informed me that I had gone too far this time. I began to defend myself, claiming that I could not be held responsible for the fight. The headteacher interrupted me to ask what I was talking about. Suddenly, I realised the symbolic significance of our playground performance: the exchange of flowers between two males was institutionally more threatening than the physical violence of the male fight. (Mac an Ghaill 1994: 1)

Girls and boys negotiate and take up a variety of femininities and masculinities; some of these confer power and prestige, while others are stigmatised and subordinate. It is evident that schools help to maintain gender-sexual hierarchies by mapping out the range of acceptable masculine identities and positioning anything associated with femininity as contaminating. However, the organisation of that spectrum of difference has resonance for the new trend that has been identified of a minority of boys being disaffected with school itself.

On 5 January 1998 Schools Standards Minister Stephen Byers articulated his concern with 'the laddish anti-learning culture' and gave details of a coordinated approach to tackle the underachievement of boys (The *Guardian* 6 January 1998). This included a requirement that each LEA address the issue of male disadvantage in drawing up its Education Development Plan. In this situation it is crucial that the approaches suggested are both sensitive to the findings of feminist and other educational works, including the multiplicity of masculinities identified by Mac an Ghaill and others. Boy-centred intervention strategies that stereotype the interests of male pupils may leave the inequalities rooted in older, traditional concepts of masculinity relatively untouched. This a major shortcoming of approaches that validate the gender gap in reading habits by investing in certain factual material on a variety of topics such as football, war, horror, action and adventure. In the long term, the failure to engage with the negative effects of hegemonic masculinities may not help those who perform less well and it is important to remember that there are still girls who are under-achieving also. Anti-sexist work might go further.

Unlike the former inner-city primary teacher disgusted at the 'cissy-culture' in many primary schools that he believes erodes boys' essential masculine natures (*The Mirror* 5 January 1998), this approach resists the re-prioritisation of the male-as-norm. More particularly, it challenges notions of hegemonic masculinities from a gender critical perspective.

Conclusion

It is notable that the 1990s have seen something of a backlash against feminist gains and policies within education amid a veritable moral panic over the prospects and performance of young males. Forget research reports of male domination of space and time in school (including overt sexual taunts); it is now the boys who are in need of care and protection from the phenomenon of Girl Power. However, the proposed educational solutions tend to be short term. They downplay higher achieving males and show little awareness of changing conceptions of masculinity and male activities in education. Interventions that legitimate the male macho culture and hold onto conventional views of domestic and waged labour do not account for the changing ways of living and working as we approach the twenty first century. In the longer term, an approach modelled on a patriarchal notion of 'back to the future' will not meet the needs of those alienated from education and facing social exclusion, whatever their sex.

Meanwhile, Girl Power has its limits. Warnings of a generation of 'Spice babies' triggered by the announcement that two of the Spice Girls were expecting babies suggest that, for some girls, having a baby can be seen as a logical response to perceived external circumstances. In the words of Judith Mullen, president of the Secondary Heads Association: 'Although girls still outperform boys, there is a particular kind of young girl who gets little encouragement at home and has low self-esteem [...] who is vulnerable to teenage pregnancy' (The *Guardian*, 8 September 1998). It is clear that, for some girls, women's domestic role is still central. Amid the current furore over male disadvantage you might be forgiven were you to forget the relative privileges of adult males. In fact, in many ways, the myth of the under-achieving boy serves to mask other differences based on ethnicity and class, as well as continuing inequalities between men and women. On the one hand, policies and practices in education and the labour market reinforce gendered trajectories. On the other, childcare is still treated by policy-makers as mothers' responsibility and this serves to perpetuate patterns to gender segregation. Women are still under-represented in the majority of jobs with any claim to status and responsibility and continuing inequalities of income have been the result.

Suggestions for further reading

Lessons for Life. The Schooling of Girls and Women 1850–1950 edited by Felicity Hunt (1987) provides an enjoyable and accessible introduction to the history of the education and socialisation of women.

For a discussion of gender issues particular to the secondary curriculum it is useful to look at Clark and Millard's (1998) *Gender in the Secondary Curriculum.* For examples of recent work on boys, men and masculinities that make clear connections with feminist and other educational works see the special issue of *Gender and Education* **9**(1) edited by Christine Griffin and Sue Lees. See the publication by Salisbury and Jackson (1996) *Challenging Macho Values: Practical Ways of Working with Adolescent Boys* for an anti-sexist way of approaching the education of boys in schools.

References

Arnot, M. (1987) 'Political lip-service or radical reform? Central government responses to sex equality as a policy issue', in Arnot, M. and Weiner, G. (eds) *Gender and the Politics of Schooling*, 309–31. London: Hutchinson.

Arnot, M. *et al.* (1996) *Educational Reforms and Gender Equality.* Manchester: Equal Opportunities Commission.

Benn, C. and Simon, B. (1972) *Half Way There. Report on the British Comprehensive School Reform.* Harmondsworth: Penguin.

Bleach, K. (ed.) (1998) *Raising Boys' Achievement in Schools.* London: Trentham Books.

Briar, C. (1997) *Working for Women? Gendered Work and Welfare Policies in Twentieth-Century Britain.* London: UCL Press.

Byrne, E. (1978) *Women and Education.* London: Tavistock.

Clark, A. and Millard, E. (1998) *Gender in the Secondary Curriculum.* London: Routledge.

Clarricoates, K. (1980) 'The Importance of being Earnest...Emma...Tom...Jane. The perceptions and categorisations of gender conformity and gender in primary schools', in Deem, R. *Schooling for Women's Work.* London: Routledge and Kegan Paul.

Dean, D. W. (1991) 'Education for moral improvement, domesticity and social cohesion: the Labour Government, 1945–1951', *Oxford Review of Education* **17**(3), 269–86.

Deem, R. (1978) *Women and Schooling.* London: Routledge and Kegan and Paul.

Deem, R. (1981) 'State policy and ideology in the education of women, 1944–1980', *British Journal of Sociology of Education* **2**(2), 131–43.

Equal Opportunities Commission (1998) *Gender and Differential Achievement in Education and Training: A Research Review.* Manchester: Equal Opportunities Commission.

Gipps, C. and Murphy, P. (1994) *A Fair Test? Assessment, Achievement and Equity.* Milton Keynes: Open University Press.

Griffin, C. and Lees, S. (1996) *Challenging Macho Values: Practical Ways of Working with Adolescent Boys.* London: Falmer.

Heward, C. (1993) 'Men and women and the rise of professional society: the intriguing history of teacher education', *History of Education* **22**(1), 11–32.

Hunt, F. (ed.) (1987) *Lessons For Life. The Schooling of Girls and Women 1850–1950.* Oxford: Blackwell.

Mac an Ghaill, M. (1994) *The Making of Men. Masculinities, Sexualities and Schooling.* Milton Keynes: Open University Press.

Miles, S. and Middleton, C. (1995) 'Girls' education in the balance: The ERA and Inequality', in Dawtrey, L. *et al.* (eds) *Equality and Inequality in Education Policy*, pp.123–39. Clevedon: Multilingual Matters in association with The Open University.

Murphy, P. and Elwood, J. (1998) 'Gendered experiences, choices, and achievement – exploring the links', *International Journal of Inclusive Education* **2**(2).

Opie, C. (1998) 'Whose turn next? Gender issues in information technology', in Clark, A. and Millard, E. (eds) *Gender in the Secondary Curriculum*, pp.80–95. London: Routledge.

Paechter, C. (1998) *Educating the Other. Gender, Power and Schooling*. London: Falmer Press.

Pascall, G. (1997) *Social Policy. A New Feminist Analysis*. London: Routledge.

Salisbury, J. and Jackson, D. (1996) *Challenging Macho Values: Practical Ways of Working with Boys*. London: Falmer Press.

Skelton, C. (1998) 'Feminism and research into masculinities and schooling', *Gender and Education* **10**(2), 217–27.

Slee, R., Weiner, G. with Tomlinson, S. (eds) (1998) *School Effectiveness for Whom? Challenges to the School Effectiveness and School Improvement Movements*. London: Falmer Press.

Stanworth, M. (1986) *Gender and Schooling. A Study of Sexual Divisions in the Classroom*. London: Hutchinson.

Summerfield, P. (1987) 'Cultural reproduction in the education of girls: a study of girls' secondary schooling in two Lancashire towns, 1900–1950', in Hunt, F. (ed.) *Lessons for Life. The Schooling of Girls and Women 1850–1950*, pp.149–70. Oxford: Blackwells.

Thom, D. (1987) 'Better a teacher than a hairdresser? "A mad passion for equality" or, Keeping Molly and Betty down', Hunt, F. (ed.) *Lessons for Life. The Schooling of Girls and Women 1850–1950*, pp.124–46. Oxford: Blackwells.

Whyte, J. *et al.* (1985) *Girl Friendly Schooling*. London: Methuen.

Chapter 9

Intercultural issues in education

Ian Menter

There was this Englishman who worked in the London office of a multinational corporation based in the United States. He drove home one evening in his Japanese car. His wife, who worked in a firm which imported German kitchen equipment, was already at home. Her small Italian car was often quicker through the traffic. After a meal which included New Zealand lamb, Californian carrots, Mexican honey, French cheese and Spanish wine, they settled down to watch a programme on their television set, which had been made in Finland. The programme was a retrospective celebration of the war to recapture the Falkland Islands. As they watched it they felt warmly patriotic, and very proud to be British.

Raymond Williams 1983: 178

Introduction

This chapter is not entitled intercultural education. This fact signals from the outset an uncertainty about the meaning of such a term. It is fascinating to trace the emergence of the term in English language writing about education (as we shall see, the term appears to have surfaced initially in non-English speaking contexts). It is only in very recent years that 'intercultural education' had made it into the titles of books (e.g. Coulby *et al.* 1997; Fennes and Hapgood 1997).

In this chapter I start by examining definitions of culture before exploring some of the possible linkages between culture and education. Following that I explore the concept of 'intercultural education', drawing on a range of experiences and a range of published sources in an attempt to determine what such an approach to education might entail. I then return to questions touched on earlier about the relationship between education, culture and identity.

It is my contention that the exploration by teachers and learners of the connections between 'cultures' is at the core of contemporary developments in education. It is in this site that we work creatively to shape the future democratic education of the world's citizens. This is no easy task; rather, it is the central and very demanding challenge that all those involved in education or the politics of education should be concerned with.

Culture

Before examining the possible meaning of *inter*cultural, I wish first to look at some definitions of culture. This is certainly one of the most difficult words in the English language (and because we will be considering other cultures, and hence other languages, we must be sensitive to the particularities of English definitions, especially in the context of education histories in this country).

Arising from the strongly class differentiated nature of English (and indeed British) society at the time of the development of mass education (i.e. the late nineteenth and early twentieth centuries) a strongly normative definition of culture has had an enormous hold throughout this century. This is the view of culture which contrasts it with anarchy (see Matthew Arnold's *Culture and Anarchy* (1869, 1932 edn)) and propounds 'sweetness and light'. Such a selective approach to culture was also famously promoted by T. S. Eliot (1948) in his short book *Notes Towards the Definition of Culture*.

However, the steady empowerment of people from working-class homes arising from greatly improved literacy standards and, indeed, the consolidation of universal state education (notwithstanding the continuing presence of a separate private education for an élite), together with the economic and social transformations which took place following the Second World War, provided the foundations for the firm establishment of a radically different approach to the definition of culture. In simple terms, this is seen as culture 'as a way of life'. In other words, culture is not a selection from the habits, artefacts and arts of a group of people, but is a comprehensive, inclusive term which is used to describe all of the behaviours and expressions of humanity which distinguish the group (family, class, nation) under discussion.

In England, work first published in the 1950s by such writers as Richard Hoggart (1957) brought into the public domain the possibility that the industrialised working class of the great English towns and cities might very well be culturally strong and distinctive. This writing emerged simultaneously with a number of other manifestations, notably in drama and literature. However, it also drew on philosophical and political theory. Historians too played their part in uncovering the past (and previously 'invisible') expressions of this broader understanding of culture (e.g. Thompson 1963).

Arguably though, the most significant, persuasive and developed work around this theme was that of Raymond Williams. Williams grew up in the border country of Wales, in a railway family and progressed from his grammar school to a scholarship at Cambridge University, itself one of the bastions of the narrow definition of culture discussed above. He demonstrated in a profound way that the relationship between society and culture is dialectical, that is, one can only really understand literary expression through a social analysis, but that simultaneously, the literature itself can provide insights to the culture. And in terms of the creative processes involved, literature is both a product of a society and has the potential at least to be a motor for change. Culture is thus dynamic, organic, a site of social struggle and change, symbolic and real (material). Williams' work amounts to a sustained critique of élitist approaches to culture which idolise the individual. The power of his critique arises in large measure from his ability to draw into his discourse deep understandings of 'high' culture (as in *Culture and Society* (1958) or *The Country and the City* (1973)) and mass culture (notably in *The Long Revolution* (1961), but also in his work on television (1974)).

Since the 1950s, a number of other key developments have occurred which have influenced and reformed this definition of culture as a way of life. The strong emergence from the early 1960s onwards of distinctive youth cultures has been documented by sociologists. These developments were sometimes closely associated with the strengthening of 'popular' culture, particularly through music, television and video, and of course as young people grow older they do not discard their earlier cultural forms or activities entirely, so that the youth culture of yesterday can become part of the 'mainstream' culture of today. We have seen a number of studies which have taken a serious anthropological or sociological look at youth sub-cultures, perhaps the most influential being that by Willis (1977).

It is immediately apparent looking at the development of cultural studies that it was dominated in its early days by men. It is also apparent that much of the focus on working-class culture was actually on working-class men. The workplace, the social club, the sports activities and so on all tended to be male activities. And yet, the strongly gender differentiated nature of the work was not systematically criticised until the wider emergence of feminism in politics and academia during the 1960s. Certainly since that time, there has been increased attention to the lives and experiences of women (young and old) and a surge of academic activity by women in this field (e.g. Griffin 1985).

A similar critique can be made of the origins of cultural studies with regard to ethnicity. Certainly there were early sociological studies of racial discrimination but the systematic development of an ethnically aware cultural studies took a considerable time to develop (Gilroy 1987).

So, if youth, gender and ethnicity have all been key features of studies in culture and society between the 1960s and 1980s, what of the more recent past? I would suggest that the key development as we approach the millennium has been a very visible 'globalisation' of culture. For centuries, there has been a world culture of trade, commerce and international relations. But the significant development in the last two decades has been the explicit introduction of cultural activities. Electronic information technologies have been a prime facilitator of this development. The ease with which communication around the globe now occurs means that it is possible not only to read about others' lives but to call up a number or electronic address and talk face to face with someone in Australia or South Africa.

In postmodern cultural theory it is often suggested that individuals may now best be described as having multiple identities. Individuals are defined and experience their lives through their ethnicity, their language, their religion, their age, their gender, their sexuality, etc. There are no longer simple correlations between these dimensions. Especially among young people we can see much evidence of complex mixtures of previously unassociated features. In educational terms the huge and increasing number of bilingual children in schools in Europe and the USA (as well as many parts of Asia, South America and Africa) is but one small part of this global picture. It has long been recognised that a person's first language is a key element in his/her identity formation. For young people growing up fluent in more than one language, it is clear that their identity is likely to be more complex.

Culture and education

If we have established now that culture is complex, dynamic and differentiated, what then of culture and education? The first important point to make is that education is part of culture. In other words, the way in which education is structured in any social setting is a key element of the culture in that setting (see Williams' chapter on education in *The Long Revolution*, 1961). The second key point is that education (depending on one's definition) may play a major part in the production and reproduction of culture (see Bowles and Gintis 1976 or Althusser 1971). And thirdly, the substance of any education system has a particular relationship with the culture. This is not just the simple but important point that a curriculum is 'a selection from the culture'. What I am arguing here is that curriculum, pedagogy and assessment – Bernstein's three message systems (see Bernstein 1975: Chapter 5) – are all inherently cultural phenomena. They do indeed convey messages. The range of pedagogical practices within a society will demonstrate such matters as the view of knowledge, understanding and skills which prevails. Also, the ways in which school students are taught will illustrate the status of children and the future orientation of the society. Assessment policies and practices will illustrate how the society views the purposes of education and the social selections which are associated with it. As we examine in the next section what might be meant by intercultural within the context of education, it is worth bearing in mind how each of these three message systems may relate to one or more cultures.

Intercultural education – does it exist?

What then might be meant by intercultural education? If we accept that societies are in fact 'multi-cultured', then what is the relationship between the education system and the variety of cultures within a given society?

Again, I would like to approach these questions by looking at the case of England. I have already alluded to the cultural selections which take place in English education (selections of pupils, selection of curricular content, for example). The history of ethnicity and education (or what Mullard (1982) called 'racial forms of education') is a fascinating study. This history is more fully covered elsewhere in this book (see Chapter 6 in this volume). For the purposes of this chapter, it will have to suffice to draw attention to the aspirations that were held for multicultural education. Put crudely, proponents of multicultural education hoped that the study of a range of cultures within the curriculum could foster tolerance and racial harmony among young people.

The idea was that through learning about 'other cultures', children would develop their understanding of other people. There were many problems with this approach and there has been very little evidence that it had the desired effect. One of the problems was that the whole approach tends to treat 'other culture' as fixed both in time and place. Cultures become rarefied and stereotyped. Troyna (Corner 1984) sardonically referred to this as 'the Three S's' – saris, samosas and steel bands – approach. Another problem inherent in this approach was the implicit promotion of congruity between ethnicity (or race) and culture. As I have already demonstrated, culture is much more variegated than ethnicity. Ethnicity is a key factor, but it is only one of many. To pose this in a different way, why was 'multicultural' education never about social class, another key factor in cultural identification?

Can an intercultural approach offer something which was not offered by multiculturalism? Davies and Rey (1998) have traced the use of intercultural education to Micheline Rey (papers written in 1991 and 1997).

> She has explained that using the word 'intercultural' means emphasising the prefix 'inter': interaction, exchange, opening up…It is vital to recognise the importance and meanings of the interactions between individuals and groups in different places and different times. There are two key aspects: the term 'intercultural' affirms explicitly the reality of interactions and interdependence as well as ensuring that these interactions contribute to mutual respect and the formation of cohesive communities rather than accentuating relations of domination and attitudes of exclusion and rejection. (Davies and Rey 1998: 183–4)

The replacement of the prefix *multi-* by *inter-* would seem to imply an exchange or at least interaction between cultures. This is to imply more than the recognition of diversity but the existence or promotion of a dynamic relationship, of some organic process. As a starting point, this would seem to be much more consistent with the understanding of culture which I have developed above.

One context in which a discourse of intercultural education is developing rapidly is that of the new Europe. This is worthy of some consideration here. The European Union has been in existence in some form or other for approximately 50 years now. Over that period, we have scene a steady move towards the reduction of political and economic barriers between the constituent states of the Union. We have also seen the steady increase in the number of Member States. And since 1989, we have seen the re-orientation of a large number of states formerly under the influence of or control of the Soviet Union towards the West.

> The Council of Europe believes that participation and the active development of a multicultural society through intercultural education and learning are key concepts for achieving a more just and more tolerant, and therefore more democratic society. Encouraging young people to take responsibility for themselves and their environment is one of the big challenges for schools today; intercultural education is the other. (Taylor 1997: 58)

The history of Europe demonstrates that boundaries and peoples have been constantly shifting. Indeed it is no simple matter to define Europe either now or at any time in the past (see Coulby and Jones 1995: Chapter 4 for a discussion of this issue). However, the current overall direction is clearly towards 'harmonisation', if not federation. The social policy makers within the bureaucratic apparatus which is attempting to manage this process has long seen education and cultural development as key aspects of successful pursuit of this goal. When we do consider European history, there is plenty of evidence of conflict and attempts at exclusion. The rhetoric of European unity has for long featured 'diversity' and 'pluralism' (in much the same way as within British society). However, it is only in more recent times that we hear the use of 'intercultural'.

What is the significance of this development? As long as the cultural element of this concept is not ossified then I believe we can argue for this as a very progressive development in society at large and in education in particular.

The growth of 'intercultural education' within the European context has been very closely associated with emerging concerns around nationalism, ethnicity and identity. There have been surges of ultra-nationalism in many western European countries, including the United Kingdom (sic), France and Germany. In the German case the situation has been related to the process of 're-unification' of East and West Germany and with continuing controversies around the explanations of the rise of fascism in the Third Reich. But in all cases the tensions which have emerged related to earlier or recent movements of peoples into 'territory' judged to belong to existing residents (see Ignatieff 1994).

Case study of Latvia

A number of the issues raised so far were very apparent in a project undertaken in Latvia during the mid-1990s (see Menter and Clough 1995 and Clough *et al.* 1995). Latvia is one of the three Baltic States which had experienced a form of colonisation by the Soviet Union for 40 years following the Second World War. When the Soviet Empire collapsed in the early 1990s these three republics (Lithuania and Estonia are the other two) found themselves independent again. Or, to put it another way, nationalist forces within these three countries were prominent in bringing about the demise of the USSR. There were very real conflicts and considerable loss of life in achieving independence. Once it had been won, however, Latvia was faced with a number of serious dilemmas. The country was populated by people from a wide range of backgrounds. About 52 per cent of the people were 'ethnic Latvians', that is their ancestors had lived in Latvia and they spoke Latvian as their first language. But following the 40 years of 'occupation' about 34 per cent of the population were Russians – that is, they themselves or their parents had arrived from Russia to take up posts in the military or in key economic positions. They spoke Russian as their first language.

In seeking to redevelop the education system in an appropriate form for a new democracy, policy-makers, teachers and teacher educators were faced with many difficult issues. Our project was concerned with teacher training in Latvia and we were working with a group of lecturers from universities across the country who were working in the field of 'civics'. Under the Soviet system the curriculum for schools and colleges had included the study of Marxism–Leninism. This created a slot on timetables which there was now a strong desire to fill with an appropriate 'democratic' replacement.

We were thus exploring, over a period of some three years, some of the issues around the democratisation of teacher education. It soon emerged in our discussions both that some of the cultural assumptions we had developed working in England were irrelevant or inappropriate in the Latvian context and also that it is impossible to work on one element of the curriculum in this way without giving serious consideration to many other matters, including the structure of teacher education and the structure and curriculum of the school system. We found on visiting a teacher training institution that students were taught on two separate pathways, one for Latvians and one for Russians. This reflected the fact that separate schools existed for Latvians and Russians. Since that visit in 1993, Latvian has been officially declared as the national language and all teacher training and schooling has been moved towards using entirely Latvian as the language of instruction. The citizenship laws which were implemented following inde- pendence disbarred those Russians and their descendants who had not been domiciled in Latvia prior to 1940 from being Latvian citizens. Thus many people born in Latvia, even as long ago as 1941, were not entitled to Latvian citizenship. If language is a dynamic expression of ethnicity and nationality, then citizenship is a fundamental legal definition of rights within a society.

What then might be the shape and purpose of intercultural education in such a context? This is a society that is changing rapidly as a result of major political upheavals. The society as a whole is redefining itself as a nation within Europe and as a 'liberal democracy'. How can education assist in the achievement of these aspirations? In discussion with our Latvian colleagues we were able to identify the significance both of studying history and of discussing human rights. Latvia was shifting from a situation where a powerful and large minority (Russians) with the support of an imperial government (the Soviet Union) had held sway in most matters political, to a situation where the majority group (Latvians) which had been disempowered and oppressed for 40 years was seeking to take control. At the centre of our discussion was the desire to define the values which should underpin social and educational development. Elsewhere we have written about some of the steps we took together (Clough *et al.* 1995). The extent of anti-Russian feeling was variable but in some settings there was severe hostility. The desire to expunge the former oppressors from the society has been a feature of many countries post- independence (cf. many countries in Africa or Asia).

The main conclusion which we came to in this work is that only an interactive developmental and dynamic approach to these issues will work. It is not appropriate to create a fixed curriculum for example, which can support the development of a democratic plural society. The teachers and indeed the pupils themselves have a part to play not just in teaching and learning but in curriculum development.

Culture, identity, citizenship ... and education

> Confronting differences, understanding our prejudices, recognizing stereotypes as what they are, finding ways to communicate – this learning is done through process, practice and reflection. There are no 'right' answers; an examination would not tell us that a pupil passed or failed. There are ways to find out about differences, to learn more about prejudices and stereotypes, to learn how to communicate effectively with others who communicate differently, to know oneself as others do. These are known as intercultural learning. (Fennes and Hapgood 1997: 2)

Returning to Bernstein's message systems, I wish to draw this discussion to a close by examining connections between intercultural approaches in education and recent policy developments within the English education system. I hope this provides the reader not only with an example of how the work of a theoretical sociologist such as Bernstein can be applied, but also more generally of a method of approaching the critique of education policy.

Taking the question of pedagogy first, it would certainly be true to say that central government had played very little part in defining teaching and learning approaches until recently. Education inspectors (HMIs) had for a number of years offered guidance on good practice in a number of their publications, but it has only really been since the creation of OFSTED – the Office for Standards in Education – in 1992, that the inspection framework was built around notions of good teaching (teaching is currently ranked on a 7-point scale by inspectors). The Government also now defines the 'standards' that should be achieved by trainee teachers in order to attain Qualified Teacher Status. Although there is some acknowledgement of equal opportunities within these frameworks, the underlying assumption is that the cultural underpinning of teaching is static. The teacher's job is to transmit the National Curriculum effectively. In the most recent development at the time of writing – the National Literacy Strategy – primary teachers are enjoined to teach daily a 'literacy hour', the structure of which is laid down in documents published by the Department for Education and Employment (DfEE 1997). There is a danger that an unthinking delivery of this hour could create a very monocultural approach to literacy and indeed literature, a danger which was forewarned by Datta (1998) who expressed concern that the needs and strengths of bilingual learners would tend to be ignored in this new centralist thrust.

Bernstein's second message system, that of assessment, is also afflicted by a strong tendency to monoculturalism. In the tests which children at the ages of 7, 11 and 13 must undertake annually (SATs) as well as with the recently introduced baseline assessment (at age 4 or 5) and in 'public' examinations at 16, it remains difficult in many subjects to identify serious acceptance of the dynamic nature of culture. The problem is perhaps not as much that the approach is monocultural, as that the dynamic nature of culture is ignored. Students are not enabled to demonstrate their awareness of the ways in which society is changing, of their awareness of European or global culture.

And finally, if we consider the curriculum itself (the third of the message systems), we are faced straight away with a probable oxymoron – an intercultural national curriculum. Is such a curriculum possible? I would argue that unless we can meet two conditions, then a national curriculum is unlikely to be intercultural or even to be sensitive to intercultural issues. The first condition is that there must be a clear contextualisation for a national curriculum, which both acknowledges the limits which must exist to the definition of the curriculum and stresses the importance of the plurality of culture within the nation, the nature of European cultures and the global nature of contemporary cultural developments. Such a contextualisation is likely to lead to a recognition of 'cross-curricular themes' such as citizenship or environmental education. Such themes were established in the first version of the English National Curriculum (from 1988) but were effectively squeezed out through the enormously detailed content and coverage of the core and foundation subjects. It is only with the review of the National Curriculum carried out in 1993 and with the change of government in 1997, that we are beginning again to see serious attention being given to some of these questions (see below).

The second condition has already been alluded to in the previous paragraph. A national curriculum which over-emphasises 'content' or 'subject knowledge' at the cost of processes and skills and to some extent understanding is one which is likely to be 'a curriculum of the dead' (Ball 1994). It is true that the programmes of study for most subjects do concern themselves with skills (e.g. using and applying maths), but, even where this is the case, the skills tend to be defined in a narrow way which does not encourage the broader skills of thinking and acting appropriately in a democratic society to be developed effectively.

Any government is faced with a number of difficult decisions in its development of education policy. Not least is the question of the extent to which government itself should intervene in the provision of education and its processes. However, given that at present in this country [England] (as in many others) we do have a very high level of national state involvement, there are real tensions between developing policy to meet the 'basic needs' of individuals (such as literacy and numeracy) on the one hand and seeing education as a vehicle for the achievement of a wider political and social agenda such as the promotion of English/British citizenship. This latter then begs the question, in the context of interculturalism, as to what extent Englishness or Britishness is to be Europeanised or globalised?

It is fascinating that the report of the Advisory Group on Education for Citizenship and the Teaching of Democracy in Schools (AGECTDS) makes very little reference to matters of culture. However there is evidence of an underlying concern with cultural issues:

A main aim for the whole community should be to find or restore a sense of common citizenship, including a national identity that is secure enough to find a place for the plurality of nations, cultures, ethnic identities and religions long found in the United Kingdom. Citizenship education creates common ground between different ethnic and religious identities. (AGECTDS 1998:17)

Fennes and Hapgood (1997) offer a theorisation of intercultural education which is broadly consistent with the ideas set out in this chapter. Their particular belief is that intercultural education can reduce intolerance and increase mutual understanding. Their book is published under the auspices of the Council of Europe. They include a range of activities which can be carried out in classrooms.

Conclusion

Gundara, drawing conclusions to the World Yearbook dedicated to intercultural education, writes:

The complex challenge for intercultural education in the next millennium is... how to protect the narrow or local identities of groups at one level, while at another developing a broader policy for more democratic civic cultures in which every citizen's human rights are protected and in which all groups have a stake. Intercultural discourses are by definition complex, particularly if they are to engage with substantive education questions...A key element in this complexity is the dominance of exclusionist and supremacist European discourses. (Gundara 1997: 209)

These European discourses are dominant both within Europe and around the world. If in the last 30 to 40 years, educationists had been faced with the challenge of educating against racism, today's challenge is to educate for intercultural awareness and understanding. The aim is to create citizens whose rights are protected, but also for those citizens to be conscious of their own power to create culture. That 'culture' is not only a matter of artistic creation (literature, music, art), nor limited to material life (housing, food, etc.) but is about the political framework in which people live their lives. Thus an intercultural approach to education will draw on all subjects of the curriculum, perhaps especially history, geography and 'English' in order to explore what it means to be a citizen in a 'democratic civic culture'.

There continue to be forces at work in all parts of the UK, Europe and the wider world which seek to undermine such cultures. The vicious racism against black people is still a strong element in Britain and must continue to be opposed. But the 'new Europe' is also revealing new forms of discrimination. At the time of writing (December 1998), refugees have been arriving in recent months from Kosovo, an Albanian enclave in former Yugoslavia, where the Serbian government based in Belgrade has sought to repress the Albanians. Numbers of Roma people from Romania have been arriving as refugees, again having experienced brutal discrimination (Veash and Bright 1998). Because some of these refugees have been temporarily accommodated by Kent Social Services in a hotel (rather than more humble bed and breakfast facilities) the English tabloid press has run some extremely vitriolic headlines. The fact that the men of the families have been 'accommodated' in prison, while investigations are carried out evokes no sympathy from these same tabloids.

The effect on the children in these families of both the original discrimination in Romania and the venom directed towards their families once in the UK is hard to imagine. But, if these children do stay in England it will not be long before they go to school. How will their teachers cope, both with accessing the National Curriculum for these children and with the animosity and/or hostility which these children may experience from the children of local longer established families?

It is an enormous challenge that faces education at the end of the twentieth century. Until we have a society that can deal with issues of migration humanely and creatively, a society that can offer a positive educational experience to pupils from all cultural backgrounds, we will not be beginning to offer an adequate education. Teachers and students must be enabled to play a part in the transformation – an appropriate education cannot be imposed from above. Certainly legislative frameworks can be established at national and international levels, but the enactment of curriculum development, pedagogy and assessment must be matters for continuing evaluation and review by those most closely connected with them – that is, the teachers and students.

Suggestions for further reading

Two books have been referred to which address intercultural education directly. One, by Coulby *et al.* (1997), presents an historical and theoretical overview and has an international perspective. The other, by Fennes and Hapgood (1997) takes a more classroom based approach and is co-published by the Council of Europe. For a thorough analysis of culture see any of the works by Raymond Williams listed in the References to this chapter. For a more recent analysis of the European context then Coulby and Jones (1995) is well worth reading.

Journals which can be recommended include *The European Journal of Intercultural Education* and *Multicultural Teaching.*

References

Advisory Group on Education for Citizenship (AGECTDS) (1998) *Education for Citizenship and the Teaching of Democracy in Schools.* London: Qualifications and Curriculum Authority.

Althusser, L. (1971) *Lenin and Philosophy and Other Essays.* London: New Left Books.

Arnold, M. (1869, 1932/1960) *Culture and Anarchy.* Cambridge: Cambridge University Press.

Ball, S. (1994) *Education Reform – A Critical and Post-structural Approach.* Buckingham: Open University.

Bernstein, B. (1975) *Class, Codes and Control, Vol. 3: Towards a Theory of Educational Transmissions.* London: Routledge and Kegan Paul.

Bowles, H. and Gintis, N. (1976) *Schooling in Capitalist America: Educational Reform and the Contradictions of Economic Life.* London: Routledge and Kegan Paul.

Clough, N., Menter, I., Tarr, J. (1995) 'Developing citizenship education programmes in Latvia', in Osler, A., Rathenow, H.-F., Starkey, H. (eds) *Teaching for Citizenship in Europe.* Stoke-on-Trent: Trentham Books.

Corner, T. (ed.) (1984) *Education in Multicultural Societies*. Beckenham: Croom Helm.

Coulby, D. and Jones, C. (1995) *Postmodernity and European Education Systems*, Stoke-on-Trent: Trentham Books.

Coulby, D., Gundara, J., Jones, C. (eds) (1997) *Intercultural Education (World Yearbook of Education 1997)*. London: Kogan Page.

Datta, M. (1998) 'Double talk', *Times Educational Supplement*, 17 July, 15.

Davies, I. and Rey, M. (1998), 'Questioning identities: issues for teachers and children', in Holden, C. and Clough, N. (eds) *Children as Citizens: Education for Participation*. London: Jessica Kingsley.

Department for Education and Employment (DfEE) (1997) *National Literacy Strategy*. London: HMSO.

Eliot, T. S. (1948) *Notes Towards the Definition of Culture*. London: Faber.

Fennes, H. and Hapgood, K. (1997) *Intercultural Learning in the Classroom: Crossing Borders*. London: Cassell.

Gilroy, P. (1987) *There Ain't No Black in the Union Jack*. London: Hutchinson.

Griffin, C. (1985) *Typical Girls? Young Women from School to the Labour Market*. London: Routledge and Kegan Paul.

Gundara, J. (1997) 'The way forward', in Coulby, D., Gundara, J., Jones, C. (eds) *Intercultural Education (World Yearbook of Education 1997)*. London: Kogan Page.

Hoggart, R. (1957) *The Uses of Literacy*. London: Chatto and Windus.

Ignatieff, M. (1994) *Blood and Belonging, Journeys into the New Nationalism*. London: Vintage.

Menter, I. and Clough, N. (1995) 'Teacher education in "the New Europe": some lessons from Latvia', *European Journal of Intercultural Studies* **6**(2), 3–11.

Mullard, C. (1982) 'Multiracial education in Britain: from assimilation to cultural pluralism', in Tierney, J. (ed.) *Race, Migration and Schooling*. London: Holt, Rinehart & Winston.

Taylor, V. (1997) 'The Council of Europe and intercultural education', in Coulby, D., Gundara, J., Jones, C. (eds) *Intercultural Education (World Yearbook of Education 1997)*. London: Kogan Page.

Thompson, E. P. (1963) *The Making of the English Working Class*. London: Gollancz/Penguin.

Veash, N. and Bright, M. (1998) 'Their men in jail, the press besieging them – they are fugitives in this hostile land', *The Observer*, 13 December, 5.

Williams, R. (1958) *Culture and Society*. London: Chatto and Windus.

Williams, R. (1961) *The Long Revolution*. London: Chatto and Windus.

Williams, R. (1973) *The Country and the City*. London: Chatto and Windus.

Williams, R. (1974) *Television: Technology and Cultural Form*. London: Fontana.

Williams, R. (1983) *Towards 2000*. Harmondsworth, Penguin.

Willis, P. (1977) *Learning to Labour: How Working Class Kids Get Working Class Jobs*. Hants: Saxon House.

Chapter 10

Comparing educational systems
Nigel Grant

Tell me good Brutus: can you see your face?
No Cassius, for the eye sees not itself
But by reflection; by some other things.

William Shakespeare *Julius Caesar*, I, ii

Introduction

The first problem that needs to be dealt with in comparative education is in deciding what it is for, both generally and in terms of the individual considering making use of it. It is quite common for government bodies to take evidence of the relevant experience of others to their own problems, such as the 1963 Robbins Committee on the expansion of higher education in the United Kingdom (Committee on Higher Education 1963).

Most students who study comparative education are not, and have no intention of becoming, specialists in the field themselves. Quite properly, they are looking to the study to give them comparative insights into some other field, whether it be a teaching subject, the curriculum, educational policy, management or whatever. This is just as well, for the capacity to provide this perspective is one of the strengths of the subject's appeal, namely its value to the non-specialist.

This raises fundamental questions about approaches to the subject. Methodological discussions are concerned with finding the most effective ways of explaining the behaviour of educational systems, and it is in this light that the relative merits of the various approaches – national case-studies, cross-cultural thematic studies, the construction of models and typologies, and the search for valid generalisations – have to be considered. For the purposes of research, there is general agreement that the study of comparative education has to progress from accurate *description* to *analysis*, and from that to the forming of *generalisations* about the working of educational systems. There are strong disagreements about the best ways of achieving this, but little dispute about the broad aims themselves. But when one considers the position of the non-specialist student, and the great majority of students do come into this category – other criteria must be thought of as well and these will influence the way in which the subject is presented.

What, then, can non-specialist students gain from the study of comparative education? To say that they can develop a 'comparative perspective' on their own special fields, while true enough, needs further elaboration. Leaving aside particular interests, one might suggest that a comparative perspective can offer the following elements at least:

Awareness of the differences between systems and their policies and practices in various countries

Whether these are more important than the similarities is arguable, but the point needs to be made that educational problems, and the ways of tackling them, can differ considerably from those with which we are familiar.

Similarities between systems also have to be made clear

If only the differences are dealt with, the impression may be conveyed that the experience of other countries is irrelevant to one's own, and the main point of pursuing such study at all is lost. (This may seem like a blinding glimpse of the obvious, but this obvious point is ignored in many quarters with surprising frequency).[1]

The importance of the context within which the educational process functions has to be stressed

It is crucial to realise that education does not work in a vacuum, but is profoundly influenced by the geographical, demographic, historical, economic, cultural and political aspects of the society which it serves. At the same time, lest the impression be conveyed that the relationship between education and society – any society – purely reflects the context, the influence of the system *on* its context also has to be examined. It has to be understood that no educational system operates in isolation, but has an intricate relationship with its environment.

The relevance of other countries' experiences to one's own follows logically from this

Otherwise, it may be felt that comparative study, fascinating though it may be for the specialist, has little to offer anyone else. Not that one would argue for the direct *application* of other systems' practices to one's own country; this may be feasible sometimes, but involves serious dangers. The experience of other systems can contribute to an understanding of one's own; indeed, it can be argued that this is the most valuable contribution of comparative education to the non-specialist.

Strategies of study

We can go on to consider various approaches as *strategies* of study. One popular method is the 'themes' approach, which starts by taking particular topics such as the curriculum, primary schools, vocational training, educational planning, and so forth, and comparing them across a number of selected systems, with the aim of formulating valid generalisations about the behaviour of educational systems in particular circumstances. A popular alternative, the 'systems' approach, examines complete educational systems as functioning units in their particular societies. These are not really disagreements about where the study should be going, but about the most effective starting point.

The themes approach has the advantage of coming to grips with the real stuff of comparative education – comparison and analysis – right from the start. But it presents great difficulties for those without much knowledge of other educational systems, for there are many temptations to make comparisons out of context and thus fall into some serious errors. The possibility of such error is large, but a few examples will serve.

Education does not necessarily mean the same thing in all societies

It may have quite different aims, operate under different conditions, and be assessed by different criteria. The differences are not absolute, or comparative study would lose much of its point. But there is much to be said for emphasising the differences, as these are likely to be overlooked or misunderstood if we go directly into cross-cultural comparison. For example: politicians and others are fond of reinforcing their arguments with assorted pieces of evidence from the experience of other countries. Many advocates of comprehensive schooling in the UK used to find much comfort in vague statements about Swedish reforms, while their opponents were equally fond of dire warnings of what they thought was happening in the USA or in the then Soviet Union. That much of this 'evidence' was wrong is not really the point; even when the information was accurate it could easily be used with little appreciation of the differences between the other systems and one's own (Grant 1968).

Advocates of greater emphasis on lifelong learning in the UK make use of Denmark, the USA and France and many other countries as models or as inspiration, supporters of bilingualism in Scottish schools point to Wales, Canada, Catalonia, Israel, Finland and The Faeroes (Haugen *et al.* 1980). Again, this is not to say that the comparisons are invalid, let alone the causes. In the latter case, the situation in The Faeroes or Catalonia, where there is a strong numerical base for the language and vigorous institutional support, does not easily transfer to the circumstances of the Gaels of the Western Isles or the Punjabi-speakers of Glasgow, where the languages are penetrated to some degree by the use of English.

This applies to some extent to all the countries mentioned; but there are areas in some, and particular initiatives, where much can be learned to support the case, for example in Scotland, for bilingual education, *provided the right evidence is brought forward and due allowance is made for contextual differences.* (The experiences of Welsh-medium schools in the South of Wales or of French-immersion courses in non-French Canada, for instance, provide a much more useful guide to the possibilities for the Gaels and the Scottish Punjabis than a broad appeal to the general phenomena of bilingual education). If the differences are not allowed for, even valid comparisons can be vitiated (Grant 1983).

The differences can be quite profound. The very word 'education' can have different connotations in different societies. Indeed, some languages are unable to make the distinctions which others find essential. In English, for example, the single word 'education' normally has to fulfil all the functions of *Bildung, Ausbildung* and *Erziehung* in German, *éducation, instruction* and *enseignement* in French, while Russian has a whole battery of words. But even when the same word is used, the associations that go with it may be different. A good example of this may be seen in comparisons between the USA and the UK; these were particularly common during discussions in the 1960s on the comprehensive reorganisation of schools in the UK, and especially in England, where the issue can still arouse more controversy than in Scotland or Wales.

Anglo–American comparisons are particularly favoured by opponents of comprehensive schooling. Put crudely (and it usually is), the argument goes thus: US high schools, being comprehensive, achieve low standards compared with English grammar schools, therefore, comprehensive schooling leads to low standards. The same arguments are made about US-style mass higher education. The implications for policy are obvious.

But, as usual, things are not as simple as that. For one thing, there are not that many grammar schools left in England, as most authorities have comprehensive systems; and where they do exist, they admit only a small minority of the age group, whereas the US high schools admit all of it, the vast majority staying on until 18. Like, therefore, is not being compared with like. Further, it is more difficult to generalise about school standards (or anything else) in the USA than in England. US education is more decentralised, and its financing is much more dependent on the resources of the particular areas where the schools are located. Standards in US schools therefore vary greatly from state to state, and within each state, and *any* generalisation thus has to be hedged about with qualifications.

But just suppose, for the sake of argument, that even broadly equivalent groups – those following academic courses to proceed to higher education – do show a marked disparity in standards (as many US educationists would readily concede). What exactly are we comparing? If we limit our attention to scholastic attainment as measured by examinations, it is quite probable that the 'college preparatory' tracks do come out worse. But few US teachers, parents or students would accept this as the only criterion of what the school is trying to do. US schools devote a great deal of time to socialisation, to the preparation of the student for life in US society, stressing the development of social and communication skills. It may be that the outward manifestations of this – the patriotic rituals, the varied social events, the morale-boosting sessions for the school football team, and so on – would strike English grammar-school staff as faintly comical. But the same could be said of a German *Gymnasium* teacher's impression of the games and character-building by which some grammar schools still set such store; and the German final school certificate, the *Abitur* or *Reifeprüfung* (test of maturity), is academically far ahead of the English General Certificate of Education (GCE) in its turn.

It is, of course, quite reasonable to argue that one set of priorities is preferable to another, but this has to be argued, not assumed. By plunging straight in and making comparisons and evaluations without allowing for the differences of priorities and values, we are in danger of misunderstanding the situation right from the start (Bell and Grant 1971).

This is an example of how even the meaning of 'education' can be affected by different sets of priorities. But many other factors determine what education is, what it can do, and how its aims are defined; these have to be considered if any useful comparisons are to be made. In countries such as the USA, France, Spain or Britain, for example, it is at least *possible* to consider leaving the choice of textbooks to the schools and the open market; the *actual* decision can be taken on a variety of grounds. But in Albania or Iceland, decisions are severely constrained by the small numbers speaking the national languages, whatever policy the authorities might prefer.

Again, the existence of substantial linguistic minorities in Russia, India, Belgium, Spain and a host of other countries raises problems that only the relatively homogeneous countries such as England or Denmark can afford to leave aside – or could, until the realisation that the settlement of immigrants and their descendants had confirmed their development into multicultural societies too. As for matters such as distance and difficulties in communication, these are not *major* factors in Denmark, Ireland, The Netherlands or most of the UK, but they *are* in a huge country such as Russia and they were in the USA when the pattern of educational organisation was taking shape, and they are in India and China.

Climate, demographic patterns, and of course economic circumstances, can raise needs or impose limitations that do not arise much in most of the systems of the developed world. In countries affluent enough to provide secondary schooling for the entire age group, for example, it is realistic to discuss whether the schools should be comprehensive or selective or some kind of compromise between the two; but in most developing countries where there are insufficient means to guarantee even universal primary schooling, and where the growth in population can nullify every hard-won advance, the question hardly arises. And so on: the background conditions are so important for the functioning of education – and even for defining it – that they must be taken into account if we are to make any sense of the systems themselves.

The parts of any educational system are interdependent, and have to be examined in relation to the whole

Many attempts to make international comparisons across several countries fall into the trap of assuming that things with the same name must have the same function. They may, but there can also be substantial differences. 'Primary school', for example, means in England and Wales a school for children between the ages of 5 and 11; but in Scotland it is from 5 to 12, and in the Republic of Ireland usually from 4 to 12. This is within an area, the British Isles, with close past or present political links; elsewhere, the difference can be greater. What is usually translated as 'primary school' or 'école primaire' or 'Grundschule' can cover the ages of 7 to 16 in Denmark and in Sweden, and so on. Various systems organise the structure differently, preferring in some cases to make the main division at mid-adolescence, the end of compulsory schooling, and in others at the point of transition from undifferentiated to subject-specialised teaching.

Similarly, the term 'secondary school' may mean the entire stage from pre-adolescence onwards (as in the systems of the British Isles or the USA), or it may be only the stage entered *after* compulsory school, as in Scandinavia. But this does not apply everywhere; in some countries, only *certain* post-compulsory schools – generally those leading to higher education – are designated as 'secondary', thus distinguishing them from vocational or trade schools (Bell and Grant 1971). The Irish Republic offers an example of what used to be a common western European practice. In some cases the nomenclature can be even more confusing. In the former Soviet Union, for example, there was a common school ('incomplete secondary') from 7 to 15 (latterly from 6 to 15, and still pursued in some areas); after that, pupils could change over to various types of professional or trade schools, or stay in the general school for the upper secondary stage (Zadja 1979; Grant 1982b).

This was generally a continuation of most common schools, which thus provided the whole course from 6 to 17; and when this happened, the term 'secondary' was applied to the *entire* school, *including its primary section.* Just to complete the confusion, there were 'secondary specialised schools' which could be entered after completion of the *general* secondary school. Further, changes may take place but old titles may remain in use. Even on official notices, they use the formal title, with the informal and old-fashioned title, which is what everyone says and had a different structure, in brackets, as in Germany. It is a dangerous business, especially when translation is involved, to pull institutions with similar-sounding titles out of context for separate examination.

But opportunities for misunderstanding do not end there. What happens at one level of a system has to be considered in the light of what happens before and after it. This can be illustrated by going back to the example of contrasting US high school and English grammar school standards (bearing in mind the dangers already mentioned). We have seen that academic attainment is only part of the picture, but even if we confine our attention to that for a moment, the comparison is still misleading, because it is incomplete.

In England (as in most European countries) the end of secondary schooling is still quite a reasonable point at which to consider what standards have been achieved. Enough of the age group stay on to make the judgement worthwhile, and too few go on to higher education to suspend judgement for one stage more. (This may change in the future.) But this is not so in the USA where something like half the age cohort proceeds to tertiary education. Some take only short-cycle courses, some of these transfer to full higher courses, others enter longer ones from the start but drop out, and some of these drop back in again, making it difficult to keep track of any particular age group, but a reasonable estimate would be that about a quarter eventually complete first degrees.

Admittedly, the standard of US degrees varies considerably. Some US universities and colleges can easily stand comparison academically with any higher educational institutions in the world, while others award degrees too mediocre to be recognised in other countries (or in the USA itself); and in between can be found almost every imaginable variety, from the admirable to the abysmal. But, with very few exceptions, even the worst could be reckoned to come up at least to English A-level standard and, of course, most go well beyond that. It follows, therefore, that in the USA a higher proportion of the population reaches at least A-level standard than was ever admitted to grammar school in England in the heyday of selective schooling. Even by the narrowest scholastic criteria, more get there in the end and unless we postulate some mystic law whereby certain standards must be attained by a fixed age, US education appears to perform more creditably than its detractors (on both sides of the Atlantic) would allow. To attempt an adequate assessment of a system, we have to look at all of it, not just a part. A similar point could be made about the age of starting primary school and the relevance of pre-school provision.

Nor need such considerations be confined to the formal school system, for other organisations can attend to 'curricular enrichment', as the Pioneers did in the former Soviet Union. That is all gone now, but there are some parallels in China and Cuba, and of course the *folkehøjskoler* in Denmark and the various Church organisations in some countries, particularly in Latin America, fulfil some needs for 'public enlightenment', especially for young adults. Many countries have youth and adult organisations in the cultural, linguistic, nature and athletic areas. The limitations of most of these are that they often lack adequate support and finance; they also tend to be fragmented, so that they touch few of the young people or children they are aimed at. But they are there, and sometimes function as a vital adjunct to the normal experience of formal schooling (Dunstan 1985).

There are other examples, but these should make the general point – *educational systems have to be examined as wholes, and in their contexts*, before cross-cultural studies can be expected to yield much benefit. Objective data on particular institutions can seem quite precise; but unless they are seen in relation to other institutions in the same system, and unless that system is examined in the light of the factors that make it what it is, we are in danger of misunderstanding how it works. Further, since the most common use of evidence out of context is to back up educational arguments at home, there is the additional danger that such misunderstandings may simply reinforce misunderstanding of one's own system. This is not what comparative education is for.

Why compare educational sytems?

Part of the answer has to do with *informing educational policy*. Individual teachers rarely feel they have much of a role to play here, but they often have more influence on the success or failure of policies than they may be aware of. In some countries they have considerable discretion in the choice of subject matter, method and even organisation, and therefore have an obligation to make thoughtful and informed choices rather than fall back on precedent or hunch. They are also involved in the larger issues in their capacity as citizens. Unless teachers are to be reduced to functionaries, the uncritical executors (however efficient) of decisions taken by someone else, wider understanding of the options available in the educational process is not only desirable but, at a time of constant educational change, necessary.

This could be said for educational theory in general, or any of its contributory disciplines. What benefits, then, can be expected for the thoughtful teacher from this particular kind of educational study?

The possibility of borrowing ideas is usually the first that comes to mind. Popularly, this is often held to be the main purpose of comparative education, and governments are all too often limited in their view of its possibilities to seeing it (if at all) as a method of identifying practices that could be transplanted to their own country. But great care is needed here. Quite apart from the risk that the other countries' practices may be misinterpreted anyway, they may be too closely bound up with their specific contexts to be applicable anywhere else.

Certainly, the exportation of practices has often had unfortunate effects. After the Second World War, for example, the new communist governments in Eastern Europe drew heavily on Soviet models. This was hardly surprising, in view of the political hegemony of the USSR; the newly-established régimes were not only inclined to display political loyalty, but were also trying to reform their traditional systems along Marxist–Leninist lines, and at that time the USSR was the only country with experience of this.

Unfortunately – but, in the political atmosphere of the time, unsurprisingly – the remodelling on Soviet lines was quite uncritical. History was taught from a Russocentric viewpoint, textbooks were modelled on their Soviet counterparts (and sometimes were straight translations), even degrees were often renamed to correspond to Soviet practice, and of course policy was modelled on that of the USSR, sometimes even to the wording, whether appropriate to local conditions or not (Grant 1969).

This led to some curious distortions, and could even be counter-productive. The short-lived attempt to reintroduce selective schooling in the then Czechoslovakia in 1969 was, in large measure, a reaction against a Soviet-style system, when anything Soviet was unpopular after the invasion of 1968. That the measure was short-lived is beside the point; so is the irony that the selective system the Czechoslovaks were seeking to revive was not indigenous either, but had been based on Austrian models from the time of the Habsburg rule. Quite apart from practical problems, one of the effects of undue reliance on Soviet models was that attitudes to them depended more on their origin than on their merits (Palouš 1969).

This was not just found in the former eastern bloc; the former British and French colonial empires are clearer illustrations of the effects of uncritical borrowing. Some of the more grotesque examples, such as African children being taught that their ancestors had been fair-haired people from across the Alps, are rarely heard of now. But most ex-colonial countries still retain their inheritance of British- or French-style school systems with examinations linked to assumptions about the relationship between paper qualifications and job expectations that are wildly out of keeping with these countries' needs and conditions. The damage caused is not so much by the persistence of inappropriately Europeanised curricula, which are changing anyway, it is rather caused by the expectation that going to school will provide certificates leading to white-collar jobs in the city, when the vast majority are certain to be disappointed at some stage. Large numbers of young Africans thus receive just enough schooling to make village life unacceptable, but not enough to fit them for anything else – an explosive situation due in part to an educational system devised in London or Paris that makes little allowance for conditions in Lagos or Bamako, let alone a tribal village (MacIntosh 1971).

Borrowing is more likely when there is some measure of direct or indirect control, but this is not necessary. In its early days, the USSR was an importer of educational practices. Some of the innovations after the Revolution were home-grown, but many came from the USA, such as the project methods of the Dalton Plan which were enthusiastically applied for a time. The trouble was that US progressive methods were developed in circumstances quite different from those of the Soviet Union in the 1920s. The most pressing needs there were for engineers, technologists, technicians, skilled workers and mass literacy (for literacy was necessary to sustain an industrial economy), and they were needed in a hurry. Under these conditions, progressive methods appeared ineffective and irrelevant. This made it easier for Stalin to stop 'irresponsible experiments' and impose a rigidly formal régime from which Soviet schools had hardly begun to emerge when the whole Soviet régime collapsed.

The process continues. In Scotland, for example, the relatively generalist curriculum is being eroded by English specialisation, not as a result of examination of its merits but in a random and piecemeal way, exacerbated by an impressive ignorance of Scottish matters on the part of the Westminster authorities (Grant 1982a). In Northern Ireland, which had an independent Minister of Education before the recent emergency, the results were no happier. For political reasons,

English practice was copied as a matter of policy, to emphasise the links with Britain and the differences from the Republic. But innovations take time, hence the ironic picture of Northern Ireland constructing a system of 11-plus selection just in time to see it discredited in its country of origin. The policy of 'keeping in step with England' turned out to be one of keeping one step behind (Bell and Grant 1977). This should change with the setting up of the Northern Irish Assembly, which will be responsible for all education in the Province.

More widely, however, we see the adoption of European and US models over much of the developing world. These systems differ greatly, of course, but they have all been devised to meet the needs of relatively affluent and highly industrialised societies, quite different from the low-income agrarian countries to which they have been exported. We have seen something of this in post-colonial Africa, but it is not just from former colonial powers that inappropriate models are received, but from the industrial world in general. It has become increasingly obvious that these models do not serve the needs of the 'Third World' countries, even if they could afford them; but as long as they offer such great advantages to those lucky enough to go through the whole process successfully, they make it difficult to devise other and more suitable models.

This is not to say that importation can never be valuable. For all the uncritical borrowing from the USSR in Eastern Europe, there were *some* valuable innovations, such as the development of systems of adult education and the breaking down of some of the more rigid class barriers between different kinds of school. On a more limited scale, there is the spread of the Danish Folk High Schools to other Scandinavian countries, and even some influence on adult education in Germany and Great Britain (Rørdam 1980).

Again, for all the unfortunate effects of over-hasty and uncritical adoption of US progressive methods, their positive contribution has to be recognised as well. 'Progressivism' may have run its course by now, but it has left its mark on practice. Whenever a primary teacher teaches capacity by getting children to pour water into cans rather than recite tables, s/he is using what at first were US 'progressive' methods. That this is rarely apparent is an indication of how far these methods have been naturalised. The adoption by the Open University in the UK of a credit system owes much to US practice, and has created a degree of flexibility hitherto lacking in British higher education. But this was not a straight copy; it was an adaptation of a US procedure to the rather different needs of part-time students in the UK, which still managed to avoid some of the problems in the USA. It could be added that the Open University in its turn is having a considerable impact on higher education in many other countries, including the USA.[2]

There are many other examples of effective borrowing, with one thing in common: they were taken from systems sufficiently like the importing ones to fit in, or were adapted to do so. This, possibly, is one of the most valuable contributions of comparative studies: not only can they set forth a range of alternative ideas and practices but, intelligently applied, they can help distinguish what can reasonably be imported from what can not and by examining educational practices in context can help indicate the kind of adaptation needed to fit them into another system.

But comparative education can render a particularly valuable service by providing a background of contrasts against which to examine our own problems. If our horizons are bounded by our own system, many of its practices may seem natural or inevitable, yet they may have arisen in circumstances that no longer obtain, and may now be unnecessary, arbitrary or even harmful. It is not impossible to examine one's own system critically from the inside, but it is more difficult without a comparative perspective. The very existence of other assumptions and practices can provide a necessary challenge to some of our own. It does not automatically follow that we *have* to change; even if we are alone in this practice or that, it may still fit our own circumstances. But the existence of alternatives obliges us to justify rather than assume, so that if we do adhere to something, there is a chance of knowing why we do it.

An example can be seen in the horizontal and vertical divisions within the school system. In most of the UK it is taken for granted that the division between primary and secondary school at 11 or 12 reflects a qualitative and necessary change in pedagogical styles, and even that it has some natural sanction. Sensible and convenient it *may* be, but it is not inevitable. The break at this point is also found in the USA, Italy, France and some German states; but in Denmark, Sweden, Spain and some countries of Eastern Europe (and in all of them before the system collapsed) the main division, and the main point of differentiation, is at 15 or 16.

The same variation applies to *vertical* division into parallel schools for the same age-group, as was common throughout Great Britain before comprehensive reorganisation. Segregation of this kind was regarded as quite unacceptable in the former USSR but as absolutely essential in most German states.[3] In the USA, the common school is taken for granted, but so is internal division (known as 'tracking'). In every case, the matter is open to argument and here the existence of alternatives can be a useful corrective to the widespread habit of taking one's own practice as the norm.

Comparative studies can also clarify our ideas of what is possible, a useful step before deciding whether something is *desirable*. International practice is frequently evoked over some of the more emotive issues such as school uniforms, sexual differentiation, and so forth, and it is true that, internationally, attitudes towards such things range from automatic acceptance to horrified rejection (Hajnal 1972). But they are often not the best examples, as they are closely bound up with a broader complex of social expectations and pressures. It would be rash, for instance, to attribute too much of the disorder in many US schools to the schools themselves; there are too many other forces in operation. But curriculum policies, for example, can profitably be looked at with an eye to what is being done elsewhere, as in the debate in the UK on specialisation versus generalisation, or the relation between school and work.

To take one example, little is expected in the English-speaking countries of average or below-average pupils in the learning of foreign languages. In the British systems, languages were formerly largely confined to the 'academic' schools or streams, and although we have advanced somewhat in the last 10 or 20 years, many teachers are still convinced that trying to teach languages to any but the most able, like the top third of the ability range, is a waste of time. Whether it is desirable that they should do so is, of course, another argument, but international evidence does not support the idea that the average child has some inherent linguistic incapacity. Bilingual and multilingual communities are common throughout the world, and even school-based learning can be extremely effective. In Scandinavia, for instance, all children learn at least one foreign language (usually English), and many more learn at least one more besides; the levels of competence vary, but are generally high. Unless we believe in some kind of inborn incapacity among the Americans and British, we have to reject the idea that 'languages for all' is *impossible*. Discussions of the *desirability* of such a policy has a chance of being considered on its own merits, then, without unnecessary presuppositions.[4]

But an international perspective can also provoke re-examination of some of our educational concepts (or slogans) such as 'standards', 'discipline', 'indoctrination', 'excellence', 'leadership', 'freedom of choice', 'general culture', and so on. We are not always clear, however, just what we mean by them, and one incentive to clarify our definitions is seeing how different they are elsewhere. For example, 'democratic education' would mean maximum curricular choice and grass-roots control to most Americans, but would suggest a centrally-determined uniform curriculum to the French, on the grounds that the child must be free of the chances of local circumstance. 'Leadership' has positive connotations in England, but in Scandinavia would sound distinctly sinister.

Teachers and academics in most countries have a fairly clear notion about what is meant by (say) 'university standard', but usually have difficulty in defining this. 'Indoctrination', in the sense of a deliberate inculcation of values, may be more obvious to someone looking at a system from outside than to someone actually in it; 'indoctrination' may turn out to be something that *other* people do, but which we prefer to call something else – 'moral education', perhaps, or 'citizenship'. Unless we are prepared simply to dismiss other interpretations as 'wrong' just because they are different, their very existence requires us to attempt a definition of *our* terms. We may, once again, decide that they are valid and useful, but at least we should have a better idea of what we are talking about.

Conclusion

Comparative education thus has the capacity to do in space what educational history does in time; it can provide the opportunity to understand better the workings of the educational process by giving us a wider view than the here and now. At a time when everyone in contemporary educational systems is faced with unprecedented challenges, as crises of resource and direction loom ever larger, and as the need to educate for future uncertainty becomes more urgent, the importance of clear and radical thinking could hardly be more obvious. This is not to say that *everything* is on the agenda for change; tribal customs may after all have their place, but it does not help to confuse them with laws of nature.

Comparative education cannot, of course, pretend to offer any uniquely valid set of answers, but can claim to be one useful tool for the better understanding of the educational process in general and one's own system in particular; and this, at a time when understanding and ideas are not exactly in over-supply, is a claim of no little importance.

Suggestions for further reading

One of the major problems in comparative education is that publications age very rapidly. For this reason, the journals are the best source for up-to-date articles. The major journals in the UK are *Comparative Education, Compare* and *Oxford Studies in Comparative Education*. Internationally, the principal journals in English are *Comparative Education Review* and the *International Review of Education*. Various other international journals exist within particular domains in education and will often carry articles of a comparative nature. There is at present no introductory text which is not completely out of date.

Notes

1   The then Scottish Education Department (now the Scottish Office Education and Industry Department), in the course of disputes with the Western Isles Council about extending the Council's bilingual education scheme, ruled that any arguments based on Welsh experience were 'irrelevant'.

2   This includes the highly profitable sale of teaching materials.

3   Even Länder with 'Unified School Systems' (*Einheitsschulen*) retain institutional differentiation within a notionally unified secondary school; in states with comprehensive school centres (*Schulzentren*), the three-track system is distinct, and often applies to staff as well as pupils.

4   The Munn Committee on the Curriculum in Scotland excluded foreign languages from the 'core', largely on the grounds that learning in this area was so far generally ineffective (rather than calling for improvement); this kind of consideration was not allowed to weigh against the inclusion of anything else. See *The Munn Report*, (SED) 1977.

References

Bell, R. E. and Grant, N. (1971) *A Mythology of British Education*. London: Panther.
Bell, R. E. and Grant, N. (1977) *Patterns of Education in the British Isles*. London: Allen and Unwin.
Committee on Higher Education (1963) *Higher Education. Appendix Five to the Report of the Committee appointed by the Prime Minister under the Chairmanship of Lord Robbins, 1961–1963. Higher Education in Other Countries*. London: HMSO.
Dunstan, J. (1985) 'Soviet education beyond 1984. A commentary on the reform guidelines', *Compare* **15**(2), 161–87.
Grant, N. (1968) 'Comparative education and the comprehensive schools', *Scottish Educational Studies* **1**(2), 16–23.

Grant, N. (1969) *Society, Schools and Progress in Eastern Europe*. Oxford: Pergamon.

Grant, N. (1982a) *The Crisis of Scottish Education*. Edinburgh: Saltire.

Grant, N. (1982b) 'Work experience in Soviet and East European schools', in Eggleston, J. (ed.) *Work Experience in Secondary Schools*. London: Routledge and Kegan Paul.

Grant, N. (1983) 'Multicultural education in Scotland', *Comparative Education* **19**(2), 133–53.

Hajnal, J. (1972) *The Student Trap*. Harmondsworth: Penguin.

Haugen, E., McClure, V., Thomson, D. S. (eds) (1980) *Minority Languages Today*. Edinburgh: Edinburgh University Press.

MacIntosh, J. (1971) 'Politics and citizenship', in Lowe, J., Grant, N., Williams, T. D. (eds) *Education and Nation-Building in the Third World*. Edinburgh: Scottish Academic Press.

Palouš, R. (1969) 'Pädagogische und soziologische Aspekte der Differenzierung im tschechoslowakischen Sekundarschulwesen', in Anweiler, O. (ed.) *Bildungsreformen in Osteuropa*. Köln: Kohlhammer.

Rørdam, T. (1980) *The Danish Folk High Schools*. Copenhagen: Det Danske Selskab.

Scottish Education Department (SED) (1977) *The Structure of the Curriculum in the 3rd and 4th Years of the Scottish Secondary School* (The Munn Report.) Edinburgh: HMSO.

Zajda, J. (1979) 'Education for labour in the USSR', *Comparative Education* **15**(3), 287–300.

Chapter 11

Access to higher education
Catherine Matheson

Once an institution throws down the structured and qualificatory barriers associated with entry to higher education, it merely reveals the fundamental social-structure barrier than lurks beneath the more ostensible pedagogic hurdles.

Neave 1976

When secondary schooling became universal after the Second World War, the discourse of access shifted from focusing on entry to secondary education onto entry to higher education. Today the discourse of access as an entitlement, replacing that of equality of opportunity, has become 'the mission for institutions of higher education, defining the character of courses and academic structures, pervading the values of institutions and transforming historic patterns of organisations' (Robertson 1992: 31). This chapter provides a historical perspective of access to British higher education within the educational discourse of equality of opportunity before looking at the discourse of widening access and increasing participation and its historical evolution in Great Britain.

Access to higher education in the nineteenth century

At the beginning of the nineteenth century the British universities were unevenly distributed. England had only two universities, Oxford and Cambridge while Scotland with only a tenth of the population had four: St Andrews, Glasgow, Edinburgh and Aberdeen. The Scottish universities had seen their student numbers rise sharply in the latter part of the eighteenth century and offered large lectures and a less developed tutorial system than Oxford and Cambridge. The two English universities were far more aristocratic and élitist than their Scottish counterparts and concentrated in the liberal education in the arts and humanities, providing mainly non-vocational courses for residential as opposed to predominantly local students. Although the University of Durham, founded in 1832, was based on the Oxford and Cambridge 'aristocratic' model of a collegiate university, University College London, established in 1827, was based on the Scottish model.

In the second half of the nineteenth century several of the industrial English cities established civic or 'bourgeois' universities which were locally supported, vocationally orientated, and closely related and dependent upon local business and industry with middle-class students living largely at home (Bligh 1990). Whether aristocratic or bourgeois, university education in the nineteenth and early twentieth century was largely a privilege for the fortunate and wealthy, especially in England.

A notable exception was the University of London, created in 1836, a purely examining body and offering only external degrees until the end of the nineteenth century for courses in technical colleges and other institutions as well as correspondence courses and which thus provided an alternative route of part-time study, distance learning and franchised degrees for non-traditional entrants such as women, mature and working-class students. A relatively unknown aspect of higher education is that in the late nineteenth century part-time students constituted the majority outside Oxford, Cambridge and Durham while residence did not become a dominant feature of higher education until the early twentieth century when the provincial colleges obtained university charters and more especially after the expansion of higher education in the 1960s (Wright 1989).

The USA was the first country to address gender discrimination in terms of access to higher education. As early as 1842 the first four women students graduated as bachelors of arts at Oberlin College in Northern Ohio (Kamm 1965) and more women in the USA had gained access to higher education at the start of the Second World War than in other industrialised countries (Solomon 1985). In England, University College London awarded the first degrees to women in 1878. Only in 1892 did the four Scottish universities start admitting women to degrees on equal terms with men and it was not until 1920 and 1948 that Oxford and Cambridge respectively did likewise. In the long struggle for women to obtain university degrees Britain, unlike the USA, blazed no trail to the extent that the countries of the British Commonwealth were also ahead of England and Scotland in opening their degrees to women, as New Zealand produced the first woman graduate in the Commonwealth in 1877 (Kamm 1965).

Access to higher education in the twentieth century

From the Renaissance until the Modern Age the most insurmountable barriers to higher education had been on the grounds of gender and also very often of religious discrimination. From the late nineteenth century these were progressively removed but the financial barrier to university education was slower to disappear. At the institutional level the idea of providing scholarships to ease the way for students of limited means developed at a snail's pace. In any case, few scholarships were sufficient to allow a student without other support to attend university, although various discretionary local education authorities grants had been available for Teacher Training since the nineteenth century. Age, whether for men or for women, was not a barrier to higher education insofar as mature students were not excluded from it and had been catered for in considerable numbers by franchised degrees from the University of London and at the provincial colleges which gained university charters in the early twentieth century (Wright 1989).

In 1900 there were seven universities for an English and Welsh population of 23 million, while the US state of Ohio with 3 million citizens boasted 37 higher education institutions (Miliband 1992). At the beginning of the twentieth century, there were about 29,500 full-time students in higher education in Britain. Most of these, around 24,000, were in universities, and the rest mainly in Teacher Training colleges with only a very small proportion in technical colleges. By 1945 the number of full-time students in Britain had risen to about 100,000 and nearly doubled by 1960 to about 180,000 (Edwards 1982). Two years later in 1962 it was still just under 200,000, while in 1970 it was just under 500,000 and in 1987 well in excess of 500,000. The current number of full-time students is now around one million and the total number of students is nearing 1.5 million (HESA 1998). There was a continual acceleration until 1955 and then a far steeper acceleration from 1955 to 1970 when the numbers increased two-and-a-half fold followed by a plateau (while in the decade 1987–97 the number of full-time students rose sharply and nearly doubled).

Equality of opportunity

Broadly speaking, before the Second World War, university education in the UK had the function of supporting and reproducing a socio-professional elite and universities were attended and staffed mainly by people drawn from the upper-middle-class. Was then the expansion of higher education the consequence of the Robbins Report of 1963 better equality of opportunity in education (the major concern of progressive politicians and educationalists since the beginning of the twentieth century), the raising of the school-leaving age in 1947 and 1973, or some other factor?

While it is difficult to determine the extent to which the raising of the school-leaving age in 1947 and then again finally in 1973 (and not in 1970 as announced) was directly linked to the explosion in student numbers, a measure such as this is unlikely to lead to a decrease in the number of students entering higher education. Indeed, a seemingly inevitable consequence of the expansion or universalisation of secondary education would be the growing pressures for higher education places. Following the same logic in order to expand even further as the present government wishes, it is imperative that more pupils stay on at school after the school-leaving age. For precisely that reason in the late 1990s, as we have moved from élitist to mass higher education, pupils in Britain are not yet legally required but only encouraged to stay on at school until the age of 18 or even 19. In 1998 Baroness Blackstone, the higher education minister, even suggested that A-levels were 'too narrow and elitist' and prevented too many young people especially those from working-class background from going on to higher education (Clare 1998: 1).

In the case of higher education the simple question of equal participation was for a long time clouded by the substitution of the question of equality of opportunity, a very elastic term and as elusive a philosophical concept as it is a practical target, which has been taken to apply to those able and willing to make use of it. Such a concept of policy culminated with the so-called Robbins meritocratic principle that anyone able to get the necessary qualifications and willing to go should find a place in higher education. Having highlighted that the proportion of middle-class children who reach degree-level courses was 'eight times as high as the proportion from working class homes' (Committee on Higher Education 1963: 46) and had remained unchanged since the 1920s, the Robbins Committee Report, a sociological analysis of the influence of class on access to the higher levels of education, argued for a massive expansion in the provision of university places within the discourse of equality of opportunity in terms of extending educational opportunity to all those qualified and willing to participate.

While the Robbins Report recommended a massive expansion of higher education in the grounds of equality of opportunity, it did not actually generate the explosion in the number of students because this exponential growth (which has so often in Britain been attributed to the Robbins Report) actually started about seven years prior to that date and was almost exactly duplicated throughout the individual countries in Europe (Edwards 1982). The age participation rates for 18-year-olds which measures the number of entrants as a proportion to the size of the relevant 18-year-old group showed a more significant increase *before* the Robbins Report than *after*, as the rate went from 3% in 1950 to 8.5% in 1962, only to reach 12.7% in 1977, 14% in 1987, 20% in 1992 and 34% in 1998. In other words, the age participation rate nearly tripled in the twelve years before the Report, rose by only about a third in the course of the following 14 years and 24 years later after Robbins it had not even doubled.

The 'sharp and internationally synchronous and uniform escalation of higher education post-1955 indicated that a sufficiently powerful change in the international climate of economic and social thinking could trigger off a rapid change in the demand for higher education' (Edwards 1982: 67), especially if the ground had been prepared by raising the school-leaving age in the previous decade. The rate of growth of students enrolments in the late 1950s and 1960s was not much influenced by variations in the total population of 18- to 21-year-olds because working-class children, who constituted the majority of this population, had very little involvement in higher education, unlike the children of the rapidly expanding professional and managerial class whose services were increasingly needed by employers to adapt to the growing economic demand for qualified human resources.

As a result, the sharp escalation in students numbers from 1955 to 1970 was not accompanied by any significant change in relative participation rates by social class since the great majority of the increased flow came from the same social class as before, in the 1970s there was still the extreme disparity of social participation to higher education in the UK. Accordingly, the liberal expansion of higher education in the 1960s led to the situation that the relative chances of young people from different background gaining access have changed only slightly and then in favour of those groups already well-off (Edwards and Roberts 1980; Halsey *et al.* 1980). In the 1970s the rate of growth of higher education slowed down. However, in the decade 1968–78, the proportion of students from professional and managerial classes expanded rapidly while the much smaller proportion from the children of manual workers correspondingly declined (Edwards 1982).

The financial barrier to higher education largely remained until 1945 and then began to slowly disappear as the number of grants awarded by local authorities increased to keep up with the rise in numbers. From the early 1960s the local authorities were required to give mandatory grants to suitably qualified full-time students accepted for university first-degrees. Notwithstanding a system of income-related mandatory grants instead of discretionary local authority grants, the implementation of the Robbins recommendations failed to significantly increase the relative participation of the working-class and higher education remained consequently deeply inegalitarian, reflecting the class structure of society by denying opportunities to working-class people and favouring those from a middle-class background. The lifting of the financial barrier did not remove the more entrenched social class divide, perhaps because of the increasing emphasis on residence ever since the early twentieth and more especially since the early 1960s, or perhaps simply because although the cost of the post-Robbins expansion was borne by all the taxpayers, the balance of reward favoured those who were already better-off (Williamson 1986).

Whether higher education plays an integral part in schooling's complicity in the reproduction over the generations of an unequal and hierarchical social and sexual division of labour or serves as a means of social empowerment is open to question, because, whereas the social exclusiveness of higher education was not showing many signs of being eroded, the gender exclusiveness was faring much better and seemed slowly to be being erased. The participation of women saw a steady increase from 1971 to 1981, reflecting a trend in the school system with more girls gaining qualifications to enter higher education. The percentage of full-time students in the universities in Great Britain was seven men for three women in 1971–72, six men for four women ten years later and five men for five women today (Williamson 1986).

Apart from social class and gender inequalities, additional barriers to higher education remained those of age, regional and race inequality. If the number of full-time mature students increased slowly but fairly steadily from 8,500 in 1971–72 to 10,200 in 1979–80, the proportion of mature students, however, fell marginally, although there was a sharp rise in the number of women over 25 and a fall in the proportion of men, especially those aged 21–24 (Squires 1981). Regional participation rate when known variations in social class composition were taken into account showed that Scotland, Wales and the North West of England were doing better than expected on the basis of social class trends, while Northern England and East Anglia were doing rather worse (Williamson 1986). When social class was taken into account, 37 per cent more Scots entered university education than would have been expected on the basis of what happened in England and Wales. This much higher participation was perhaps the result of a different educational system in which the transfer from secondary to higher education takes place a year earlier and which has a broader upper-secondary curriculum. The better than expected performance in Wales and in the North West of England was not explicable in such terms and points, particularly in the case of Wales, to the importance of general and political attitudes towards education (Farrant 1981). The extent to which this remains true is currently the subject of ongoing debate and controversy. Osborne (1999) suggests that Northern Ireland is now doing somewhat better than the rest of the UK in terms of participation by lower social classes and that Scotland is now lagging behind (Wojtas 1999), though the differences are minimal.

Widening access and increasing participation

As higher education in the UK has moved from an élite to a mass system, its overall participation rate has increased more than eleven-fold from 3 per cent in 1950 to nearing 34 per cent half a century later. The percentage of male and female participation in higher education is now more or less equal, while the age participation rate was, and still is, unequally distributed according to social class divisions and to age and, to a lesser extent, geographic situation.

Access and participation are now among the major policy issues in post-school education in the UK (Fulton 1981, 1989; Williams 1997a; Davies 1994; Parry and Wake 1990) and worldwide (Halsey 1992; Davies 1995). In Britain and in many industrialised countries 'the impact of the idea of access has arguably been felt most keenly in the last decade or so [since the mid-1980s] and then in the sectors of, first higher education and then, more recently higher education and training' (Tight 1996: 131).

As the concept of access to higher education has undeniable political resonances and has to do with who gets educational opportunities and who does not, it is worth bearing in mind that the question as to who should have access depends on what higher education is for and on the advantages it brings, both for the individual and for society. This is a point returned to in the next chapter. In the UK, the concept of wider access and increased participation in higher education is not infrequently deemed to raise fears about lowering of standards and credential inflation as well as fears that a graduated system of institutions and courses would still privilege an élite.

Because the motivations behind the major policy issue of widening access and increasing participation were both the uncertainty caused by the demographic decline and fluctuations of the traditional entry cohort of the 16 to 19-year-olds and a desire to open up opportunities for more and different people closely related to the former, it is useful to examine how the government and funding bodies have approached the issue of access since the mid-1970s.

Two Labour Government documents at the end of the 1970s, a 1978 Green Paper (Department of Education and Science (DES) and Scottish Education Department (SED) 1978) and a 1979 Report (DES 1979) looked at the impact of the projections of an increasing 18-year-old population in the early 1980s followed by a rapid decline in the second half of the decade which would leave the system with considerable spare capacity. The immediate concern was to prevent a too-rapid expansion in the early 1980s while attempting longer-term planning by suggesting measures against a severe pruning of higher education because of a projected demographic fall in the traditional entry cohort. Because of predictions that between 1981 and 1996 the number of people aged between 30 and 44 would increase by about 1.6 million, the number aged over 44 by about 0.3 million, and the number aged between 16 and 29 would decrease by about 0.6 million, the effect of the two Government Papers was to make many academics and institutions much more aware of the potential of mature student entry because they suggested ways of avoiding the impending fall in student numbers for the best reasons: expansion and equalisation of educational opportunities (Squires 1981).

Indeed, for many, mature students were beginning to be seen as the way to save higher education from decline in the 1990s. Although the 1978 Green Paper had suggested that a way of coping with the demographic fall was to increase the number of mature students, especially those from a working-class background and to further increase the participation of women, there were many obstacles to the effective implementation of these ideas, not least of which was the arrival of a Conservative Government in May 1979 led by Prime Minister Margaret Thatcher.

In the summer of 1981 the Conservative Government announced a programme of cuts in public expenditure in the universities which was to reduce their income by about 20 per cent in real terms in the next two years. The government let it be known that the major objective of the squeeze was to reduce the number of students entering higher education. The financial disincentive for not meeting target numbers had a rapid effect on institutional behaviour of the universities. Because the polytechnics were funded within a local authority system, the impact of reduced unit costs on their institutional finances was not as immediate as it was with the universities. The polytechnics consequently expanded as fast as possible, reasoning that their unit costs would have been even further reduced if other HE institutions had expanded and they had not.

The attempted squeeze of higher education provision in the first half of the decade was therefore marked by an unprecedented expansion in student number (30 per cent increase) along with reduced unit costs (25 per cent decrease) in the polytechnics and colleges which saw students denied university places flocking to them. In 1984 the funding bodies (University Grants Committee (UGC)/National Advisory Body for public higher education sector (NAB)) each produced two strategy documents as well as a joint statement which, by stressing 'ability to benefit' from higher education, raised awareness and changed forever the climate for access and continuing education (UGC 1984a, 1984b; NAB 1984a, 1984b). The following year came the government's response in the form of a Green Paper (DES 1985) which grudgingly accepted the 'ability to benefit' as long as it was greater than the costs and not at the expense of standards. In other words, the Green Paper stressed efficiency and a rather élitist concept of quality (Wagner 1989b). The 1987 White Paper (DES 1987) nevertheless widened the criteria for entry even further by saying that 'places should be available for all with the necessary qualities [and not qualifications] to benefit from higher education' (DES 1987b: 7).

In 1989, in a speech at Lancaster University, the Secretary of State for Education and Science urged that the participation rate among the 18-year-olds should double from 15 per cent to reach 30 per cent within the next 25 years and that in the latter part of the 1990s the expansion of higher education should see an increase in participation from the conventional student age group and from the 'new patterns of recruitment among non-conventional students' (Wagner 1989b: 156). By the time the 1991 White Paper (DES 1991) was published the participation rate of the 18 to 19-year-olds was one in five and the anticipation was that the number would be one in three by the year 2000. The binary divide between the universities and the polytechnics (established from 1967 onwards with the majority in the early 1970s and financed by the local education authority except in Scotland where they were funded by the Scottish Education Department (SED) but had close relationships with the local community) was removed with the 1992 Further and Higher Education Act when the funding bodies, the status of which had already been changed by the Education Reform Act of 1988 to increase public accountability, were simultaneous divided geographically according to the nations of the UK while being united across the higher education sector.

From 1964 the history of higher education has been, along with the discourse of widening access and increasing participation which followed that of equality of opportunity, one of decreased financial commitment and increased control. This is further illustrated by the fact that the whole system of mandatory grants was gradually replaced from 1990 by a part-grant, part-loan scheme, a measure already tentatively contemplated by various governments since the late 1960s. Although the present government took things even further in terms of decreased financial commitment by introducing tuition fees in 1998 and in removing maintenance grants in 1999 when loans will be available to part-time students for the first time. There is an apparent paradox in the Government's attitude to access. On the one hand, there are fees and loans and, on the other, the Government's acceptance of Dearing's (1997) recommendation that

> increasing participation [...] must be accompanied by the objective of reducing the disparities in participation in higher education between groups and ensuring that higher education is responsive to the aspirations and distinctive abilities of individuals (NCIHE 1997: 101).

The Governments response to Dearing admitted that the current student support arrangements have not encouraged students from lower socio-economic groups to enter higher education, whether on full-time or part-time courses (DfEE 1998a).

From Robbins to Dearing the issues of widening access and increasing participation have progressively become central policy concerns for a rapidly expanding, and, from the late 1980s, an exploding, mass higher education system. The proposed 1998 White Paper, which was downgraded to the 1998 Green Paper *The Learning Age* in February (DfEE 1998b), aims to expand further and higher education to provide for an extra 500,000 people by 2002 and to widen participation in, and access to, learning in further, higher, adult and community education and through the University for Industry.

Entry requirements to higher education

Except for the Open University, created in 1970, which opened its doors the following year and provides the majority of part-time university first-degree courses in the UK for which no formal qualifications are necessary provided the applicant is over 21, the normal entry requirement for higher education since the 1950s has been performance in England and Wales at the Advanced level of the General Certificate of Education and in Scotland at the Higher level of the Scottish Certificate of Education.

The application for entrance to higher education is through a central clearing house, the Universities and Colleges Admission Service (UCAS) which deals with all the applications to enter higher education for full-time first degree courses or HNDs. The requirements for entry to a degree-level course vary according to the institution and are not part of any governmental regulation. The applicants are selected by each institution, faculty and department according to their own criteria and their own procedures, but following general guidelines. Traditionally, entry has been highly competitive, but increasingly, universities, especially the newer ones, have recognised alternative routes provided mainly by the further education sector such as vocational qualifications, in England formerly Business and Technical Education Council (BTEC) National Awards now General National Vocational Qualifications (GNVQs) with subject areas and pass levels, in Scotland formerly Scottish Technical and Vocational Educational Council (SCOTVEC) Awards now Scottish Vocational Qualifications (SVQs), and in both England and Scotland accredited Access courses.

Access courses and alternative routes to higher education

The broad idea of wider access has different ideological roots and is not to be confused with the narrower concept of Access courses designed for mature students without formal qualifications to gain specific entry to further and higher education and which offer an alternative to established examination systems designed for adolescents whether A-levels or Highers or vocational qualifications. While some mature students follow the traditional route and return to college or school to study A-levels or Highers, a steadily growing minority of students now enter university via the above-mentioned alternative routes.

Although there had always been older people studying for degrees, the admission of mature students without the conventional entry qualifications was given a boost in the mid-1970s when the grant regulations were changed to make such students, if they were studying full-time, eligible to receive mandatory awards as opposed to awards at the discretion of local education authority. In 1978 the first government recognition of Access courses occurred when the Department of Education and Science asked seven selected local authorities to provide special courses for people who had 'special needs which cannot be met by existing educational arrangements' and who possessed 'valuable experience but lacked the qualifications required' (DES 1978). Although there is a higher drop-out for mature students as opposed to their younger fellow students, the performance of those who graduate is comparable to non-mature students and this whatever the entry route (Woodley 1991).

The 1985 Green Paper welcomed Access courses provided that 'the challenge of non-standard entry is to maintain a reasonable degree of openness for late developers, and for those who for whatever reason did not enter higher education earlier, while ensuring that academic rigour and standards are maintained' (quoted in Brennan 1989). The 1987 White Paper and subsequent government pronouncements have placed increasing emphasis on extending access and have seen Access courses as playing an important role in it by recognising them as one of three entry routes, the other two being A-levels or Highers and vocational qualifications. Although the number and range of access courses has grown exponentially since 1978, they are only one of the recognised route of access to further and higher education for mature students over the age of 21. Access to higher education by other alternative routes does also exist and includes long-standing diverse and flexible methods such as examination or assessment, through liberal adult education provision, through assessment of prior (experiential) learning, through probationary enrolment and through open entry schemes (Tight 1996).

Over the years Access courses have gained increasing recognition among politicians and others as providing an answer to problems of participation in higher education in the 1990s. Arguably, the more broadly-based Access courses which offer a closer matching of requirements than A-levels or Highers because they tend to be linked to a particular institution and which emphasise continuous assessment rather than final examinations, provide an alternative more flexible route while emphasising equality of opportunity (Stowell 1992).

Access courses are often perceived by providers and recipients as a form of positive action targeting disadvantaged minority groups and seeking to increase their representation in higher education. Yet while it is 'undeniable that they have helped many individuals to pursue their education further than they might otherwise have been able to do, Access courses have yet to make a major impact upon the social make-up or the assumptions of higher education' (Tight 1996: 132). This particular criticism of Access courses perhaps explains, or is perhaps explained by, the fact that they tend to over-emphasise higher education as a destination and thus help sustaining conventional perceptions of higher education rather than seeking to change them (Tight 1996).

Access to higher education in the twenty-first century

Paradoxically, one benefit of the funding squeeze in the 1980s and the shift in funding towards a focus on students numbers has been a greater openness on the part of many institutions to mature, part-time and other 'non-traditional students'. In 1991 a quarter of university entrants were classified as entering via 'non-traditional' routes and in 1995 one third of undergraduate entrants were over 21 (HEFCE 1996). This has in some way reflected the desire of higher education institutions to maintain numbers during a demographic decline of the traditional cohort, but also reflects some determination to offer new opportunities to previously under-represented groups (Miliband 1992). Although the White Papers of 1987 and l991 (DES l987, 1991) talked less about qualifications and more about 'qualities' required to enter higher education and stressed flexibility and accessibility they did not outline specific measures for coherent reform. Whereas the expansion of higher education in the 1980s and 1990s saw significant improvements in relative participation rates for women, most minority ethnic groups and mature students the exact position of social class is not fully known because of shortcomings in available data. Although the data is extremely problematic and tends to relate only to full-time students on first degree courses (Davies 1997), it would neverless seem that ratios of participation from lower socio-economic groups have remained fairly constant and there still remain a disproportionate number of students from professional and managerial background as opposed to partly skilled and unskilled background (HEFCE 1996, 1997a, 1997b; NCIHE 1997; CVCP 1998).

A recent HEFCE (1997b) report found that young people from very high-income professional neighbourhoods in exclusive areas had 75 per cent chance of getting to university; those from middle-class families in owner-occupied suburban semi-detached houses 35 per cent and those from low-income semi-skilled and unskilled families living in areas of high unemployment 7 per cent (Carvel 1997). Recent figures show that 8 per cent of young people from lower socio-economic groups enter higher education compared with 16 per cent of middle-class origin and 39 per cent from managerial and professional families (Metcalf 1997). 'The expansion of higher education since 1987 has been unable to shift the balance of opportunities between most social groups' (Robertson 1997: 10).

Although the changes in higher education since the 1960s, and especially since the late 1980s, were embedded in a discourse, espoused by the access movement, underpinned by an ideology of social justice and equity (Wiliams 1997b), national policies have nevertheless seemingly tended to be driven by a preference for numerical growth and not by a concern for social justice and equity. In particular, expansion and structural changes and even the recognition of alternative routes have failed to a great extent to challenge the culture of élitism and consequently how higher education is perceived among the underrepresented groups. If expansion has yet to produce the culture change normally associated with the shift to a mass system, it is because British higher education is a 'mass system in its public structures', but nevertheless still 'an élite system in its private instincts' (Scott 1995: 2). Many of the practices in British universities 'remain rooted in an élite past', that is, in subtle and stealthy socialisation and acculturation rather than explicit intellectual formation and skills development which are recognisably élitist (Scott 1995: 23).

Many believe that it is insufficient that access to higher education be simply widened to increase participation without thinking of ways to change the internal barriers that are personal inhibitions (linked to social class, gender, ethnicity, age) and the public barriers to graduate employment that are gender, ethnic and age discrimination as well as transforming higher education itself which needs to provide more short courses, part-time courses, modules and credit-based learning, facilitate a mix-and-match approach and transfer from one institution to another, take courses outside its walls and to the people, use Accreditation of Prior Experiential Learning (APEL) to select students, offer courses for professional groups, activities and learning methods for mature students. Higher education can no longer mean only a full-time three-to-four-year residential engagement with a narrowly focused learning experience, at the expense of the state and with socially-advantaged élite (Robertson 1992). Hopefully the élitist system, which has reinforced rigidly a class system that is arguably the main cause of inequalities and economic malaise in society, will evolve into a more egalitarian one of mass and perhaps universal higher education as learning opportunities are being radically altered by the impact of increased participation, declining resources, changes in institutional governance, changes in post-compulsory education, European and international harmonisation and the development of educational and philosophical concepts such as Lifelong Learning, the Learning Society and the Learning Age. There is therefore a need to stimulate demand for higher education from under-represented groups through raising expectations and improving attainment by measures such as community outreach and promotion, information, advice and guidance and development of progression routes. Higher education will need to diversify creatively and open up opportunities where none previously existed and meet the challenge of the twenty-first century, whereby the right of access to higher education should be available to potential learners throughout their lives.

Suggestions for further reading

Bligh's *Higher Education* (1990) presents a very comprehensible but clear picture of the structure and history of higher education and is highly accessible and easy to read. *Access and Institutional Change* edited by Fulton (1989) looks at the processes of selection for, and exclusion from, higher education and at the effect of the internal processes of higher education on 'non-traditional' students. Also highly pertinent are Scott (1995) *The Meanings of Mass Higher Education* and Williams (1997) *Negotiating Access to Higher Education*.

Bibliography

Ball, C. and Eggins, H. (1989) *Higher Education into the 1990s: New Dimensions*. Milton Keynes: The Society for Research into Higher Education and Open University Press.
Bligh, D. (1990) *Higher Education*. London: Cassell.
Brennan, J. (1989) 'Access courses', in Fulton, O. (ed.) *Access and Institutional Change*. Milton Keynes: The Society for Research into Higher Education and Open University Press.
Carvel, J. (1997) 'University intake startlingly biased towards the rich', The *Guardian*, 19 April.

Clare, J. (1998) 'Universities told to make entry easier', *The Daily Telegraph*, 18 September.

Committee on Higher Education (1963) *Higher Education. Report of the Committee under the Chairmanship of Lord Robbins*, Cmnd 2154. London: HMSO.

Committee of Vice-Chancellors and Principals (CVCP) (1998) *From élitism to inclusion: Good practice in widenng access to higher education*. Summary Report. London: CVCP.

Davies, P. (1994) 'Fourteen years on, what do we know about adult students? Some reflections on national statistical data', *Journal of Access Studies* **9**(1), 45–60.

Davies, P. (ed.) (1995) *Adults in Higher Education: International Experiences in Access and Participation*. London: Jessica Kingsley.

Davies, P. (1997) 'Number crunching: the discourse of statistics', in Williams, J. (ed.) *Negotiating Access to Higher Education: the Discourse of Selectivity and Equity*. Buckingham: Society for Research into Higher Education and Open University Press.

Department for Education and Employment (DfEE) *Higher Education for the 21st Century: Response to the Dearing Report*. London: DfEE.

Department for Education and Employment (DfEE) (1998) *The Learning Age: a Renaissance for a New Britain*. London: The Stationery Office.

Department of Education and Science (1978) Letter of invitation to Chief Education Officers. London: DES.

Department of Education and Science (DES) (1979) *Future Trends in Higher Education*. London: HMSO.

Department of Education and Science (DES) (1985) *The Development of Higher Education into the 1990s*. Cmnd 9524. London: HMSO.

Department of Education and Science (DES) (1987) *Meeting the Challenge*. Cmnd 114. London: HMSO.

Department of Education and Science (DES) (1988) *Advancing A Levels*. London: HMSO.

Department of Education and Science (DES) (1991) *Higher Education: A New Framework*. London: HMSO.

Department of Education and Science and the Scottish Education Department (DES/SED) (1978) *Higher Education into the 1990s: A Discussion Document*. London: HMSO.

Edwards, E. G. (1980) 'British Higher Education: long-term trends in student enrolment', *Higher Education Review* **12**(2), 7–43.

Edwards, E. G. (1982) *Higher Education for Everyone*. Nottingham: Spokesman.

Edwards, R., Sieminski, S., Zeldin, D. (eds) (1993) *Adult Learners, Education and Training*. London: Routledge.

Farrant, J. H. (1981) 'Trends in admissions', in Fulton, O. (ed.) *Access to Higher Education*. Guildford: The Society for Research into Higher Education.

Finch, J. and Rustin, M. (1986) *A Degree of Choice? Higher Education and the Right to Learn*. Harmondsworth: Penguin.

Finegold, D. *et al.* (1992) *Higher Education, Expansion and Reform*. London: Institute for Public Policy Research.

Fulton, O. (ed.) (1981) *Access to Higher Education*. Guildford: The Society for Research into Higher Education.

Fulton, O. (ed.) (1989) *Access and Institutional Change*. Milton Keynes: The Society for Research into Higher Education and Open University Press.

Halsey, A. H. (1992) 'An international comparison of access to higher education', *Oxford Studies in Comparative Education* **1**(1), 11–36.

Halsey, A. H. (1993) 'Trends in access and equity in higher education: Britain in international perspective', *Oxford Review of Education* **19**(2), 129–40.

Halsey, A. H., Heath, A. F., Ridge, G. M. (1980) *Origins and Destinations: Family, Class and Education in Modern Britain*. Oxford: Oxford University Press.

HEFCE (1996) *Widening Access to Higher Education: A Report by the HEFCE's Advisory Group on Access and Participation*. Executive Summary. Reference M9/96 April 1996. Bristol: HEFCE.

HEFCE (1997a) *The Participation of Non-traditional Students in Higher Education*. Summary Report. Bristol: HEFCE.

HEFCE (1997b) *The Influence of Neighbourhood Type on Participation in Higher Education*. Interim Report. Bristol: HEFCE.

HESA (1998) *Students in Higher Education Institutions 1996/7*. Cheltenham Higher Education Statistics Agency.

Kamm, J. (1965) *Hope Deferred*. London: Methuen.

Metcalf, H. (1997) *Class and Higher Education: The Participation of Young People from Lower Social Class Backgrounds*. The Council for Industry and Higher Education.

Miliband, D. (1992) 'Introduction: expansion and reform', in Finegold, D. *et al. Higher Education, Expansion and Reform*. London: Institute for Public Policy Research.

National Advisory Body (NAB) (1984a) *Report of Continuing Education Group*. London: NAB.

National Advisory Body (NAB) (1984b) *A Strategy for Higher Education in the late 1980s and Beyond*. London: NAB.

National Committee of Inquiry into Higher Education (NCIHE) (1997) *Higher Education in the Learning Society: Report of the National Committee (The Dearing Report)*. London: HMSO.

Neave, G. (1976) *Patterns of Equality*. Windsor: National Foundation for Educational Research.

Osborne, B. (1999) *The Institutional Distribution of Young People from Low Income Groups*. Address to a joint meeting of the Quantitative Studies and Access Network, Society for Research into Higher Education, 9 February.

Parry, G. and Wake, C. (1990) *Access and Alternative Futures for Higher Education*. London: Hodder & Stoughton.

Robertson, D. (1992) 'Courses, qualifications and the empowerment of learners', in Finegold, D. *et al. Higher Education, Expansion and Reform*. London: Institute for Public Policy Research.

Robertson, D. (1997) 'Growth without equity? Reflections on the consequences for social cohesion of faltering progrsss on access to higher education', *Journal of Access Studies* **12**(1) 9–31.

Scott, P. (1995) *The Meaning of Mass Higher Education*. Buckingham: The Society for Research into Higher Education and Open University Press.

Solomon, B. M. (1985) *In the Company of Educated Women*. New Haven & London: Yale University Press.

Squires, G. (1981) 'Mature Entry', in Fulton, O. (ed.) *Access to Higher Education*. Guildford: Society for the Research into Higher Education.

Stowell, M. (1992) 'Equal opportunities, access and admissions: tensions and issues for institutional policy', *Journal of Access Studies* **7**(2), 164–179.

Tight, M. (1993) 'Access not access courses: maintaining a broad vision', in Edwards, R., Sieminski, S., Zeldin, D. (eds) A*dult Learners, Education and Training*. London: Routledge.

Tight, M. (1996) *Key Concepts in Adult Education and Training*. London: Routledge.

University Grants Committee (UGC) (1984a) *Report of the Continuing Education Working Party*. London: HMSO.

University Grants Committee (UGC) (1984b) *A Strategy for Higher Education into the 1990s*. London: HMSO.

Wagner, L. (1989a) 'Access and standards: an unresolved (and unresolvable?) debate', in Ball, C. and Eggins, H. (eds) *Higher Education into the 1990s: New Dimensions*. Milton Keynes: The Society for Research into Higher Education and Open University Press.

Wagner, L. (1989b) 'National policy and institutional development', in Fulton, O. (ed.) *Access and Institutional Change*. Milton Keynes: The Society for Research into Higher Education and Open University Press.

Williams, J. (ed.) (1997a) *Negotiating Access to Higher Education: The discourse of Selectivity and Equity*. Buckingham: The Society for Research into Higher Education and Open University Press.

Williams, J. (1997b) 'The discourse of access: the legitimation of selectivity statistics', in Williams, J. (ed.) *Negotiating Access to Higher Education: The Discourse of Selectivity and Equity*. Buckingham: Society for Research into Higher Education and Open University Press.

Williamson, B. (1986) 'Who has access?', in Finch, J. and Rustin, M. (eds) *A Degree of Choice? Higher Education and the Right to Learn*. Harmondsworth: Penguin.

Wojtas, O. (1999) 'Scots class myth debunked', *Times Higher Education Supplement*, 29 January.

Woodley, A. (1991) 'Access to what? a study of mature graduate outcomes', *Higher Education Quarterly* **45**(1), 91–108.

Wright, P. (1989) 'Access or exclusion: some comments and future prospects of continuing education in England', *Studies in Higher Education* **14**(1), 23–40.

Chapter 12

The university
David Matheson

PROFESSORS: But, Professor, where will the students sleep?
GROUCHO: Where they always sleep. In the classroom.

Horsefeathers (1932)

Introduction

The aim of this chapter is to discuss what the term 'university' might mean and sets out to do so by comparing the origins of the university with its situation in modern times. The meaning of the 'university' is gaining in importance as we see universities expanding rapidly in terms of both institutions and students. We also see them diversifying in their types and even, it seems, in their goals.

It is undeniable that institutions bearing the name 'university' have been in existence for a long time. Their age has given rise to myths and tales which try to make them even older (Curtiss 1967). The range of these myths may span from notions of freedom to notions of greatness of teaching. An implication, if not direct assertion, of these myths is that throughout the ages universities have always fulfilled the same task and that this task is the same now as when the name of the institution of the university was conceived. The fallacy of the myth of greatness of teaching is shown by universities competing for students with schools from their inception until as late as 1882 (Bell and Grant 1974).

Knowledge and subjects

The idea of the university arguably has echoes from the Library in Alexandria, from Plato's Academy, the monastic schools and the Arab *medressa* (sometimes termed 'mosque universities') (van Ginkel 1994), but the actual amount of knowledge available in Medieval Europe was very limited, consisting of the bare elements of grammar, rhetoric, logic and the still barer notions of arithmetic, astronomy, geometry and music, which did duty for an academic curriculum (Haskins 1923). It was feasible in Europe, and this remained true until at least the Renaissance, for a person to learn at least major parts of everything that was judged worth knowing.

Europe in the Dark Ages had effectively lost most of what we now might term its academic knowledge, except for what was conserved by a few monasteries, especially in Ireland. The return to Europe of the works of Aristotle, Plato, Euclid and the Greek physicians, which came mainly via Arab scholars in Spain, together with various texts on Roman Law and Arab treatises on astronomy, philosophy, architecture and algebra (itself an Arabic word) changed the situation dramatically. Add to this the importation of Arab numerals, of which the most important is the zero (if you find this hard to believe, try doing multiplication or division with Roman numerals!) and we have a situation where not only is a vast amount of knowledge suddenly available but there is also a growing merchant class with a need for clerks, scribes, and strategic planners, and which was equipped with the wealth needed to pay for this.

In other words, knowledge and the *need* to have knowledge available are essential prerequisites to having the university at all. This dependency on knowledge and its transmission has continued to be its major mission, in theory at least. So much so that John Henry Cardinal Newman (1852) defined the university as being a place to teach universal knowledge. Newman's name is associated with the idea that a university education is simultaneously an end in itself and one whose acquisition develops habits of mind which are useful throughout life in almost any sphere of activity.[1]

Even at levels beyond the basic curriculum, the Medieval university's monopoly on teaching was relative. Many lawyers and doctors were trained 'on the job' (Verger 1981) as were many clergy. However, the autonomy and prestige that came to be associated with the university saw to its survival and at least some development. Research was not part of the original mission. Research was certainly carried out and ideas shared, but the form that it took is open to question.

In the modern world, universities are now freed from competition with schools; the demand for university courses often outstrips supply, especially in the most prestigious faculties such as medicine (Gerbod 1981). Lawyers, doctors and most clergy receive at least their initial training in universities. This now long-standing tradition of training such professionals in universities gives lie to the notion that vocational courses in universities are a new invention. Nonetheless, an on-going controversy persists whereby we hear courses such Media Studies being decried as 'sexy' (*sic*) since they have popular appeal and are directly related to employment while courses in medicine, for example, which also have popular appeal and are directly related to employment, are an accepted part of the university scene. This is perhaps related to what is judged to be acceptable knowledge. Yet, it is only in fairly recent times that the University of Oxford, for its part, decided that medicine, now the most prestigious of all university courses in the UK, was an acceptable domain to teach. It is not only knowledge which changes, but perceptions of knowledge also change, just as do professions and trades and the perceptions of these. We no longer, for example, expect our barber to double-up as a surgeon or as a dentist as was once the case and these last two activities have gone from being despised and distrusted to being highly respected.

The name 'university' has also been used for institutions not of advanced learning but of dancing or institutions in which one can buy a piece of paper marked 'degree' (e.g. Bob Jones' University where $50 will buy a degree in, for instance, Spiritual Theology). There is now a plan afoot to develop a 'University for Industry' (UfI) in the UK which will encompass not only advanced business management but also basic literacy and numeracy. This confuses the issue even further. The inclusion of basic skills has distinct echoes from earlier times. However, the UfI is a single case and perhaps the fact that the UK government has seen fit to term it 'university' is simply indicative of the prestige attached to the name.

Defining the university

Verger (1981) defines the university of the Middle Ages as:

(i) taking students from outwith its immediate locality;
(ii) being an institute of advanced teaching in at least one 'higher' faculty (Theology, Law or Medicine); and
(iii) being administratively autonomous.

Criterion (i) is taking on new meanings as distance universities develop but even in traditional, campus-based universities there are always students who come from beyond commuting distance. Criterion (ii) is loaded with value judgements and the criteria and state of the art of the period. Criterion (iii), as we see later, is relative: autonomy is arguably in the eye of the beholder.

One of the most important innovations in the Medieval university which persists to this day is 'the notion of a curriculum of study, definitely laid down as regards time and subject, tested by an examination and leading to a degree' (Haskins 1923: 35). This curriculum followed essentially two steps: grammar and rhetoric as a basic introductory course followed by classes in one of up to three higher faculties. Some universities were reputed for one faculty over the other two while at Oxford medicine was totally absent.

The function of the basic introductory course was perhaps similar to that performed at present by secondary schools in preparing young people for entry to university. The examinations in grammar and rhetoric served to decide the fitness of the student for higher study. Similarly, examinations such as Highers (in Scotland) and A-levels (in the rest of the UK), together with their equivalents elsewhere in the world, are now used to decide fitness to enter university.

The teaching in the Medieval university was largely oral and usually took the form of *lectio* and *quaestio*. In the *lectio*, 'the lecturer read the text paragraph by paragraph, and at the end of each one commented on its content' (Curtiss 1967: 70). With the passage of time, the commentaries became more and more profound with the literal sense of the work being only the first step; lecturers strove to extract 'real scientific problems from texts' (Verger 1981: 297). In the *quaestio*, the master would invite discussion on a problem and would preside over the bachelor answering difficulties raised by other masters, bachelors and scholars. This might last a day, with the master's determination coming the next day. This was where he 'grouped the arguments and objections proposed the previous day and then ... announced his own solution, quoting some authoritative text in support of it' (Curtiss 1967: 72).

The *quaestio* may have declined with the years but it is only with the post-Second World War expansion in the world's student population that

> the master's court lectio with its dogmatic nature and historical tradition has complemented or even rivalled by the appearance of directed work, practical work, seminars (these are perhaps the descendants of the quaestio) ... The nature of student work has been in part modified: team work, collective research have often come to complete the classical personal work of lectures and the assimilation of bookish learning. (Gerbod 1981: 448)

Obviously, with the appearance of readily available books, there was no longer the need for the lecturer to read through a text in class nor was s/he necessarily confined to one text at a time for a particular course. This has allowed, in theory at least, for a course to be an entirely personal creation of the lecturer or his/her department.

Academic standards

Perhaps the first attempt to lay down examination standards was through the seeking of a Papal Bull which granted the masters of the university 'the right to teach anywhere in Christendom' (Curtiss 1967: 58). How many universities actually received the Bull is open to question - for example, Curtiss' (1967) assertion that Oxford received its Bull in 1254 is flatly denied by Verger (1981) who claims that Oxford never in fact got the Bull at all. However, once granted, the privileges of the Bull never seem to have been withdrawn. Thus, at the end of the Middle Ages the standard of teaching, in many cases, could decline to mediocrity and some universities vegetate at a low level while still being able to grant their *licentiae*, or degrees.

In modern universities, maintenance of standards is attempted, in the British case, by a system of external examiners, mutually exchanged between the universities. The extent to which uniform standards are maintained is open to question and is the subject of regular and on-going debate, but it is interesting to note Bell and Grant's contention that high academic standards are a relative novelty in British universities:

> It was only the intervention of Parliament in the 1950s which produced the lavish supply of student grants which was so to increase the demand for

university places that the universities could institute rigorous selection procedures which have made them *for the first time* places of generally high academic standards. (Bell and Grant 1974: 101, emphasis in the original)

The availability of the university

The availability of university education in the modern world is usually in marked contrast to that in the Medieval. When student grants appeared in the UK (for example) and systems of loans and grants were introduced in many other countries, the main criteria for entry into university shifted largely from financial to qualification. Hence, the band of population seeking university entrance widened and this allowed states to cap numbers entering higher education either nationally, as in the UK and Germany, or for certain courses (as happens in medicine and the *grandes écoles* in France) (Gerbod 1981). (The *grandes écoles* are prestigious schools of engineering, administration and war studies. Graduation from them virtually guarantees a high-status job.)

As we shall see later, the expansion of higher education in the 1960s and 1970s was, in many industrialised countries, a mere taster of what was to come in the 1980s and 1990s.

The division of Medieval society into clearly visible layers in which the vast majority were in the economically lowest, coupled with widespread illiteracy (and no state support for students) and serfdom, meant that university education was only open to those with the cash, mobility and at least some prior knowledge (or who were willing to go into the Church as a means of elevating their station). Thus, the land-bound serfs were excluded; the artisans were unlikely to be able to support a child at university. So, in general, only the merchant class and aristocracy (and, of course, the Church) were able to take advantage of the educational opportunities offered by the universities.

Academic organisation

The number of courses on offer would appear severely limited by modern standards. However, the aim of the university in the Middle Ages was 'the inculcation of a limited knowledge and precise intellectual techniques, sanctioned by a degree and aiming to prepare the student, if not for certain jobs, at least for certain activities' (Verger 1981: 297). But the Medieval universities rarely pretended to teach encyclopaedic knowledge. Besides, those areas left out of the programme (Science, Literature, and History to name but three) were frowned upon by the Church.

In the modern university, the number of faculties has certainly increased. The preparation for higher education now being done in schools, the Arts faculty has expanded its range of activities, an expansion which began at the end of the fourteenth century (Verger 1981). This, however, has not meant encyclopaedic knowledge being taught – British and Swiss university students, for example, tend to focus on small areas comprising perhaps only two or three subjects with one or two being taken to a higher level (over 75 per cent of students in the UK take Honours degrees, the UK being one of the few countries offering different levels of undergraduate degrees). North American universities offer broad-based general programmes for the first one or two years which act as a form of orientation cycle and may also fill in gaps in high school education. Overall, in the modern world, the tendency is one of width at the beginning and depth at the end and in this way is an echo of the Medieval where the relatively wide Arts course led into the relatively narrow Law, Theology or Medicine.

In the twelfth and thirteenth centuries, we see emerging those features of organised education with which we are most familiar: instruction represented by faculties and courses of study, examinations and academic degrees (Verger 1981). The degree began life as the *licentia ubique docendi* to which was later added the Bachelor and Doctorate (Curtiss 1967). Incidentally, a good many degrees, such as those in Dentistry, were, until recently entitled Licentiate, while in Francophone countries a first degree is usually termed *licence* (the high school diploma which gives right of matriculation to university being the *baccalauréat* or bachelor's qualification).

In British, French and US universities, the three-step ladder of Bachelor, Master and Doctor operates (the UK has also DLitt and DSc but their award is comparatively rare) while in Switzerland an effectively two-tier system exists, there being nothing between the first degree and Doctorate. However, such comparisons at best confirm or deny that the Medieval three-step ladder has some name equivalents in the modern university but no further comparison is possible without examining the role of each kind of graduate in each society and also how the level of knowledge of each graduate compared with that of graduates bearing similar titles from other universities. An examination of the perceptions of and about the graduate would also be in order. As these go beyond the horizon of this chapter, I shall not venture into them.

Academic freedom?

The university 'is entitled ... to freedom to teach and publish without censorship and freedom to make appointments without political or other interference' (Swann in Bell and Grant 1974: 96). This ties in with the last part of Verger's definition of a university: that it must be administratively autonomous. That the Medieval university was never free is aptly demonstrated by Haskins when he talks of the ever-present Inquisition and its threats to those tempted. For 'a mind that played too freely about a proposition [and] might easily fall into heresy' (Haskins 1923: 72) the Inquisition offered a series of cures that needs no elaboration. This said, some were willing to risk life and limb to study the forbidden. Between 1210 and 1263 Aristotle was banned in Christendom and yet studied in some Faculties of Arts

(Curtiss 1967). Interference in what was taught often came in the form of *censures*, the content of which could vary from matters of fundamental dogmatic importance to Latin verb constructs. Haskins, though, makes the point that 'accepting the principle of authority as their starting point, men did not feel its limitations as we should feel them now' (Haskins 1923: 72). This, of course, did not stop them being limitations.

Compare this principle of authority with that of the Soviet Union where not only had everything, where possible, to be taught from a Marxist–Leninist standpoint, but all university curricula were either prescribed or at least approved by the republic of USSR Ministry of Higher Education (Grant 1979). In the UK 'universities are [generally] financed from treasury funds... [but] despite this financial dependence, those who run universities have a great deal of autonomy in terms of what they teach and how it is assessed, and also in selecting undergraduates' (King 1977: 100). There are however incidences, albeit rare, of university teaching staff being censured or even losing their posts for advocating points of view which were judged unwelcome by those in authority. This includes, at its most extreme, cases which supported paedophilia and racial discrimination. It does however raise the question of academic freedom and the extent to which this freedom, like all other freedoms, has to be balanced with responsibility. One must also ask whose responsibility it is to see that the academic respects the rights and liberties of others.

Graduates, students and power

Medieval graduates generally served in supportive roles in society which allowed them to display their intellectual competence but 'the graduate appeared more frequently in the service of the ruling class than he formed part of it' (Verger 1981: 300).

In the modern world, 'going to university is valued as the entry to high status occupations although... graduates from working and lower middle-class backgrounds do not enter quite such high status jobs as others, keeping class of degree constant' (King 1977: 103).

The pattern described by King continues unabated and so the children of today's ruling class aim to remain in that group while the rest, although aspiring to status, tend to remain in supportive roles. There is doubtless much more social mobility now than in the Middle Ages, aided by accessibility of higher education to the masses but still graduates are a group with strong social class linkages.

Given the economic and intellectual realities of the time, it is unlikely that Medieval universities had often to turn away students on the grounds of being full. The fact that the teacher's pay usually depended directly on the number of students s/he could attract would mean little selection on any but financial grounds. This meant that students potentially could wield great power, but this depended on whether theirs was a university of masters or of scholars. In the former, the Arts students were ruled out of all participation in university government while students in higher faculties took part (as they were already Masters of Arts) and the university government seems to have been quite democratic. In the latter, the students formed themselves into a university of scholars which hired masters each year and put each 'under bond to live up to a minute set of regulations which guaranteed his students the worth of the money paid by each' (Haskins 1923: 15). However, the apparent subjugation of the masters reduced neither their prestige nor the high incomes they could enjoy. Thus, regardless of the type of university, all but possibly the Arts students had some say in how the institution was run.

In the modern university, the participation of students in university government is, by and large, limited. In some of those universities which were founded as universities of scholars, there is still a rector elected by the students as the titular head of the university, but what real power does s/he wield? The kind of people often nominated for the Rectorship at Glasgow University, for example, ranging as they do from sports commentators to imprisoned dissidents of one kind or another, generally (although not always) serve to reinforce the idea that the rector is just a figurehead. Students may be found on departmental committees, on Academic Boards, occasionally on Senate. They can influence decisions even sometimes at the highest levels but they are always in the minority, both numerically and in terms of the power they can wield.

It is often over the lack of effective say in the running of their education that students have clashed with authority. They may protest, sometimes violently, against university reforms (as happened in the People's Republic of China in the 1980s) or against the introduction of a general *numerus clausus* (capping of student numbers) (as happened in France in the same decade). Were students given a share of decision-making in and about their universities such protests might become less common although the politically-based protests would continue. Whether students *should* get such a share is another issue.

Clashes between Medieval students and society seem to have been based on more mundane notions such as food and lodging.

The universities of scholars were formed by students as protection against profiteering by townspeople who saw in the influx of students a fine opportunity to bump up the prices of rooms and necessities (Haskins 1923). The most famous town and gown[2] clash began in Oxford on St Scholastica's Day, 10 February 1354, and culminated the next day in the deaths of many students (Curtiss 1967).[3] Such clashes remained focused on a particular cause for complaint. There was never any great escalation of the disturbance, unlike in May 1968 when a student protest in Paris ended in a general strike throughout France and the downfall of the government. Medieval students were never, in Lenin's words, the vanguard of the revolution, but remained committed to the sustaining of the *status quo* as witnessed by how few of them took part in the popular revolts of the fourteenth and fifteenth centuries. The universities and their students were, especially towards the end of the Middle Ages, increasingly committed to the established social order (Verger 1981).

This support for the *status quo* is, it seems, common to most modern universities and their students although 'in some countries, they are the only source of critical comments on any government initiative and practice' (Omari 1991: 202).

It may only be in university and in church that dissenting voices can be heard. But, in general, although students may grumble about politics and society, it is rare for any to go beyond grumbling and most will end up working within and in support of society. Were this not so then governments would not find that 'investments in "grey matter" show themselves both paying and necessary in the national politics of agricultural, industrial and commercial development' (Gerbod 1981: 446) as is actually the case. Indeed, to within a few exceptional cases, student action has generally moved away from the wider actions of, for example, the 1960s onto specific, single-issue actions. The indication is that political awareness is still there but that it no longer identifies itself so much with political parties and movements as once seemed to be the case. Perhaps in this respect the wheel has swung back towards the Medieval students' attitude where single issues galvanised them into (occasional) action.

The modern student tends to do battle less with local townspeople than did the Medieval, although s/he may clash from time to time, depending on the country, with police and army who, in theory at least, act on behalf of the people. Instant communications and widespread news coverage enable protests to spread more widely and more readily, but competition for news space compensates to some extent for this. And, in the end, like his/her Medieval counterpart, the modern student still has to go out into the world to earn his/her living. The world, however, may not regard the student with as much awe and suspicion as it did in Medieval times. Through the media, the general public now has some idea of what goes on inside the university and however erroneous or stereotyped that idea might be, it presents more of a reality than the widespread ignorance felt in the Middle Ages would allow. The importance of the student's social life is one aspect which has remained right through the history of the university. Drinking to excess as a sort of undergraduate rite of passage has 'an enormous international history across, for example, the European universities from the Middle Ages to the twentieth century' (Silver and Silver 1997: 112).

The enduring nature of the university

There have been some important, fairly recent innovations in the realm of the university and these deserve mention. The first is the generalised move, across much of the industrialised world since the Second World War and accelerating in Europe since the 1980s, towards mass higher education. In the UK, for example, the number of students in higher education rose from just over 400,000 in 1969/70 to over 1.5 million by 1994/95 (Connor *et al.* 1996) and has continued to rise. The natural corollary of the comprehensive school in its various guises was an increasing demand to open the doors of higher education to a degree heretofore undreamt of. This brought with it problems of funding and space. In France, as in some other countries, the response was to overfill classes and increasingly anonymise the student body. In others, such as Switzerland, the response has been to develop the higher levels of what is termed non-advanced tertiary education, i.e. higher level vocational education. There are also criticisms of the curricula on offer:

> One of the major causes of failure is that universities, in the process of 'massification', have become too much like secondary schools in their programmes and in the behaviour not only of the staff but also of the students ... We have packed our programmes with knowledge but there is not much to motivate or to educate students to pose the right questions or to find the right solutions. (van Ginkel 1994: 81)

This view is echoed by Sampson (1997) who insists that time constraints on both teachers and students now discourage the cultivation of educated scepticism at undergraduate level. If so, then the university has failed in one of the missions that Newman (1852) ascribed to it: that of philosophising which nineteenth century Scottish academics saw as the key *raison-d'être* for higher education (Beveridge and Craig 1989). But the university is now seen as having a major role to play in the wider world.

The university is not content to simply maintain and transmit knowledge: it is seen as a major player in stimulating reflection, research, experimentation and cultural activities (Bassand 1990). It is also rediscovering its importance in international cooperation (Delors *et al.* 1996). These areas give rise to debate as to what the functions of the university actually are. In this light, let us consider teaching and research and the growth of open and decentralised universities.

Founded, as we have seen, to provide teaching, with research being done to stimulate that teaching, it is often the case in universities that research has come to be the more highly regarded of the two. Thus, undergraduates may be taught by postgraduate students in order to free lecturers to conduct their own scholarly activity. Lecturers achieve academic status among their peers by publishing research-based writing in academic journals and books, not usually by teaching. Indeed, staff may be selected for posts uniquely on the basis of their publications as these often have a direct bearing on the allocation of departmental research funding (as happens with the Research Assessment Exercise in the UK). 'Research is [now] the prime currency of academic competition' (Sampson 1997: 160). The underlying assumption seems to be that *anyone* can teach, all one needs is the knowledge, and the techniques for its successful transmission will follow. This reduces the status of teachers at all levels but it is a notion which is being increasingly challenged.

More and more universities are establishing a department of pedagogy. In the UK these frequently bear the title of *Teaching and Learning Service* but the aim is essentially the same everywhere: to demand that new teaching staff receive some form of training in teaching and to encourage established lecturers to evaluate and update their skills. Simultaneously, students are increasingly seen as consumers (Silver and Silver 1997), and having to pay more and more for their education. As such, they are less content to be forced to endure lecturers who put them to sleep or who appear completely uninterested in them or the subject. The whole relationship between the teacher and the learner in higher education is undergoing a major re-evaulation and, in this respect, there are interesting times ahead.

Conclusion

The university was long seen as a fixed, urban establishment. It was always important in maintaining the dynamism and prestige of the town and urban area which hosted it (Bassand 1990). Yet since the 1960s we see the beginnings of a change in this relationship. There has been the creation of various kinds of open university. These range from the high-tech versions (such as in the UK) through to very low-tech varieties (such as is found in British Columbia). Open universities may demand entry qualifications or be open to all-comers up to some eventual limit on numbers. The essential point about all open universities is that they offer their courses by distance education and hence increase the geographical accessibility of university education (Matheson 1996). At the same time, there has been a growth in the decentralised university which was initially conceived for scattered island populations. The UK will shortly see its first decentralised university in the shape of the University for the Highlands and Islands (UHI), a consortium of 13 existing colleges scattered over an area equal to one fifth of the total surface of the UK, which hopes to receive its University Charter in 2001. Using the Internet, the UHI already offers franchised courses for institutions such as Aberdeen University and attracts interest from as far afield as Finland, Austria and Ireland (Highlands and Islands Enterprise News Release 1996). The notion of the franchised course is already well-established and one frequently finds colleges of further education the length and breadth of the UK offering whole or part courses on behalf of universities, blurring the edges between higher and further education.

The university is in mutation. As we have seen in Chapter 11, the age profile of its students is changing as increasing numbers of adults enter, or return to, higher education. The range of courses never ceases to increase. The university is finding an increasing role in lifelong education. Yet, in all this evolution, echoes from the past remain and in many respects the more things change the more they stay the same. Verger's definition of a university, however simplistic, probably fits many modern universities better than ever and this is as true of the decentralised university, be it open or not, as it is of the more traditional, fixed variety. Universities have grown and necessarily changed through the centuries but every change, deliberate or otherwise, freely chosen or forced, has the past as its backdrop, since 'once a given form of education exists it exerts an influence on future educational change' (Archer 1979: 3). This is probably true of any facet of society: alternatives are a reaction to it; attempts to change it are affected by it and change is a change of it. The slate cannot be wiped clean and experience cannot be removed. Thus the modern university descends from the Medieval as one complex organism can stem from another by allowing for adaptation to new demands and circumstances. Some characteristics remain; others have evolved; new ones have been introduced. But the university has retained its function of (usually) sustaining society and of providing trained brainpower necessary for that sustenance, while contributing to pushing back the frontiers of knowledge. Even with the advent of the virtual university, based entirely in cyberspace, it will probably continue to do so.

Suggested further reading

Since universities have formed such an important (and money-hungry) part of the educational scene for so long, it is hardly surprising that the literature, both as book and as journal, is vast. What follows therefore is merely a taster, in English, of what the debutante in this domain might seek out next. Full references for each are given in the References below. Newman (1852) contains a detailed argument on the need for Liberal Education and, while the style is not the easiest to follow, is essential reading for anyone interested in what the university *might* be. Haskins (1923) is one of the best accounts yet of the invention of the university and its subsequent development in the Middle Ages. For an evaluation of the modern UK university, Connor *et al.* (1996) not only present a well-argued critique and evaluation of the current university scene but also give a wealth of statistical data in easily assimilable form. Matheson (1996) presents a brief outline and critique of the various types of open university currently available in the world. Silver and Silver (1997) is a paradigm of lucidity and clarity on an often neglected area, i.e. students, while Delors *et al.* (1996) situates higher education within the wider contexts of society in general and lifelong education.

Notes

1   An editorial in *The Times* of 15 August 1998 claims that philosophy graduates are the most employable of all graduates with the exception of medical graduates.

2   It is still common in some of the oldest universities in the UK that students wear academic gowns while on campus.

3   Cobban (1988) puts the riot one year later in 1355.

References

Archer, M. (1979) *Social Origins of Education Systems*. London: Sage Publications.
Bassand, M. (1990) *Culture et Régions d'Europe*. Lausanne: Presses polytechniques romandes.
Bell, R. and Grant, N. (1974) *A Mythology of British Education*. St Albans: Panther.
Beveridge, C. and Craig, R. (1989) *The Eclipse of Scottish Culture*. Edinburgh: Polygon.
Cobban, A. B. (1988) *The Medieval English Universities*. Aldershot: Scolar Press.
Connor, H., Pearson, G., *et al.* (1996) *University Challenge: Student Choices in the 21st Century*. Brighton: The Institute for Employment Studies.
Curtiss, S. J. (1967) *History of Education in Great Britain*. London: University Tutorial Press.
Delors, J. et al. (1996) *Education – The Treasure Within*. Paris: UNESCO/HMSO.
Gerbod, P. (1981) 'L'enseignement supérieur', in Mialaret, G. and Vial, J. (eds) *Histoire Mondiale de l'Éducation Tome 4*. Paris: Presses universitaires de Paris.

van Ginkel (1994) 'University 2050: The organisation of creativity and innovation', in *Universities in the Twenty-First Century*. London: National Commission on Education.

Grant, N. (1979) *Soviet Education*. Harmondsworth: Penguin.

Haskins, C. (1923) *The Rise of Universities*. New York: Henry Holt.

Highlands and Islands Enterprise News Release 31/96J (1996) *Highlands and Islands University takes a step closer*.

King, E. (1979) *Other Schools and Ours*. Eastbourne: Holt, Rinehart & Winston.

King, R. (1977) *Education*. London: Longman.

Matheson, D. (1996) 'An examination of some of the difficulties of establishing an open university in a small linguistic area: the case of Suisse romande', *International Journal of Lifelong Education* **15**(2), 114–24.

Newman, J. H. (1852 reprint 1968 with introduction and notes by M. J. Svaglic) *The Idea of a University*. New York: Rinehart.

Omari, I. M. (1991) 'Innovation and change in higher education in developing countries: experiences from Tanzania', *Comparative Education* **27**(2) 181–206.

Sampson, G. (1997) *Educating Eve*. London: Cassell.

Silver, H. and Silver, P. (1997) *Students*. Milton Keynes: Society for Research into Higher Education.

Universities in the Twenty-First Century. London: National Commission on Education.

Verger, J. (1981) 'Universités et écoles médiévales de la fin du XIe à la fin du XVe siècle', in Mialaret, G. and Vial, J. (eds) *Histoire Mondiale de l'Éducation Tome 1*. Paris: Presses universitaires de Paris.

Chapter 13

Lifelong learning
David Matheson

When planning for a year – sow corn.
When planning for a decade – plant trees.
When planning for a lifetime – train and educate people.

Kuan Tsu, 3rd century BC

Introduction

We began this *Introduction to the Study of Education* by looking at pre-school and then moved through various issues surrounding especially school education before looking at access to higher education and the university. We have examples of how learners may be advantaged or disadvantaged by their circumstances. But throughout, the concentration has been on areas of formal education which in most cases lead either into more formal learning or hopefully into work of some sort. It is therefore perhaps appropriate that we round off this collection by considering a domain of educational theory and practice which takes the learner beyond formal education (although it can encompass it) and can last until the end of one's life: lifelong learning.

'Learning, like breathing, is something everyone does all of the time' (Tight 1996: 21). It is an inevitable part of life that humans learn continuously unless some major physical or psychological trauma interrupts the process. Even when we are asleep, we learn. Indeed, it is increasingly believed that some aspects of learning can even take place in the womb. Babies learn to associate certain rhythmic sounds with a calm, soothing environment and, once born, will respond positively to such sounds being played to them. From cradle to grave, we are acquiring knowledge, skills and attitudes. We pick up incidental bits of information, we are influenced in manners sometimes subtle, sometimes evident. From this it becomes clear that the concept of lifelong learning must concern itself with something more than simply learning throughout life. Otherwise it is a mere tautology and is hence beyond elaboration. Instead it must concern itself with purposeful learning, be this formal, non-formal or informal. We might want to term this *education* but then there is the other problem of deciding when learning constitutes education and when it does not.

Learning itself can be defined in terms of outcomes, competencies and/or in terms of process. Indeed at the heart of the lifelong learning debate, which was relaunched with the 1972 report *Learning to Be* (Faure *et al.*), lies the question of whether it is the end that counts or the means. However we choose to define learning, one thing remains clear: the notions of lifelong learning, lifelong education and the learning age have caused more ink to be spilled over the last few years than possibly any other topic of educational theory. These terms have tripped off politicians' tongues with ease; they have been the indirect and sometimes direct subject of television soap operas. For example, on Channel 4's *Brookside* we saw in 1998 a main character, Jimmy Corkhill, return to study after a long interval and consequently start a new career as a school teacher. Similarly, characters from the BBC's *EastEnders* have returned to study but notably none of these characters undertake any courses which do not result in qualification. In other words, what might be termed *liberal education* is displaced in favour of vocational study. The possible significance of this stance may become clearer as we go on.

A few myths surrounding teachers and learners

Like many other human activities, education in all its various forms has developed its own myths and mythology. Sometimes these have a basis in truth, sometimes not. By way of reorientation, if needs be, let us look at a few educational myths and check their validity.

Teachers are old and learners are young is perhaps a view which we maintain from those days in which we were young and our teachers were not so young as us. In other words, we were at school. We were most likely segregated from the rest of the learning population. We learned from our teachers and were blissfully unaware of any learning we might be giving them. Learning was seen as a one-way street, a unilateral process. Concomitant with this notion are the ideas that *teachers teach children* and *education equals school*. The latter notion clearly denies the educational validity (or even existence) of non-school education, but we dealt in Chapter 1 with some of the difficulties in the use of *school* and *education* as interchangeable terms. The former notion is patently ridiculous unless the sharing of knowledge, understanding, skills and attitudes which teachers outwith school engage in is somehow not really teaching. The notion that teachers teach children is further undermined when one considers famous teachers from history. An initial list might well include the following: Confucius, Lao-Tse, Esther, Moses, Jesus, Mohammed, Buddha, Plato, Socrates. Every one of them was a teacher of adults and none taught in a school as we know it.

It is commonly believed that *learning gets harder as you get older*. But what evidence is there for this? Anecdotes? Common sense? Or is this just another manifestation of the pro-school bias in the widely-held view of what education is?

One thing is clear: adults have generally greater demands on their time and energies than do young people. Adults often have higher levels of responsibility. In these senses, there are potentially more distractions for the adult than for the young person. But what do these hurdles tell us about the capacity of an adult to learn? Precisely nothing. At best we can say that adults are better at making excuses *and in believing them* than are young people. Certainly there are some mechanical tasks for which a younger person might well have greater suppleness in, for example, the fingers but beyond these there does not seem to be much of a case for not being able to *teach an old dog new tricks*. Besides, one thing which adults have in greater measure than young people is life experience. Consequently they have a greater context within which to situate their learning.

The current fervour over lifelong learning might lead one to believe that it is a new phenomenon, notwithstanding the teachers we have just mentioned. Yet as Gelpi tells us, 'the concept and practice of lifelong learning belongs to the world history of education and cannot be confined only to the culture of one country or a single period of history' (Gelpi 1994: 344). As our short list of teachers demonstrates, lifelong learning has a long history. Indeed it was Confucius who said that 'life is limited, while learning is limitless' (Xie 1994: 272).

The concept of lifelong education

The movement towards mass education has gained much momentum over the last two hundred years – to attend school as a child for example is now considered the international norm. So much so that Faure felt inclined to write that, between 1960 and 1968, by not being able to attend school 'every year some 2 million or more children (aged between 5 and 14) were denied the right to an education' (Faure *et al.* 1972: 38).

Of course, other than those missed entirely by schooling one must also consider the drop-outs, the school failures (although whether a child fails school or is failed by it is open to conjecture), the unemployed, the misorientated, etc. The list is vast of those categories of people for whom skills and knowledge acquirable at school might be of use. To this must be added skills and knowledge acquirable outside school which might help an individual be educated. The result is certainly an enormous mass of people who could benefit physically, mentally or financially from furthering their education and widening their knowledge and understanding.

The background notions in lifelong education as defined by UNESCO are a mixture of old and new. A basis for the idea comes from Erasmus who wrote: 'We are not born human, we become human or rather...we make ourselves human' (Margolin 1981: 172). Compare this with the following quotes used by Faure as 'the major argument in favour of lifelong education'; Lapasade: 'One never ceases to enter life', and Fromm: 'The individual's entire life is nothing but a process of giving birth to [her/]himself; in truth we are only fully born when we die' (Faure *et al.* 1972: 158).

Despite the span of several centuries the ideas are shades of the same thing. However, there remain problems in defining the concept of lifelong education. For example, according to Dave 'the learning process is the key to all education' (Dave 1972: Concept Characteristic 10) while for Faure education is conceived of as a vector – 'the path to learning is irrelevant; only what is learnt or acquired has any importance' (Faure *et al.* 1972: 185). The contradiction between these standpoints is clear but there is also a major contradiction within Faure; in lifelong education the end is, by definition, death. Therefore, unless the path to learning is seen as part of the learning there is little point in learning at all as the path to learning begins at birth and ends at death. Besides, there is a distinct lack of logic in viewing final products of an educative process (short of death) as identical on the basis only of what has been learned or acquired. If the experience has been different then the product must be also. Faure, however, characteristically hedges his bets by employing the word 'acquire' instead of some stronger term.

According to Gelpi: 'the hypothesis of lifelong education [is] that the educators need not necessarily be professionals' (Gelpi 1979: 19). This is essential for Dave for whom:

> Lifelong education seeks to view education in its totality. It covers formal, non-formal and informal patterns of education and attempts to articulate all structures and stages of education (Dave 1972: 35).

For Skäger, 'lifelong education is not a concept or a thing but a set of basic principles' (Griffin 1983: 156). This effectively says nothing and may even contradict itself, depending on how strong a meaning is taken of concept or principle. Besides, is not a true concept in fact a set of basic principles? Cropley takes an almost equally spurious tack when he writes that 'lifelong education is an orientation, concept or principle, not a tangible thing' (Cropley 1979: 113). Unfortunately Cropley does not define his meaning for tangible upon which his argument hinges. The *Shorter Oxford Dictionary* admits three meanings that encompass both the concrete and the abstract. *Assuming* that Cropley means that lifelong education is not concrete then he agrees with Lengrand who insists on the indefinable nature of lifelong education remaining forever so:

> Lifelong education is still at the conceptual stage. As with other principles such as freedom, justice and equality, it will doubtless retain indefinitely that certain distance in relation to concrete achievements which is in the nature of concepts. (Lengrand 1978: 98)

Thus Lengrand places the question 'what is lifelong education?' on almost the same footing as a moral philosopher might put the question 'what is good?' This doubtless raises the philosophical status of lifelong education but does nothing to expedite its implementation, unless of course it can be argued that there is a moral imperative to lifelong education as might be claimed for 'good'.

For De'Ath, lifelong education is of anthropological importance in that it 'could be instrumental in not only preserving all kinds of cultural diversity but also in placing a positive value on individual and collective difference' (De'Ath 1972: 247).

All these writers demonstrate the lack of rigour that Lengrand warns of when he writes: 'the term lifelong education is used haphazardly and loosely in a variety of situations and realities' (Lengrand 1979: 29).

Conceptually there is very little to grasp in the lifelong education debate that consists of anything more than very fine straws or collections of undefined terms and hurrah words such as those used by Cropley and De'Ath above. What there is consists of:

(a) an attempt to view education as not confined to school but as consisting of purposeful and process learning undertaken wherever and whenever;
(b) a view of education as a whole-life activity which ought to be facilitated by the state and in which some may take longer than others to achieve their goals but no-one is deemed a failure.

There are immediate problems with this facilitation, especially when one sees lifelong education as an activity driven by economic need. At this point, and especially where the long-term unemployed are concerned, facilitation may easily turn into compulsion as we now see in some of the Welfare to Work programmes in the USA which are being considered for adoption in various European countries including the UK.

Lifelong learning today

We live in the era of perhaps the most rapid change known to humanity. The paradigms our parents knew (and that perhaps we ourselves grew up with) are being steadily swept away. Notions such as, a job for life, are all too clearly obsolete except perhaps for an élite cadre of highly skilled, highly paid workers (Longworth and Davies 1996) while the rest are left, if they can find a job at all, with the realisation that in our possibly postmodern world there is a dearth of permanent, decent jobs (Aronowitz and Giroux 1993). Politicians talk about educating the workforce, by which they generally mean training them and training itself is held up as the great panacea. As an editorial in *The Observer* of 21 July 1996) commented, training is:

> The great palliative of our time. All parties support it and none asks what work there is for the trainees when the training ends. As a policy, it has the immense advantage of being far cheaper than building homes or creating jobs.

Mixed in with this rhetoric is increasing talk about lifelong learning from politicians. The Labour opposition in the UK promised before the 1997 General Election that lifelong learning would be the subject of a White Paper (Labour Party 1994) (while the then-Conservative Government (DfEE 1996) contributed to the debate which led to the publication in 1996 of *Learning: the Treasure Within*)

(Delors *et al.* 1996) this being a consultative document leading to a Bill before Parliament. Less than one year into office and the promised White Paper had appeared as a Green Paper (DfEE 1998), in other words, merely a consultation document which need not lead to anything else. The debate goes on but where it will lead to remains to be seen. There persist, however, the conceptual problems with lifelong learning which show no sign of resolution.

Lifelong learning is what Knapper and Cropley (1985: 20) term 'a utopian idea – an elastic concept which means whatever the person using the term wants it to mean'. As Lengrand (1986: 10) reminds us:

> There is no single centre of thought from which this idea has been disseminated, nor is there a code of propositions that would enable the faithful to be distinguished from the heretics.

Nonetheless, it is a powerful idea which captures the public imagination and makes it sound as though the interlocutor wants to actually do something positive.

Lifelong learning and school

Strictly speaking, any account of lifelong learning ought to contain an examination, if not of the first learning experiences that a person has, then at least with the first formal learning experiences, such as those that occur in pre-school and in school itself. We have seen earlier some of the influences and effects that can occur in pre-school and school that affect self-esteem and growing self-concept. Influences such as whether one attends pre-school at all, the effect of social class or of one's gender, 'race' and racialisation, the younger learner's needs and the adult's responsibilities in satisfying those needs. We have seen how some of these influences carry over into affecting whether a person seeks entrance to higher education, be it immediately after school or after an interval. School is an undeniably formative influence on a learner's perception of him/herself and also on his/her perception of him/herself as a learner.

It is in school that learners generally have their first introduction to formalised learning strategies. School introduces to learners the essential skills without which all further attempts at purposeful learning are impeded. These basic essential skills are generally held to include for example reading, listening, sifting information. It is worth mentioning in passing, however, that both Freire and Illich[1] question whether reading is such a basic skill as we in the industrialised countries claim it to be. Nonetheless,

> Schools...have to start a dynamic process through which pupils are progressively weaned of their dependence on teachers and institutions and given the confidence to manage their own learning, co-operating with colleagues, and using a range of resources and learning situations. (Abbott 1994: 108)

The extent to which schools succeed in this 'weaning' is very much open to debate. In this respect it is worth reflecting on one's own learning from school and judging how much of one's autonomy as a learner is due to influences from school and conversely how much of one's dependency is due to influence from the same source.

Lifelong learning implies by its very nature that learners have become equipped with basic learning skills, that they know how to learn, that they have gained the equipment, the skills and the attitudes needed to pursue their own learning. Learners have to have moved from a dependency stance to one of autonomy, to have developed a sense of self-direction, to have, in the terms of Malcolm Knowles, moved from needing pedagogy to demanding andragogy; in other words, they have to have moved from needing the security which comes from being told what to do, when to do and how to do it to being able to define their own educational goals and the pathways to them (Knowles 1998). The question arises as to when the learners assume this level of autonomy. One might also ask whether all learners *should* assume such a level and consider some possible ramifications. Let us keep these thoughts at the back of our minds as we continue.

As Howe puts it:

A person who leaves school ill-equipped with the competencies required for learning independently throughout the remainder of a life is at a severe disadvantage. (Howe in Claxton 1990: 165)

Much of the literature which appeared in the wake of *Learning To Be* (Faure *et al.* 1972) assumed tacitly or overtly that being properly equipped with learning tools was a necessary condition for lifelong learning. Its starting point is generally that:

Today no one can hope to amass during his or her youth an initial fund of knowledge which will serve a lifetime. The swift changes taking place in the world call for knowledge to be continuously updated. (Delors *et al.* 1996: 99)

We witness daily the truth of this statement as we rush forward in technology (and leave many old certainties behind) and in itself it implies a need for schools to instil lifelong learning skills in their pupils. Examples of how dismally schools fail in this task are not hard to find. It is unfortunately true, for example, that the rate of borrowing books from public libraries is in constant decline; employers everywhere complain about how difficult their recruits find mastering new skills; teachers in higher education complain about the declining levels of autonomy they see among their students. We should, I feel, take some of these complaints with a small pinch of salt but not dismiss them entirely. Nostalgia is not what it used to be, but nonetheless perceptions breed perceptions on the part of both the observer and the observed, roles which interchange constantly.

Despite this however, anyone who manages to get a job has to assume that the skills they begin with are almost guaranteed to become outmoded and will require updating or even replacement. Even the most apparently unchanging of occupations are altered by technology and countless others have changed beyond all recognition in the last 20 years while a multitude of other, new professions, particularly relating to Information Technology, have come into existence.[2]

However, as Stoikov (1975: 114) (and many other writers besides) points out, 'it is usually those who already have a good educational and training background who volunteer for additional education and training'. In *Learning: the Treasure Within* (Delors *et al.* 1996) we find the same message:

> Adults' further participation in educational and cultural activities is related to the level of schooling already received: [so] the more education you have then the more education you want. (Delors *et al.* 1996: 101)

In other words, it is no new phenomenon that the educated educate themselves the most. If ever there was an argument for wider initial education then this is it. It is also worth noting that Blackledge and Hunt (1985: 170) remind us: 'Educated parents equip their children for a successful career in education.' So if we want formal education to be a real agent for social mobility then we ought to be pressing for adults to increase their level of education in order to encourage their children to increase theirs. In this respect, we find echoes of Paolo Freire and his attempts at teaching literacy. It is well known that Freire despaired of teaching children to read when their parents were illiterate and so he set about teaching their parents, but using materials and learning circumstances which were of relevance to them. As Furter (1999) puts it, he tried to move people from mere literacy to cultural development.

Lifelong learning and economics

In an ideal world, in a true learning society, any person would be free at any time to learn anything that lay within their intellectual capabilities and would feel supported and nurtured in taking such initiatives. Unfortunately simple economics removes this option immediately. All activities, be they formal or non-formal, must be paid for. Each subsidy must be argued for and the formal, initial domain of education clearly and indisputably has first priority. In most countries it would be unthinkable to levy general charges on primary school children although this is increasingly demanded for some artistic activities; similarly, in lower secondary, although paying some fees for upper secondary school is quite common across Europe. Education beyond upper secondary has to play second fiddle: after all it applies to a smaller and smaller proportion of the population. Indeed as we move up the age range of the target population, the greater the likelihood of fees being applied in one way or another. There are, however, exceptions such as courses aimed at the long-term unemployed which might be funded at 100 per cent by central government or via unemployment insurance. In this last respect, the challenges laid by the economy are performing exactly as d'Hainaut and Lawton

(1981: 37) predict when they say that 'the economy serves as a powerful stimulus to education in general and to lifelong education in particular'. A cynic might say that it gives the government and its agencies something to do with the unemployed. In this light, we might think back to training and the palliative effect that it has.

It is worth bearing in mind that 'by its very nature, lifelong learning involves a change in the distribution of activities over time and among members of the population, and such a redistribution has implications for the future social structure' (Stoikov 1975: 7). This obliges us to ask the extent to which we, as a society, want to maintain the *status quo* or whether we want to encourage social development.

If lifelong learning is to become the perceived norm then there is clearly an essential need for major subsidy of those who cannot pay the fees. Otherwise it will serve as further reinforcement of economic stratification as equivalent to cultural stratification. The 'better-off' have access to most culture (by dint of having more cash to pay for it, by generally having more education with which to appreciate it), but should this necessarily be so? Is there not a role for lifelong learning in offering cultural openings to those whose purse strings cannot usually stretch that far?

However, fine as this is in theory, in practice it means the poorer student having to submit to some kind of means test to decide the fee to be paid. There is also the concomitant problem of over-subsidising learning experiences, since it is all too often the case that when something is perceived (by the consumer) as costing nothing, it may be seen as being worth nothing.

For those who can afford courses there are the dire warnings of Ohliger and Dauber that: 'concomitant to lifelong education is lifelong students, condemned to perpetual inadequacy' (Cropley 1977: 156). This is a certain problem: how can learners be encouraged to seek purposeful lifelong learning without feeling that their need for learning (for there must be such if they are to seek learning) is witness to a deeper feeling of inadequacy? It remains to be seen what will be done, if anything, to reduce or to avoid this. However there is always 'the spectre of uselessness' (Ranson 1998: 255) which hangs over workers feeling insecure in their employment.

Lifelong learning: leisure or education?

This brings us to our next point: is lifelong learning to be a leisure activity or an educational activity? If the former, then s/he who cannot partake of it for whatever reason may not perceive the loss or lack as so great as if it is the latter. The danger is that in attempting to raise the value of lifelong learning its providers, especially to secure funding, may downplay the leisure side with the concomitant risk of creating a sort of education addict, forever driven from course to course by an insatiable appetite whetted and fuelled by inadequacy. If this became generalised through lifelong learning becoming the perceived norm, then how much more inadequate will be those denied access?

On the other hand, if lifelong learning is perceived as leisure then not only is its social value decreased but it is also seen as nothing more than an optional extra, as a luxury to which only some may be expected to aspire. As a leisure activity, it loses any moral *right* to funding which an educational activity may claim. In this light, we must consider blurring boundaries.

We are used to a society which separates work from play, 'non-work' from 'work' (which often means that activities which do not lead to a wage are diminished in social status terms), learning from work (although the one may impinge on the other). We are also, perhaps most importantly, used to defining ourselves by our work. If I answer your question as to what I 'do' by describing myself as 'lecturer in education' then you would probably consider this quite normal. Were I to respond by saying that I enjoy cooking and baking and trying to play jigs and reels on the fiddle, then you might well look askance. The definition of me by my work is acceptable. The definition of me by non-salaried work or by leisure pursuits is not so readily acceptable. This apparent digression reveals its importance when we consider the lack of permanency in many, if not most, jobs. As John White (1997: 71) puts it, 'Education for unemployment may become a fixed part of the vocational landscape.' In other words, instead of education being conceived as a precursor to work, it may be construed as equally a precursor to non-work, or to leisure, to meaningfully filling one's days.

It is well documented that 'working-class' persons tend to eschew education and training which does not immediately impinge on work or the possibility of obtaining work. Education and training are seen as purely, or least largely, instrumental. What is most easily qualified as intrinsic learning, adult education classes, are dominated by 'middle-class' persons. We have different cultures perceiving education and training according to different terms. This would suggest that, unless lifelong learning is just going to reinforce existing social divisions, it will have to cross the divide between work and leisure. It will have to bridge the cultural and perceptual gaps which exist. How it does so is another question but it is arguable that a change in attitude at the level of the school might help if it abolished the arbitrary divide between work and play, the former being currently seen as serious, the latter frivolous and often confused with fun; in this respect the quote from Montaigne, with which Chapter 4 in the present volume opens, is most appropriate. Our postmodern world seems to strive to break down boundaries. The gaps between education and leisure, work and play, and work and non-work are just a few more to be tackled.

Conclusion

Lifelong learning, lifelong education, the learning society and the learning age have been high on the political agenda for over a quarter of a century. They have built on a long heritage and an ever-increasing literature. Each of the terms can be best construed as a hurrah word. However each can also mean whatever the interlocutor wishes it to mean. For the present UK government, it means lifelong training. Quality of life, previously a key feature in lifelong learning, now seems to have faded from the discussion. 'Workers require lifelong learning' (*Times*

Higher Education Supplement of 19 December 1997) and 'Lifelong learning: they're making it work' (*The Independent* of 21 May 1998) demonstrate the direction that the rhetoric has taken. However, even in the versions from the 1970s, a number of potentially important elements were missing, namely: emotion, moral development and spirituality. These are vaguely subsumed under quality of life but are never actually highlighted. It is almost as if humans were seen as not needing those very parts which are arguably those that make them human.

Yet we stand at a moment in time when Western society has lost its old paradigms and, most importantly, lost a large measure of its faith in the future. In this respect, we have an occasion to define the goal of lifelong education in a manner not evident in the 1970s. We have the possibility of moving beyond the present confusion of the hurrah word and the insecurity which is its undertone towards placing humans and their feelings at the centre. Let us propose that the aim of lifelong education be to restore and to maintain hope. We can term this *consciencisation* if we wish but with this simple goal in mind we have at our disposal the means of developing a concept which not only hangs together but which we can explain to our political masters and to the public at large in terms which are meaningful to them and which stand some chance of loosening purse-strings. Failure to do so will result in lifelong education continuing to be a political buzzword destined to mean whatever an orator wishes it to mean. Failure to actualise lifelong education will mean even more social stratification, more situations where those who have shall receive (in this case education and wealth) while those who have not must content themselves with the droppings from the rich man's table.

Suggested further reading

A good point in the lifelong learning debate to start is in Ranson (1998) which presents a wide ranging series of essays and articles on the topic. *The Learning Age* (DfEE 1998) gives an insight into the manner in which a government interprets the idea. The adult learner is discussed in depth in Knowles (1998) while Tight (1996) offers clear and concise explanations of a number of terms used frequently in the lifelong learning debate. Glendinning (1985) is an interesting account of learning beyond retirement, an area which can only grow as the population ages.

Notes

1   Both Illich and Freire began to question the intrinsic value of literacy when they observed in their work in Latin America that the rural poor may have nothing to read and yet their cultures have evident value (Pierre Furter, personal communication).

2   As time goes on, it will be interesting to observe the effect that computer-based communications have on spelling. As anyone who habitually uses e-mail can testify, the smallest mistake in the address and the communication does not go where it is supposed to go. At this point, immense care must be taken. On the other hand, the actual message is often marked by a complete insouciance for grammar, spelling and syntax.

References

Abbott, J. (1994) *Learning Makes Sense.* Letchworth: Education 2000.

Aronowitz, S. and Giroux, H. (1993) *Postmodern Education.* Minneapolis: University of Minnesota Press.

Bélanger, P. (1994) 'Lifelong Learning: the dialectics of "Lifelong Education"', *International Review of Education* **40**(3–5), 353–381.

Blackledge, D. and Hunt, B. (1985) *Sociological Interpretations of Education.* London: Routledge.

Claxton, G (1990) *Teaching to Learn.* London: Cassell.

Cropley, A. J. (1977) *Lifelong Education: A Psychological Analysis.* Oxford: Pergamon.

Cropley, A. J. (1979) 'Lifelong learning: issues and questions', in Cropley, A. J. (ed.) *Lifelong Education: A Stocktaking.* Hamburg: UNESCO Institute of Education.

Dave, R. H. (1972) 'Foundations of lifelong education: some methodological aspects', in Dave, R. H. (ed.) *Foundations of Lifelong Education.* Oxford: Pergamon.

De'Ath, C. (1972) 'Anthropological and ecological foundations of Lifelong Learning', in Dave, R. H. (ed.) *Foundations of Lifelong Education.* Oxford: Pergamon.

Delors, J. *et al.* (1996) *Education – The Treasure Within.* Paris: UNESCO/HMSO.

DfEE (1996) *Lifetime Learning.* London: HMSO.

DfEE (1998) *The Learning Age: A Renaissance for a New Britain.* London: The Stationery Office.

Faure, E. *et al.* (1972) *Learning To Be.* Paris: UNESCO.

Furter, P. (1999) *From Literacy to Cultural Development.* Northampton: Nene-University College School of Education Occasional Paper.

Gelpi, E. (1979) *A Future for Lifelong Education.* Manchester: Manchester Monographs.

Gelpi, E. (1994) 'L'Education permanente: principe révolutionnaire et pratiques conservatrices', *International Review of Education* **40**(3–5), 343–351.

Glendinning, F. (ed.) (1985) *Educational Gerontology: International Perspectives.* London: Croom Helm.

Griffin, C. (1983) *Curriculum Theory in Adult and Lifelong Education.* Beckenham: Croom Helm.

d'Hainaut, L. and Lawton, D. (1981) 'The sources of content reform geared to lifelong education', in d'Hainaut, L. (coordinator) *Curricula and Lifelong Education – Education on the Move.* Paris: UNESCO.

Knapper, C. J. and Cropley, A. J. (1985) *Lifelong Learning and Higher Education.* London: Croom Helm.

Knowles, M. (1998) *The Adult Learner.* Houston, TX: Gulf Publishing.

Labour Party (1994) *Opening Doors to a Learning Society: A Policy Statement on Education.* London: Labour Party.

Lengrand, P. (1978) *An Introduction to Lifelong Education.* Paris: UNESCO.

Lengrand, P, (1979) 'Prospects of lifelong education', in Cropley, A. J. (ed.) *Lifelong Education: A Stocktaking.* Hamburg: UNESCO Institute of Education.

Lengrand, P. (1986): 'Introduction', in Lengrand, P. (ed.) *Areas of Learning Basic to Lifelong Learning.* Oxford: UNESCO/Pergamon.

Longworth, N. and Davies, W. K. (1996) *Lifelong Learning.* London: Kogan Page.

Margolin, J-C. (1981) 'L'éducation au temps de la Contre-Réforme', in Vial, J. and Mialaret, G. (eds) *Histoire Mondiale de l'Education.* Paris: Presses universitaires de France.

Ranson, S. (ed.) (1998) *Inside the Learning.* London: Cassell.

Stoikov, V. (1975) *The Economics of Recurrent Education and Training.* Geneva: International Labour Office.

Tight, M. (1996) *Key Concepts in Adult Education and Training.* London: Routledge.

White, J. (1997) *Education and the End of Work.* London: Cassell.

Xie Guo-Dong (1994) 'Lifelong education in China: new policies and activities', *International Review of Education* **40**(3–5).

Index